Failed
Multinational
Ventures

Failed Multinational Ventures

The Political Economy of International Divestments

Leon Grunberg
University of Puget Sound

LexingtonBooks
D.C. Heath and Company
Lexington, Massachusetts
Toronto

Library of Congress Cataloging in Publication Data

Grunberg, Leon.
    Failed multinational ventures.

    Bibliography: p.
    Includes index.
    1. International business enterprises. 2. Corporate divestiture. 3. International business enterprises—Case studies. 4. Corporate divestiture—Case studies. I. Title.
HD2755.5.G783   338.8'8   80-8364
ISBN 0-669-04032-0   AACR2

Published simultaneously in Canada

Printed in the United States of America

International Standard Book Number: 0-669-04032-0

Library of Congress Catalog Card Number: 80-8364

To Sonia

Contents

List of Tables

Acknowledgments

It is a pleasure to be able to express my gratitude to the people who helped me in the preparation of this book. Christopher Vanderpool, Fred Waisanen, Bo Anderson, Kevin Kelly, and Bruce Mann were kind enough to spend many hours discussing various issues with me. I am especially indebted to William Faunce and Richard Hill who, by their friendship and intellectual stimulation, continually supported and extended me.

The nature of the research on which this book is based meant that I was continually dependent on the assistance and cooperation of many people in public life. Although many of their names are not mentioned in the book, I acknowledge their substantial contribution here.

I would also like to thank the following for permission to use copyrighted material: the *Sunday Times,* London, for permission to quote from an article by John Fryer and George Armstrong, © *Sunday Times*; Jagdish C. Sachdev for permission to quote from his "A Framework for the Planning of Divestment Policies for Multinational Companies," Ph.D. dissertation, University of Manchester, 1976, pp. 121 and 125; and the *Spectator* for permission to quote from Geoffrey Robinson, "Italian Fiasco," 6 December 1975, p. 721.

Finally, I am happy to thank those who gave me moral and material support. They include Michigan State University and the University of Puget Sound, each of which provided financial assistance; Rogina Olds and May Blau who typed the manuscript; and my parents, friends, and colleagues who kept promising to buy the book if I ever finished it. I hope they now keep their word. Above all, I thank Sonia Grunberg who has spent almost as much time as I have reading, discussing, and thinking about the book. Her many suggestions were extremely helpful and her affection and good humor made the writing less of a lonely and arduous task. I dedicate the book to her.

1
The Problem in Context

It is the inequalities, the injustice, the contradictions, large or small, which make the world go round and ceaselessly transform its upper structures, the only really mobile ones. For capitalism alone has relative freedom of movement. . . . Faced with inflexible structures ("those of material life and, no less, of ordinary economic life"), it is able to choose the areas where it wants and is able to meddle, and the areas it will leave to their fate, incessantly reconstructing its own structures from these components, and thereby little by little transforming those of others.

That is why . . . it is the source or characteristic of all great material progress and of all the most burdensome exploitation of man by man. Not only because of the appropriation of the surplus value of man's labour. But also because of that disproportion in strength and position, on a nationwide as well as a worldwide scale, which means that at the whim of circumstance there will always be one position more advantageous to adopt than the rest, one sector more profitable to exploit. The choice may be limited, but what an immense privilege to be able to choose. —Fernand Braudel[1]

There can be little doubt that we live in a world dominated by giant organizations. One particular species of the form that has stamped its mark on our lives has been the multinational company. Powerful, flexible, even restless, it has by its mobility helped to connect thousands of inflexible communities and millions of relatively rooted workers in a system dominated by its economic rationality. Driven by competitive processes to continually seek out profitable opportunities around the world, the multinational company also, in this unceasing process, continually produces and reproduces uneven development—that is, as some communities and workers reap the material and social benefits (and costs) that accompany the presence of multinational companies, others experience the economic and social dislocations of their departure.

This book focuses on one aspect of the mobility of international capital—namely, the divestment behavior of multinational companies. It explores the causes of international divestments and describes some of their consequences with an in-depth analysis of two cases of international divestment and one case of attempted divestment. The cases involve British Leyland divesting its Italian subsidiary, Leyland Innocenti, in 1975-1976; Litton Industries, a U.S. conglomerate, divesting its British subsidiary, Imperial Typewriters, in 1975;

1

and Chrysler Corporation, one of the giant but frail U.S. automobile manufacturers, attempting to divest its British subsidiary, Chrysler U.K., in 1975.

Two central dynamics are seen to be at work in the cases. One is the
tendency for more and more economic activities to become internalized
within these large multi-unit companies, a process that propels them toward
long-range strategic planning. The other is the resurgence of fierce international
competition. These two dynamics are, at this historical conjuncture, in a relation
of tension—that is, whereas internalization and planning provide some stability
for these giants, international competition undermines this stability and breeds
acute insecurity in them. How this tension will eventually be resolved is unclear.
What is clear at this time is that the tension manifests itself in extensive divestments. Large multi-unit companies absorb and react to competition or to what
Schumpeter called "the perennial gale of creative destruction"[2] by restructuring
themselves (that is, by closures, sales, acquisitions, and the movement out of old
products and into new ones).

The implications of these findings are twofold. Theoretically, they add some
support to the Galbraithian view of the economy without fully undermining the
heavy emphasis placed on competition in conventional and Marxist economics.
Politically, they raise several questions about the power of these mini-soviet
economies. If more and more economic decisions are being taken by "visible
hands," then how open should the decision-making process be, how are those
decisions to be made, and what voice or representation should those presently
excluded from the process (for example, workers and people living in local
communities) have?

Plan of the Book

The plan of this book mirrors the steps I took in researching the problem. I
have tried, in as far as it is possible after the event, to let the reader share in
the process of discovery that I experienced in this research. In fact, a movement
takes place from the general and speculative (chapters 1 and 2) to the concrete
and specific (chapters 4, 5, and 6) and then back to the general (chapters 7 and
8). Chapter 1 introduces the problem of international divestment and places it
in the context of the cyclical and structural changes that have been taking place
in the international economy. We will see that divestments have been on a rising
trend and that recessions and structural readjustments have probably been major
contributors to that trend.

Chapter 2 begins by reviewing the scant literature on the causes of international divestment and proposes, in schematic form, an explanation for divestments by multinational companies. The argument is that multinational
companies are currently engaged in a fierce competitive battle for market
shares. Because the competition among them is of an oligopolistic kind, they are

engaged in a constant struggle to gain cost advantages. They will, therefore, tend to locate their capital—that is, invest and divest—according to comparative cost conditions in an unevenly developed world. Chapter 2 also reviews the literature on the consequences of divestments and describes the damaging effects that closures can have on workers and communities.

In chapter 3, I describe the rather novel research strategy that I was forced to employ to investigate the problem of international divestments. To avoid some of the obstacles that other researchers on divestments have confronted, I undertook what I call the "long-march" approach—that is, I began data collection at the bottom and periphery of the companies and step by step worked my way up to the top and into the center. This turned out to be a very fruitful research strategy.

Chapters 4, 5, and 6 comprise the meat of the book. Readers not interested in my speculations and generalizations can usefully read these chapters alone. Although it would be misleading to suggest that a point of view has not guided the selection of data or matters of emphasis, I have, as far as is possible, tried to let the cases stand on their own by describing and analyzing them in the language and concepts of the participants.

What the case studies illustrate is the difficulty in saying that subsidiaries have been divested because they have failed in the market. Subsidiaries are seen to exist in two competitive worlds: (1) the market and (2) what I call the "internal-political economy". The Leyland Innocenti case is particularly interesting in that it contains verbatim accounts of the internal conflicts and controversies that preceded and followed the closure crisis. It demonstrates, in management's own words, the ways in which the fate of subsidiaries is vitally connected to parent decisions on such crucial things as transfer prices, product policy, and access to export markets. It also demonstrates how a well-organized group of workers can mount a massive, innovative, and successful campaign to save their jobs.

The chapter on Chrysler U.K. adds support to the emerging thesis of the importance of the internal-political economy in determining the fate of subsidiaries. It describes the internal conflicts that surrounded decisions on intergration, product development, and access to export markets—decisions that went against Chrysler U.K. and helped seal its fate. A primary reason for Chrysler U.K.'s defeat in the internal battle for resources was that it had a more-intransigent labor force than its major rival, Chrysler France, had. A postscript to the chapter briefly considers the recent troubles at Chrysler Corporation for, ironically, five years after it threatened to withdraw from Britain, it was itself on the verge of bankruptcy. In both instances, their threatened collapse compelled their respective governments to bail them out.

In the Imperial case, the parent, Litton Industries, is a multinational conglomerate. The evidence presented suggests that Imperial's life was subject, at every point, to the strategic plan of Litton. It is argued that, in 1975, Litton

systematically dismantled Imperial, killing off the production side of the subsidiary while ensuring that the marketing network was maintained for the
benefit of Triumph-Adler, its German subsidiary. The chapter also records that,
despite a spirited occupation of the factory by some of the workers, the government refused to intervene. In contrast to the Chrysler case, Imperial, with a
much smaller work force, was considered expendable.

In chapter 7, I begin the move back toward the general and away from the
specific. The three cases are compared in their essentials, and the findings are
analyzed in terms of the conceptual framework presented in chapter 2. I conclude that although I underestimated the importance of the internal-political
economy, the emphasis placed on competition was not erroneous but merely
one-sided. After all, each case demonstrates in its own way that even the very
largest companies can be rendered vulnerable, sometimes to the point of bankruptcy, by the intensity of international competition. The large multi-unit
companies, therefore, despite their structural flexibility and their strategic-
planning capacities, have done no more than increase their degrees of freedom
within an unplanned and highly competitive world environment.

Finally, chapter 8 concludes the book with a brief discussion of the concrete and ideological conflicts between workers and capital over closures and
capital mobility. I argue that as the market becomes demystified and as visible
hands are seen to be at work, economic relations will increasingly become
repoliticized.

International Divestments—The Magnitude of the Problem

This section pulls together the scattered and limited information on international divestments and tries to assess the magnitude of the problem. Before
I examine the data on divestments, a definition of this imprecise term is
necessary. *Divestment* has been used to designate the closure, full or partial
sale, expropriation, or nationalization of an operation. In this study the term
is used interchangeably with *withdrawals* and refers to the voluntary closure
or sale of a producing operation by a multi-unit company that causes some
significant production and employment effect.[3] In other words, I do not consider the closure or sale of independent businesses. These also produce significant production and employment effects but are beyond the scope of this
study. However, given our concern with employment effects, the definition
is still unsatisfactory for it does not capture the gradual contraction of an
operation as a result of parent decisions over the allocation of resources.
Starving a subsidiary of investment funds, or drawing profits away and rein-
vesting them elsewhere, may have serious employment and production
consequences that unfortunately cannot be detected in aggregate data. This
type of gradual contraction of an operation should perhaps be referred to by

the term *disinvestment*. One advantage of the case-study approach adopted in this book is that such gradual disinvestment can be uncovered more easily.

There is a truly remarkable dearth of reliable data on divestments. Official agencies, as a rule, have shown little concern for collecting disaggregated data on the various forms of capital mobility. Only by the laborious effort of several private researchers do we have any knowledge of the magnitude of the problem, either in its national or international dimension. However, it should be noted that these researchers do not restrict the term *divestments* to closures or sales that cause a significant production and employment effect. Nevertheless, what the data show is that divestments by multinational companies occur in large numbers and that their incidence has been increasing over time. For example, Torneden, after examining 515 U.S. companies (the *Fortune* 500 plus the 15 largest retailers), uncovered 561 cases of divestment of foreign operations during the 1967-1971 period. Ignoring nationalizations, which he includes under the definition, the number drops to 537.[4] Vernon, looking at 180 large U.S.-based multinational companies, discovered 717 cases of sales or liquidations of manufacturing subsidiaries between 1968-1974.[5] Sachdev, after a heroic sifting of some 3,500 documents, compiled a list of at least 532 cases of voluntary divestment by British-based multinational companies for the period 1968-1974.[6] Finally, Business International reported that divestments by foreign investors in Japan rose from 6 in 1972 to 26 in 1975 and 15 in the first half of 1976.[7]

These absolute figures as they stand are hard to interpret in a meaningful way. When related to the number of existing or new manufacturing subsidiaries, the following picture emerges. Torneden, using a figure of 3,238 newly formed foreign subsidiaries in the same period, arrived at a rate of divestments as a percentage of new subsidiaries of 15.9 percent.[8] In fact, he noted an increasing trend of divestment activity. For example, in 1967, 10.9 new establishments were formed for every divestment, whereas in 1971, the ratio was 2.7 to 1.[9] Vernon places the 717 withdrawals he discovered in the context of a total population of 6,500 manufacturing subsidiaries owned by U.S. multinationals, although he does not say what happens over time.[10] Sachdev also notes that divestment activity is on the increase, although he does not give comparative figures for existing or new subsidiaries.[11] Finally, the data on one country confirm the consistency of the pattern. Multinational companies of various parent domiciles closed 106 subsidiaries and established 447 in the 1970-1976 period in Belgium, giving an overall ratio of 4.2 to 1. The ratio narrows over time.[12] Moreover, data showed that multinational companies tended to divest more frequently than did local firms.[13]

The case of Belgium is particularly interesting since it is one of the few countries wherein the government collects data on company closures. The government figure for the number of closures in the 1975-1976 period was 50, whereas the independent research of Van Den Bulcke uncovered 108 cases in the same period, essentially by sifting through various publications.[14] The difference is substantial and illustrates the difficulties involved in monitoring the activities of private capital.

Data on the form of divestments, fragmentary and inadequate as it is, suggest the following pattern. Whenever multinational companies decide to withdraw, they usually choose to do so completely—that is, by a full sale of their ownership or a liquidation.[15] Not surprisingly, they tend to prefer a sale of their ownership share, though if necessary, they do not hestitate to liquidate and close subsidiaries.[16] However, these data, garnered from the responses of multinational companies to a questionnaire survey, mask a more-complex reality. Some multinationals probably dissect the subsidiary, liquidate parts that are no longer useful to them, and maintain or create others that will be.[17] Also, no data exist on the fate of the subsidiaries that are sold—whether they are maintained as going concerns, whether they produce the same products with the same number of workers, or whether they remain dependent on the multinational company for various services. Such questions are germane given the dependent nature of the relationship of many subsidiaries to the group.

We can conclude from the admittedly limited data that withdrawals are an established part of international production and that the increasing trend in their incidence was well established before the recession of 1974-1975. Moreover, this problem does not seem to be confined to the sphere of international production. Recent research by Bluestone and Harrison shows that a massive and continuous turnover of capital occurs within national boundaries. A careful examination of data for the New England region of the United States reveals that in the 1969-1976 period, 72,925 operations started up and 95,131 closed, resulting in an overall net loss of jobs.[18] Interestingly, multi-unit companies of the conventional and conglomerate type accounted for only 15 percent of the closings but 50 percent of the resulting job loss.[19]

In summary then, late capitalism is characterized by substantial and probably accelerating rates of capital mobility. Reasons for this are systematically laid out nowhere in the literature and are still a matter of speculation. What is becoming clear is that, though much of the turnover of capital is the result of the large number of small-business start-ups and failures, much of the large-scale turnover and mobility of capital increasingly will occur within the shifting boundaries of a relatively small number of large multi-unit companies.[20]

The International Context

To fully understand the increase in international divestments, we must situate them in the context of an international-political economy that was undergoing severe cyclical and structural transformations. The relevant period of our investigation, 1966 to 1976, was one of profound transition. It was a time when the capitalist world moved from fast to slow or no growth, from low to high unemployment, and from undisputed U.S. economic domination to unstable rivalry among the major capitalist powers. It also presided over the beginning, but not the full accomplishment, of a reversal in the advances the labor movement had made in several countries.[21]

The most visible transformation was the emergence of the capitalist world from the long postwar boom into the deepest recession since the 1930s. For example, the gross domestic product of the countries in the Organization for Economic Cooperation and Development (OECD), essentially comprising all the advanced capitalist countries, rose from $1.9 trillion in 1968, to $2.4 trillion in 1974, and then fell by $43 billion in 1975 (calculated at 1970 prices and exchange rates). Industrial production followed a similar pattern. It rose by over 65 percent in the period 1963 to 1973, leveled off in 1974, and fell by varying amounts in all countries in 1975.[22] Not surprisingly, unemployment in the OECD countries rose to a postwar high of 15 million. In the previous 1969-1971 recession, the figure was 10 million. A small decline also occurred in world trade, after the rapid growth in its volume in the preceding years.[23] Theories to explain this downturn, and business cycles in general, are complex and controversial and I cannot enter that field here. What I can do is to describe two important trends that were associated with this downturn.

First, a significant decline in rates of profit took place in most of the capitalist countries. In the United States, the rate of profit fell from a before-tax high of 16.2 percent in the period 1948-1950 to 12.9 percent in the 1966-1970 period to 10.5 percent in 1973 (the after-tax figures were 8.6 percent, 7.7 percent, and 5.4 percent).[24] In Britain the rate had fallen from 16.5 percent in the 1950-1954 period to 11.7 percent in the 1965-1969 period to 9.7 percent in 1970 (the after-tax rates being 6.7 percent, 5.3 percent, and 4.7 percent).[25] Japan, West Germany, France, Sweden, and Italy also witnessed long-term declines in the rate of profit in the postwar period.[26]

Second, several national economies had a "regular increase in excess capacity in industry."[27] Thus, while capacity utilization always decreases in recessions, the trend in the 1960s and 1970s was toward a lower rate of utilization of capacity in each successive cycle. For example, in the U.S. manufacturing industry, the rate went from 92 percent in 1966 to 78 percent in 1968, from 86.5 percent in 1969 to 75 percent in 1971, and from 83 percent in 1973 to 65 percent in March 1975, the trough of the last major recession.[28]

These trends, of course, did not operate equally in all capitalist countries or in all large companies. However, the three multinationals that are the object of this study did experience both a decline in profitability and an excess of capacity. As one would expect, these were contributing factors in their decision to divest. Of course, it is usually true that variations in the magnitude of business failures and divestment activity tend to correspond to movements in the business cycle. In the severe recession of the mid-1970s, the incidence of business failures and divestments increased, and the rate of investment activity decreased.[29]

Alongside this cyclical reversal, several important structural developments occurred in the international economy. First, the rate of technological change (innovations) probably accelerated, subjecting many products and processes to quicker obsolescence.[30] Companies were increasingly compelled to introduce better machines and new products or to fall behind in the race. Whole industrial sectors were in decline (for example, textiles, shipbuilding, steel) as demand stagnated and competition from developing countries increased and as new industrial sectors expanded (for example, computers and electronics).

Second, a change in the relative economic strength and power of various national capitals occurred. This change is expressed in a whole range of economic figures that show that countries like West Germany and Japan are increasing their share of economic activity, while others, notably Britain, find their share decreasing.[31] The U.S. position as undisputed leader is certainly threatened, though its lead in many areas is still relatively secure. Japan, Germany, and to a lesser extent, other European countries have been catching up with higher rates of labor-productivity growth. For example, while the United States had an average annual rate of labor-productivity growth in manufacturing of 2.7 percent in the period 1960-1975, Japan's was 9.7 percent, West Germany's was 5.7 percent, France's was 5.6 percent, and Britain's was 3.8 percent.[32] Allied to these differential rates of productivity growth, differences in unit labor cost between the United States, Japan, and West Germany were narrowing.[33] One consequence of this convergence was that non-U.S. multinationals were growing more rapidly than were U.S. ones, and the dominance of U.S. multinationals "declined consistently over the decade 1963-1972."[34] An additional manifestation of this relative shift in strength between the U.S. and non-U.S. multinationals was the sharp rise in the latter's penetration of U.S. industrial sectors either by the establishment of new companies or the takeover of existing ones.[35]

Third, the growing internationalization of capital, the rise of some Third World countries as industrial producers, and the relative equalization of strength among the large companies of the capitalist world have all combined to intensify the competitive struggle internationally. For despite the trend toward a greater concentration and centralization of capital nationally,[36] internationally the share of production and sales accounted for by the top three of the top twenty companies in many industrial sectors has fallen.[37] Associated with this intensification of competition, the large, typically multinational companies experienced a decline in profitability over the 1967-1972 period.[38]

Fourth, and to a large extent as a result of these other trends, structural or long-term unemployment became a serious problem in Europe for the first time since the 1930s. Thus in the post-1975 upswing, unemployment levels did not diminish but increased to 16.3 million in 1976 and to about 17 million in 1977 in the OECD countries.[39] The labor movement, which had made political and economic gains in several European countries in the late 1960s and early 1970s, was forced onto the defensive as the recession increased unemployment and as the accompanying fiscal crisis produced cutbacks in social programs.

The evolution of the three cases we discuss took place in this unique conjuncture in the history of late capitalism. In many ways each case represents, in microcosm, the playing out of these trends. Increased competition (in particular from Japan), stagnant demand, excess capacity, declining profitability, technological change, and worker resistance all, to varying degrees, acted on the multinationals and contributed to the increased incidence of divestments.

Notes

1. Fernand Braudel, *Capitalism and Material Life 1400-1800*, trans. Miriam Kochan (New York: Harper & Row, 1976), p. 445.

2. Joseph A. Schumpeter, *Capitalism, Socialism and Democracy* (New York: Harper & Row, 1950), p. 84.

3. This definition is similar but not identical to the one used by Boddewyn in Business International S.A., *International Divestment: A Survey of Corporate Experience* (New York, 1976), p. 5.

4. Roger L. Torneden, *Foreign Divestment by U.S. Multinational Corporations: With Eight Case Studies* (New York: Praeger, 1975), pp. 20-21.

5. Raymond Vernon, *Storm over the Multinationals: The Real Issues* (Cambridge, Mass.: Harvard University Press, 1977), p. 100.

6. Jagdish C. Sachdev, "A Framework for the Planning of Divestment Policies for Multinational Companies" (Ph.D. diss., University of Manchester, 1976), p. 135.

7. Cited in Business International, *International Divestment*, p. 3.

8. Torneden, *Foreign Divestment*, p. 22.

9. Ibid., p. 34.

10. Vernon, *Storm over the Multinationals*, p. 100.

11. Sachdev, *Framework for Planning of Divestment Policies*, pp. 135-136.

12. *Business International, Weekly Reports,* 15 July 1977.

13. See D. Van Den Bulcke, "Existing Data," in *Investment and Divestment Policies of Multinational Corporation in Europe* (ECSIM, Saxon House, undated), p. 47.

14. Ibid.

15. Torneden, *Foreign Divestment*, p. 27.

16. Ibid., p. 25. Sixty-three percent of the 558 divestments were sales and 33 percent were liquidations.

17. Business International, *International Divestment*, p. 51.

18. See the important recent study by Barry Bluestone and Bennett Harrison, *Capital and Communities: The Causes and Consequences of Private*

Disinvestment (Washington, D.C.: Progressive Alliance, 1980), tables 3 and 4 on pp. 35 and 38.

19. Ibid., p. 60.

20. Both Torneden and Sachdev found that a small number of large companies accounted for a disproportionate number of all divestments. Thus, 34 U.S. companies in the upper quartile of the *Fortune* 500 accounted for 226 or 48 percent of all cases of divestments, and 49 British companies in the top-100 rank accounted for 343 or 54 percent of the cases of divestments. This indicates multiple divestments by some large multinationals, which of course, could simply be because large companies have more subsidiaries.

21. Throughout this section, I rely heavily on Ernest Mandel, *The Second Slump* (London: New Left Books, 1978).

22. Ibid., p. 14; and OECD, *Main Economic Indicators* (Paris, 1976).

23. Mandel, *Second Slump*, p. 19.

24. Ibid., p. 22. The rate of profit is on the capital employed by nonfinancial companies and is calculated after eliminating gains from reappreciation of inventories.

25. Ibid., p. 23. The rate is calculated on net holdings of industrial and commercial companies.

26. Ibid., pp. 23-25.

27. Ibid., p. 26.

28. Ibid.

29. Ibid., p. 106. Mandel cites figures showing declines in investment activity in West Germany, Japan, and the United States. Interestingly, there was virtually no change in the figures for Italy and Britain.

30. See Ernest Mandel, *Late Capitalism* (London: Verso, 1978), chapters 7 and 8.

31. Mandel, *Second Slump*, pp. 48-49. For example, Britain's exports, which were ahead of France's exports and equal to Japan's exports (in value terms) in 1970, were 20 percent behind both by 1975.

32. Ibid., p. 106.

33. Ibid., p. 109.

34. J. Dunning and R.B. Pearce, Profitability and Performance of the World's Largest Industrial Companies (London: Financial Times, 1975), p. 47.

35. Mandel, *Second Slump*, p. 107.

36. On increased concentration levels in Europe, see European Economic Community, *Reports on Competition Policy* (Brussels, 1973; 1975).

37. Dunning and Pearce, "Profitability and Performance," p. 45.

38. Ibid., p. 60.

39. Mandel, *Second Slump*, p. 88. Unemployment is now (1980) close to 23 million and rising.

2 The Causes and Consequences of International Divestment

Causes

As anyone familiar with the topic of multinationals knows, an inordinate number of words have been written on the subject, mostly in a speculative vein. Yet, until very recently, there has been a virtual silence in the literature on the causes of international divestments or, for that matter, on the causes of any kind of divestments. Perhaps one of the reasons for the silence is the difficulty associated with trying to research this sensitive subject. Another reason may be that the causes of international divestment are considered to be obvious by conventional economists. After all, they could argue, it does not take extensive theoretical or empirical work to establish that companies divest subsidiaries because they have failed in the marketplace. More precisely, conventional economic theory predicts that divestment would occur either when losses are being incurred or when a higher return on investment can be earned elsewhere.[1] This view of the matter is certainly promulgated by executives of multinational companies.

In three separate survey studies, executives have portrayed their companies as deciding to withdraw when subsidiaries become a financial handicap to the whole group, either because they were making a loss or were not contributing an acceptable return on the investment.[2] Yet, neat as this sounds, we cannot just leave it at that. We need some guidance on what to look for and what to expect in the case studies. Perhaps we can construct a more-detailed explanation for international divestments after we briefly examine the literature on multinational companies and international investments.[3]

No overriding consensus exists in the literature on the reasons for foreign direct investment or for (what amounts to the same thing) the existence of multinational companies. What we can safely conclude, however, is that multinational companies typically originate from advanced capitalist countries, reside in oligopolistic industries, and tend to be technologically advanced.[4] Some seem to go overseas to exploit fully any advantages they possess,[5] and others follow the pioneers, not so much because they possess clear advantages but to keep up with the industry leader.[6] The advantages that pioneering companies possess (which can range from brand names and favored access to finance to patents on special technology and products),[7] enable them to earn additional monopoly profits in a new location. This ability threatens the competitive relationship between the firms in the industry and prompts them to "follow the leader" or to "checkmate" each others' moves in order to share in the gains and reestablish some form of competitive equilibrium. This type of behavior helps explain the so-called bunching of overseas investments that some researchers have un-covered.[8] In the early phases of overseas expansion, the competitive imperative among these oligopolistic-type companies was to ensure that each carved out a secure niche in the richest and fastest growing markets.[9]

One consequence of these waves of overseas expansion was to widen the arena of competition by connecting previously segregated markets. Whatever oligopolistic equilibrium may have existed in various markets and industries was disturbed in the intensified scramble for market shares. In several indus-tries—the automobile industry can act as an exemplar here—previously stable relations between national producers were rudely upset by the internationaliza-tion of capital. Although a new and oligopolistic equilibrium may be restored, this is still some way off.[10] The present phase is marked by battles among multinational companies seeking to establish positions in the relatively virgin markets of fast-growing societies such as Spain, Iran, and Brazil and, under the challenge of European and Japanese latecomers, to emerge successfully out of the redivision of market shares that is taking place in the older markets of Europe and North America.

The nature of the competition among these multinationals can be expected to take a nonprice form, but it will be no less severe because of that.[11] These international giants are still subject to what Barnet and Muller call the "exis-tential terrors of oligopolistic competition,"[12] which compels them to contin-ually seek to gain an advantage over their rivals or to close a gap that has opened up between them. Since the price weapon is rarely used in this struggle, these giant companies will seek to win market shares through the marketing effort, broadly defined—that is, they will try to differentiate their product by adver-tising, or to develop a better distribution and after-sales service than their rivals, or to outspend them on research and development in an effort to improve existing products or create new ones. However, if this is the visible side of oligopolistic competition, the more-hidden, and perhpas more-fundamental, struggle will revolve around production costs. For those companies that can gain a cost advantage will be able to earn higher profit margins than rival sellers (assuming no price competition) and will be able to outspend them on the marketing effort.[13]

To the extent that this explication is correct, we can expect that the prob-ability of international divestment will be related to the success or failure of subsidiaries in the cost battle. Most obviously, subsidiaries that experience a serious deterioration in their cost position because of some internal problems will find themselves at a severe disadvantage relative to their rivals and will, sooner or later, fail in the marketplace. The deterioration could be due to any number of factors peculiar to the subsidiary. For example, the subsidiary could experience a sharp and unique worsening of its labor situation relative to its competitors.

There will also be an external dimension to the cost battle. Some subsidiaries may be divested even if no deterioration occurs in their cost position because the parents, in the search for above-average profits, will relocate to lower-cost production sites. Although such aggressive relocations are undertaken by all types of companies, they are likely to be more feasible for multinational companies because of their global-scanning capacities and their organizational flexibility. Such offensive moves on the part of some parents can produce a *relative* deterioration in the cost position of rivals. This can result in divestments either because the rival parent seeks to follow the leader or, if it cannot do that, because the subsidiary becomes uncompetitive. We can expect, therefore, that in the later phases of the internationalization of production, when multinational companies have established a foothold, if not always a secure one, in the world markets, that the contest between them will increasingly revolve around "matching one another's production cost curves on a worldwide basis."[14]

Many factors influence the relative production costs of multinational companies—for example, comparative raw material, energy, transportation, finance, and labor costs, as well as comparative economies of scale.[15] The importance of each will vary according to the nature of the industry and the products produced (for example, whether the industry is labor or capital intensive, the size of the product, and so on). To the extent that international markets exist for some of these factors (raw materials, energy, finance), then their costs will tend to be similar for the multinational competitors. What can be expected to differ significantly are what Marxists call the "relations of production" and what conventional economists refer to as the "government-induced business climate."

I cannot give either of these two notions an extended treatment here but will merely indicate how each could be associated with divestment.[16] The relations of production (capital/labor relations) will influence performance in the cost battle through their effect on unit labor costs (the relation of labor costs to productivity). Labor costs refer not only to wages but also to what is known as the social wage, and these will be determined by the state of the labor market and the balance of class forces politically.[17] The productivity of labor, insofar as it is influenced by the behavior of labor (which is still a contentious matter), will be affected by the docility or the militancy of the work force at the point of production.[18] A militant work force can, for example, seriously impair the ability of management to alter the mix of machines and labor and to reorganize the labor process to increase productivity. Therefore, we can expect that some subsidiaries will be divested because their unit labor costs are seriously out of balance with the competitive average, or because aggressively minded multinationals will relocate in the search for cheaper and more-docile labor. What this implies, of course, is that the existential insecurity that such competition engenders among managers is transmitted to, and felt by, the workers.

Government policies can also influence production costs and profitability either indirectly through their effects on such factors as wages, worker strength, and the cost of money or directly through taxation, regulations, incentives, and subsidies. Multinational companies will tend to divest from countries in which a deterioration in the business climate occurs, most obviously when the government threatens to impose a heavy tax on profit repatriation or when it actually does so. However, divestments may also occur independently of any one government's actions. If, for example, a company discovers that it can find greater government incentives or a better business climate in another country, it may pull out of its present location and move to another regardless of the actions of the original government.

However, I must point out that though this sort of aggressive relocation is possible, it is much more likely that multinationals would bargain with governments or work forces on the basis of such a threat. The threat is of enormous significance precisely because the multinational can compare labor markets and government policies on a worldwide basis. Workers and governments, because they depend on capital (national and international) for the satisfaction of various needs, will tend to compete for the location of the subsidiaries of multinational companies. In such circumstances, multinationals can invoke the threat of divestments to strengthen their bargaining position, whether it be with labor or government. Of course, actual divestments tend to confirm the potential force of the threat. Most multinationals faced with an intransigent labor force, or less often, an uncooperative government, will not just pack up their bags and leave, but will first use the threat of divestment as a tactic to discipline the labor force or to bring about more-favorable government policies.[19] However, if the threat does not work, the multinational may gradually run down investment in that subsidiary to the point at which it eventually fails in the marketplace. Although this type of gradual divestment is hard to detect, it is probably quite frequent.[20]

Underlying this whole analysis has been the dynamic influence of competition. Competition will cause some subsidiaries to fail and some multinationals to seek more-favorable locations and to pull out of others. Although I have stressed that in this period of late capitalism, international competition is very fierce, we must remember that variations will exist in its intensity across industries and markets. The more intense the competition, the more compulsion there will be on companies to cut costs and/or to achieve some marketing breakthrough. Some of the more-important factors that will affect the intensity of competition are the degree of concentration in the industry, how well protected the market is, how rapid technological developments are, the degree of saturation in the market, and what is happening to the level of demand over time. Moreover, variations will exist in the strength of the competing multinationals. We can expect the companies that have smaller financial reserves, lower levels of capacity utilization, and lower economies of scale to be less able to withstand intense competition and to be more likely to divest subsidiaries.

In this discussion I have emphasized the factors that would influence multinational companies, acting in an economically rational manner, to divest subsidiaries. Some evidence, however, raises doubts about whether multinationals always act in this manner. Caves and Porter, for example, were so struck by the existence of low-return enterprises in multi-unit companies that they proposed that "barriers to exit" exist. They found evidence that various aspects of managerial behavior (for example, loyalty to a subsidiary and an unwillingness to lay off workers), and the difficulties associated with selling intangible assets such as brand names and trademarks, acted to inhibit exit from low-return operations.[21] The research of Torneden and Sachdev also suggests that organizational and personal factors may be more important in a divestment situation than purely economic considerations.[22] For example, Torneden found that divestments were often preceded by changes in top management.[23] The business journals also provide circumstantial evidence to support the barriers-to-exit thesis by actively encouraging managers to make the divestment decision a "routine," "integral," "planned," and "profitable" policy option.[24]

The case studies will not, of course, provide a test for the ideas presented in this section. Hopefully, they will indicate whether we are on the right lines and perhaps point out areas that we have missed altogether. As we shall see, they will raise fundamental questions about the meaning of competition and market failure when applied to the subsidiaries of multi-unit companies.

Consequences

If we ended the last section with the suggestion that not as many divestments take place as economic rationality would dictate, we have also seen in chapter 1 that many divestments actually occur and that their incidence is on an increasing trend. Perhaps one of the most glaring deficiencies in the burgeoning literature on multinational companies is the absence of empirical research on the effects of divestment on the well-being of workers, their families, local communities, and national economies.[25] Again, this may have something to do with the world view that dominates the economics and business literature.

Conventional economists, in their zeal to persuade us of the overall benefit that flows from the dynamism of a market economy, often overlook the burden that divestments impose on people. Even when they recognize that divestments require adjustment by all parties concerned (investors, workers, and so on), they fail to emphasize that the costs and meaning of adjustment for various groups are not commensurate. In their view, an aggregate net benefit will accrue to society if a continuous restructuring occurs in the economy in response to changes in demand, technology, and comparative advantage. To ossify the flows and motion inherent in capitalist economies is to condemn an economy to stagnation and ultimate decay. Such economists will point out, for example, that a company that continues to produce products few people want, with outdated, inefficient technology, ties up resources (labor, capital, and management skill) that could be more-productively employed elsewhere. Moreover, the company will sooner or later be judged a failure by the market, and only private or public subsidies will keep it going, which is considered a wasteful use of resources. Thus, at an ideological and policy level, divestments and their consequences are accepted, and the burden placed on those affected is to adapt, often with the support of government assistance.[26] The rationality of this prevailing wisdom is critically reconsidered in chapter 8.

Here I explore what the likely consequences of a divestment are for the multinational company, the workers and their families, and the local and national community. Framing the issue in this way will, I hope, accentuate the differences in the consequences of market failure for capital and communities. For the multinational company, the most important and potentially damaging consequence of withdrawal is that the loss of a source of supply could lead to a loss of markets in the country from which it is withdrawing and in countries to which it exported from that base. A prudent multinational thus will attempt to ensure a continuation of supply to its existing markets. This might mean increasing production elsewhere and then exporting to the market, or it could mean some form of licensing arrangement with a national company.

Other possible costs revolve around the process of withdrawal itself. An urgent sale may mean a selling price close to the book or liquidation value rather than a price based on some future earnings projections.[27] Liquidation can also be an expensive affair. The magnitude of the costs to multinational companies depends on a series of particular factors—for example, the accounting procedures they adopt to deal with liabilities, the type of taxation procedures in existence that may permit them to write off losses against future taxes on profit, and so on. A slightly less-tangible cost is the effect of bad publicity on the image of a company that will continue to do business in the country. On the positive side, withdrawal can enable the multinational to prune less-profitable subsidiaries, thereby freeing up various resources that can be used elsewhere.

We can examine the effects of divestments on workers and their families by looking at the growing research on the consequences of closures and layoffs in a national context. Once workers are laid off it certainly will make little difference to them whether this was done by a national or a multinational company. The findings of this research are in broad agreement.[28] The duration of the unemployment period varies according to the state of the local labor market, the age and skills of the workers, and their job-search behavior. Older and less-skilled workers suffer longer periods of unemployment. Some of them never again hold a full-time job. Workers find employment more quickly when the labor market is tight and when the job search is urgent and extensive. Some workers voluntarily leave their jobs before the ax falls in order to leave the sinking ship and to get some extra cash in hand if severance pay is due. These workers tend to have shorter periods of unemployment.[29] Despite government relief programs, the period of unemployment imposes a monetary cost on the workers, although the extent of the loss of income varies by country according to the type and level of state support.[30] Workers who do find work tend, on the whole, to find themselves in lower-paying and less-satisfying work.[31]

In addition to these economic costs, personal and social consequences of a nonmonetary kind exist. The few studies that have explored this area all show that closures and the resulting job loss reek severe psychological and physiological damage on those involved. For example, a study conducted in the late 1950s by Aiken, Ferman, and Sheppard found that "the loss of economic integrity" resulted in a sense of failure, which led to less contact with friends and to a sense of political alienation (but not apathy).[32] They also noted individual reactions that ranged from resignation, resentment, and bewilderment to fear and anxiety.[33]

A study by Cobb and Kasl into the psychological and physiological consequences of plant closures and job loss is unique in that it was able to compare workers who had been laid off with a control group of workers of similar charateristics who were still working. They found changes in cholesterol levels, glucose, body weight, and serum uric acid among the laid-off workers and noted, "in a larger sample, diabetes, peptic ulcer, and gout might have appeared as unduly frequent." They also found a higher incidence of suicide, dyspepsia, joint swelling, hypertension, and patchy baldness among the laid-off workers than among those in the control group. They concluded: "In the psychological sphere, the personal anguish experienced by the men and their families does not seem adequately documented by the statistics of deprivation and change in affective state."[34] More recently, work by Harvey Brenner has linked unemployment to increased incidences of alcoholism, child and spouse abuse, and mortality.[35]

Turning now to the effect of withdrawal on local communities and national economies, the first obvious point to note is that the extent of the impact will depend in large part on the importance of the subsidiary in the environment in which it is located. A community with limited alternative sources of employment will be severely affected by a withdrawal. No short-term solution is feasible except for the workers and their families to move or for many members of the community to become recipients of government aid. Even in larger areas the impact of withdrawal can be severe if the area is already depressed and if multiplier effects exist because of the linkages of the operation within the local economy.[36] At a national level, several fiscal effects can be identified, and again they will be more significant the larger the withdrawal. For example, tax revenues, both from the company and the workers employed, will be lost. In addition, expenditures on unemployment benefits and other social security payments will increase. Also, some balance-of-payments effects may result in a loss in exports and a rise in imports.

If there is one redeeming aspect to the suffering and dislocation that closures and mass layoffs produce, it is that, increasingly, workers and their allies are struggling to develop a counterrationality that challenges the private, unregulated, and abrupt nature of capital mobility. It is here, perhaps, that the character of multinationals may have had an unintended positive effect. The very size and seeming permanence of these companies makes divestment that much harder to accept as inevitable. A small- or medium-sized company that fully goes bankrupt may be more-readily accepted as a market failure than a subsidiary of a giant multinational company. One business journal, specifically directed at international business, has noted what it calls the "growing quest for permanent employment" in Europe and claims that because of their size, multinationals are being singled out as where it should all start.[37] Responding to the mounting struggles against closures in the mid-1970s, the journal warned multinationals that they could no longer make mistakes, "close down an operation, chalk everything to experience, and throw people out of jobs because workers nowadays are not prepared to suffer for your mistakes."[38] They even went so far as to advocate that multinationals consider treating labor as a fixed cost.[39]

The struggles against closures that characterized the 1970s rarely prevented the withdrawal of a multinational. Much as the workers tried to tie the hands of multinationals by the occupation of factories and by attempts at crossborder solidarity, in the end they had to rely on the political pressure they could direct at government to save their jobs.[40] As isolated communities of workers, they did not have the political power to counteract the economic power of internationally mobile capital.

Notes

1. See, for example, Matityahn Marcus, "Firms Exit Rates and Their Determinants," *Journal of Industrial Economics* 16 (1967):10-22.

2. See Roger L. Torneden, *Foreign Divestments by U.S. Multinationals: With Eight Case Studies* (New York: Praeger, 1975), pp. 128-30; Jagdish C. Sachdev, "A Framework for the Planning of Divestment Policies for Multinational Companies" (Ph.D. diss., University of Manchester, 1976), p. 203; and Business International, *International Divestment: A Survey of Corporate Experience* (New York, 1976), p. 12.

3. For a more-extensive review see Leon Grunberg, "International Divestments and the Multinational Company: Three Case Studies" (Ph.D. diss., Michigan State University, 1979), chapter 2.

4. See the data in United Nations, *Multinational Corporations in World Development* (New York, 1973).

5. Stephen Hymer, *The International Operation of National Firms: A Study of Direct Investment* (Cambridge, Mass,: MIT Press, 1976), p. 42.

6. See F. Knickerbocker, *Oligopolistic Reaction and the Multinational Enterprise* (Cambridge, Mass.: Harvard University Press, 1973); and the more-recent discussion in Raymond Vernon, *Storm Over the Multinationals: The Real Issues* (Cambridge, Mass.: Harvard University Press, 1977), pp. 67-68. Companies may also go overseas when their export markets are threatened by rising local competitors who have been attracted into the market by the high profits.

7. Charles P. Kindleberger, *American Business Abroad, Six Lectures on Direct Investment* (New Haven: Yale University Press, 1969), pp. 15-27.

8. Knickerbocker found that companies in certain industries tended to locate their foreign investments in the same location within a short space of time. He called this "bunching." See *Oligopolistic Reaction*, p. 60.

9. This helps explain why some two-thirds of foreign direct investment is located in the developed capitalist countries. See United Nations, *Multinational Corporations,* p. 8.

10. Some signs of this coming equilibrium are evident as more and more multinational companies enter into cooperative collaborative relationships. The business press is daily announcing some new agreement. To name just a few, collaborative relationships exists between Chrysler and Peugeot, Renault and American Motors, Isuzu and General Motors, and British Leyland and Honda.

11. See the discussion on this form of competition in Paul A. Baran and Paul M. Sweezy, *Monopoly Capital* (New York: Monthly Review Press, 1966), pp. 52-72.

12. This phrase is used by Richard Barnet and Ronald E. Muller in *Global Reach: The Power of the Multinational Corporations* (New York: Simon and Schuster, 1974), p. 364.

13. Baran and Sweezy, *Monopoly Capital,* pp. 67-72.

14. Knickerbocker, *Oligopolistic Reaction,* p. 203.

15. For brief reviews of the importance of comparative production costs in the relocation decision see Richard B. McKenzie, *Restrictions on Business Mobility: A Study in Political Rhetoric and Economic Reality* (Washington, D.C.: American Enterprise Institute, 1979), pp. 42-46; and Barry Bluestone and Bennett Harrison, *Capital and Communities: The Causes and Consequences of Private Disinvestment* (Washington, D.C.: The Progressive Alliance, 1980), pp. 168-98, 211. Bluestone and Harrison, however, believe that too much emphasis has been placed on comparative cost factors in explaining spatial investment behavior. They propose that unionization is the more-important factor.

16. For a more-extended discussion see Grunberg, *International Divestments*, chapter 1.

17. The social wage refers to such things as health, pension, vacation, and other benfits that workers receive in addition to their wage.

18. A careful study on this subject notes that the most important determinants of productivity are factors such as rate of output, length of runs, and age of the plant and equipment. See C.F. Pratten, *Labor Productivity Differentials within International Companies* (Cambridge: Cambridge University Press, 1976), pp. 60-61.

19. Numerous examples are cited in the press of this tactic's being used against labor. For example, Commodre Business Machines has threatened to pull out of Britain and move to Taiwan rather than give recognition to the union (*Manchester Guardian*, 30 June 1977), and Grundig has repeatedly used the threat of closure in response to industrial-relations difficulties at its Irish subsidiary (*Manchester Guardian*, 8 March 1979).

20. For example, one study found that multinationals tend to make their structural modifications by the transfer of future rather than actual production. See G.B.J. Bommers, *Multinational Corporations and Industrial Relations: A Comparative Study of West Germany and the Netherlands* (Amsterdam: Van Goreum, 1976), p. 108.

21. Richard E. Caves and Michael E. Porter, "Barriers to Exit," in *Essays on Industrial Organization in Honor of Joe S. Bain,* eds. Robert T. Masson and P. David Qualls (Cambridge, Mass.: Ballinger, 1976), pp. 39-69.

22. Sachdev, "Framework for Planning of Divestment Policies," p. 138.

23. Torneden, *Foreign Divestments,* pp. 104-06.

24. See Harry W. Wallender III, "A Planned Approach to Divestment," *Columbia Journal of World Business* 8 (1973):33-37; and F.D. Hollingworth, "Divestment—It's Tough to Bite the Bullet," *Business Quarterly* 40 (1975): 29-32.

25. As I suggest in note 11, chapter 3, this deficiency is being remedied as a result of union pressure and the willingness of sympathetic academics to research this problem.

26. For discussions of government's role in alleviating the impact of unemployment see Santosh Mukherjee, *Through No Fault of Their Own: Systems for Handling Redundancies in Britain, France and Germany* (London: MacDonald, 1973); and John Greenwood, *Worker Sit-Ins and Job Protection: Case Studies of Union Intervention* (London: Gower Press, 1977).

27. A full discussion of the costs of divestments from the multinational company's perspective can be found in Business International, *International Divestment.*

28. Such findings are reported in, for example, Frank Herron, *Labour Markets in Crisis: Redundancy at Upper Clyde Shipbuilders* (London: MacMillan, 1975); and Stephen S. Mick, "Social and Personal Costs of Plant Shutdowns," *Industrial Relations* 14 (2):203-08.

29. Herron, *Labour Markets in Crisis,* p. 98.

30. Ibid., p. 60; and OECD, *Economic Outlook* (Paris, 1975), pp. 3-22.

31. Bluestone and Harrison, *Capital and Communities,* p. 66.

32. M. Aiken, L.A. Ferman, and H.L. Sheppard, *Economic Failure, Alienation and Extremism* (Ann Arbor: University of Michigan Press, 1968), p. 103.

33. Ibid., p. 22.

34. Sidney Cobb and Stanislav V. Kasl, "Termination: The Consequence of Job Loss" (Study prepared for the U.S. Department of Health, Education, and Welfare, 1977), p. 180.

35. As reported in *U.S. News and World Report*, 28 June 1980, p. 68.

36. For a discussion of some community effects see Robert N. Stern, K. Haydn Wood, and Tove Helland Hammer, *Employee Ownership in Plant Shutdowns: Prospects for Employment Stability* (Kalamazoo, Mich.: W.E. Upjohn Institute For Employment Research, 1979).

37. *Business International Weekly Reports*, 24 October 1975, p. 337.

38. *Business Europe Weekly Reports,* 23 March 1975, p. 161.

39. *Business Europe Weekly Reports,* 28 November 1975, p. 380.

40. The 1970s witnessed an upsurge in the occupation tactic as workers tried to prevent closure and to show the public that they were willing and able to work. For example, some 102 factory occupations were counted in Britain between 1971 and 1974. See Ken Coates, *The New Worker Cooperatives* (Nottingham: Spokesman Books, 1976), p. 11.

3

The Long March: Collecting Data on Multinational Companies

The experiences of myself and other researchers clearly indicate that researching divestments by multinational companies is extremely difficult. Multinational companies have erected a remarkably prickly shell to protect the details of their divestment behavior. It seems that few topics are as sensitive and secretive in the business world, and the reason for this sensitivity is not difficult to discover. Divestments, because of their typically damaging effects on workers and communities, are, to use the words of a former British prime minister, "the unacceptable face of capitalism." Neither companies nor governments are particularly anxious to expose that face to rigorous scrutiny.

My original intention in this study was to collect both aggregate data and case-study material. Statistical manipulation of the former would enable some generalizations to be made on the causes and consequences of divestment, and the case-study material would hopefully bring to life the factors and processes involved by in-depth description. I was forced to abandon the first approach because of the dearth of available data. Even in countries with sophisticated data-collection capacities, the published data on flows of foreign investment are not sufficiently disaggregated to distinguish cases of withdrawals as defined in this study.[1] Also, as a rule, the subsidiaries of multinational companies are not specially categorized in manufacturing censuses. Rather, they are treated as indigenous. The few Western governments that conduct special censuses or surveys of multinational companies do not publish data on divestments, even if they collect such data. Such information is classified as confidential.[2]

I considered and rejected the option of employing the survey method to build my own aggregate-data base for two reasons. First, a high probability existed of a very low response rate. Second, the obtained responses would tend to eschew detailed answers and would be difficult to check for reliability. The experiences of Sachdev and Torneden emphasize the strength of these problems. For example, Sachdev compiled a list of 143 multinationals that appeared to have divested subsidiaries. His request for cooperation received a positive response from 21 companies, 29 did not respond, and 87 refused.[3] Similarly, Torneden contacted 189 U.S. multinationals that had experienced one or more divestments and received a response from only 38 companies.[4] Moreover, each researcher experienced difficulty in obtaining detailed answers to important questions in the interviews. Sachdev notes that executives had little reserve in discussing the matter in general terms but were "cautious over the question of giving specific statistics such as the profit or loss figures in the period before disinvestment, the extent of the disinvestment operations, and proceeds of disinvestment."[5] Torneden, for several years an executive for a U.S. multinational company, commented along the same lines:

> It was found that good interviews were generally obtained from corporate executives who were my business acquaintances, while interviews held with executives who were previously unknown to me generally produced incomplete and superficial findings.[6]

A review of Sachdev's experience in interview situations gives the reader the strong impression that somewhere deep in the cases lurked some secret waiting to be uncovered. For example, Sachdev reports that "before each interview the author was virtually asked to take a pledge not to make any information public or give any indication whereby a company could be identified."[7] He adds that he was occasionally grilled as to his plans and aims for the study and describes the atmosphere during the interviews as "frequently tense and diffused" and clouded by an air of suspicion.[8] At the conclusion of the interviews he noticed also that executives "frequently appeared relieved . . . and in almost every case expressed the desire to be informed of the study as soon as possible."[9]

The virtual nonexistence of aggregate data on divestments and the protectiveness and discomfort that multinationals exhibit when researchers delve into what they seem to consider their private domain compelled me, of necessity, to concentrate on the case-study approach. As the research progressed, I became convinced that in the current primitive state of our knowledge, the case study was in fact the most appropriate and fruitful approach.[10]

The next decision centered on the number of cases to research and what selection procedure to adopt. As almost always is the case, such decisions are strongly guided by the constraints of available resources. Within these constraints, and following the principle that more than one case is analytically preferable, I opted to research three cases. A plurality of cases invites comparative analysis by bringing into relief similarities and differences on several dimensions and leads toward generalization. Again, resource constraints prevented the development of a fine scanning mechanism to catch most of the cases of withdrawals, to categorize them meaningfully, and to select a handful of cases representing specific types. More pragmatically, I selected three cases that were important and significant enough to have been widely reported on and that differed on several dimensions that could be relevant in analyzing the causes of international divestment. For example, differences exist in the nationality of the parents and subsidiaries, in the organizational structure of the multinationals, in the industrial structures in which they operate, and in the outcomes of the three cases. The selection of important cases could be a source of bias, tending to portray divestments as important economic and political events surrounded by extraordinary publicity and controversy. This aspect will have to be kept in mind, though from an extensive reading of the press, most cases of divestments apparently are perceived as important and controversial, especially in Western Europe and increasingly in the United States.[11]

Two data-collection tactics were available for researching the three cases: (1) I could go directly to the top of the decision-making hierarchy, the center of the cases—that is, the parent—or (2) I could begin at the bottom and periphery and work up to the top and into the center—that is, from worker representatives and local politicians to subsidiary management and to parent executives. I call this tactic the "long-march" approach because it suggests that getting inside knowledge of how large companies operate is usually a long, slow, step-by-step process. The advantage of the first tactic is that it avoids wasting time pursuing unnecessary or irrelevant lines of inquiry and would, as it were, get at the story in one fell swoop. The disadvantages, however, are more substantial. Least serious was the possibility of rejection since the other option remained. More important was the following dilemma: On what basis could I, as an outsider, form specific and penetrating questions, and what credibility could I attach to the answers given? The second approach promised a way around these problems. The long march would lead to an accumulation of details from a wide variety of sources that could be employed both to generate specific questions for executives to answer and to corroborate their responses. Moreover, such detailed knowledge would act as a powerful lever on executives to grant frank interviews so as to present their side of the case. In this way, I hoped to obtain a detailed, balanced, and comprehensive picture of the cases.

I began by forming an overall picture of the cases by scanning newspapers, journals, government documents, and other publicly available material, as well as by interviewing a few journalists and academics who in one way or another had some familiarity with the cases. I then contacted involved persons who would be the least likely to be nervous and secretive about the issues. Trade-union officials, shop-floor-worker representatives, and politicians were all forthcoming and eager to tell their side of the story. An invaluable source of information proved to be ex-executives of subsidiaries who were employed prior to, and at the time of, the withdrawal attempt. These men possessed enormous quantities of highly detailed and sensitive information, which they were sometimes willing to divulge. Perhaps a useful rule of thumb for researchers is to expect conflicts to have occurred within the multinational company between various management enclaves and to try to exploit them to obtain specific information. I also contacted the current management of subsidiaries. Armed with a great deal of detailed information, questions, and positions and views of various parties, I approached the parent. I expected them to be more willing to participate in order to present their side of the case and more forthcoming to someone who had accumulated much data. My experience with this tactic proved fruitful. In one case I did try, as a small experiment, an early and direct approach to the parent. I received no reply after several attempts at contact. Much later, after extensive research and interviews with ex-executives, I tried again and this time received an eager acquiescence to meet, though I had the impression that the purpose was to find out how much I knew rather than to provide me with additional information.

The reader will nevertheless become aware as the case studies are read that an unevenness exists in the depth and range of material presented, both in an overall respect and in particular aspects (for example, transfer pricing, industrial relations, product strategy). This is an unavoidable corollary of the case-study approach. Sometimes one penetrates deeply at one point and shallowly at another depending on a combination of factors, not least among them being luck. For example, in the case of Imperial Typewriters, which was completely closed in 1975, it was very hard to trace executives of the liquidated subsidiary, and when one was, he refused to cooperate.

Much of the information collected in this research was from primary records and firsthand verbal accounts. I was fortunate enough to gain access to several company and government documents that had not been prepared for public circulation. In such cases, the information obtained is likely to be highly reliable for it is unlikely that either companies or governments would engage in self-deception. I also conducted thirty interviews in person and several less-important ones by telephone and letter (I received two refusals, one of which was later reversed).

In the interviews I tended to avoid general questions and concentrated on specific and concrete questions. In this way I hoped to avoid empty posturing and philosophizing, resolve discrepancies in the data, fill in gaps in knowledge that existed from the documentary phase of the collection, and elicit the fine inside details and flavor of the cases. I found that the quantity and quality of data I elicited bore a close association to the degree of knowledge of, and sophistication about, the cases I was able to project. Once I had gained access, the interviewees were usually helpful and open. The interviews lasted, on average, two hours. None was less than one hour long, some took the better part of a day, and some spanned several days. Additional information or clarification was often requested by follow-up letter and/or phone call. I rarely used a tape recorder, mainly to avoid the sense of unease that a tape recorder can create. Contrary to the experience of Sachdev, the issue of confidentiality rarely came up, primarily, I suspect, because my previous legwork had rendered the issue inapplicable. Occasionally during an interview, I was asked to note something "off the record," and this I did. Otherwise no assurance of confidentiality was offered and none sought. Nevertheless, I have not identified the names of the interviewees or their specific job titles because of the delicate nature of some of the material. This is the only aspect of the cases that is disguised.

I was confronted by a serious problem when I came to evaluate the quality of the data I had collected from these primary sources. The nature of divestments is such that it encourages a high degree of special pleading from management and workers. Management often claimed that market circumstances, worker intransigence, and government policies were responsible for problems at the subsidiary that was chosen to be divested, and bypassed issues such as transfer pricing, insufficient investment, bad management, and so on. Workers emphasized precisely these neglected aspects and ignored others such as, for example, a decline in demand and low productivity. Workers and their allies also tended to defend their position by attacking, sometimes unfairly, the performance records of other subsidiaries in the group. For example, one aspect of their defense strategy was to show that no exceptionally problematic situations existed at their subsidiary. If both sides can be accused of bias and selectivity in the public presentation of their respective cases, we should, in all fairness, take note of the vastly different circumstances compelling each to do so. Multinational companies typically decide to divest after a long and careful review process often carried out by "special divesting units." These groups prepare for the withdrawal by developing strategies and battle plans, sometimes to the point of engaging in mock question-and-answer sessions to simulate anticipated difficulties with government, the press, and unions.[12] All this is done to safeguard the image of the company as a socially responsible actor or, as one manager put it, to allow the multinational to withdraw "looking beautiful and smelling like a rose!"[13] In contrast, workers often have to prepare their initial defense in a matter of hours, with the purpose of preventing closure and saving jobs.[14] I point this out not to argue that different standards of verification should be applied to each group but to help us understand the asymmetry in their respective situations.[15]

I tried to overcome the problems created by the special pleading by at all times subjecting the data to the normal verification procedures. Where relevant documentary data existed, I cross-checked interviewees' answers to reconcile discrepancies. I also cross-checked data in documents from various sources. Crucial and sensitive pieces of information gained in one interview were cross-checked by bringing them up for comment in another interview and sometimes at different times within the same interview for consistency. However, some points inevitably could not be cross-checked and on some issues conflicting positions were evident. Such problems are indicated in the text. Having experienced the prickly shell at first hand, I can only echo the recommendations and demands of many other researchers, politicians, and worker representatives. Legislation is urgently needed to expose the inner world of multinational companies to public scrutiny.

Finally, I add a word about the presentation format adopted in the next three chapters. Each case is presented in a fairly straightforward and chronological manner, beginning with an overview, according to the following format:

Reasons for investment;

Factors affecting the development and performance of the subsidiary:
    Competition,
    Product strategy (including research and development and marketing),
    Industrial relations,
    Transfer pricing,
    Profitability.
Reasons for the decision to withdraw;
Process of withdrawal;
Consequences of withdrawal.

I have used this format to enable readers to follow the development of the cases, as far as is possible, as they occurred. However, although I have tried to present as much of the evidence as possible, I have not avoided interpretation.

Notes

1. The U.K. census of overseas transactions, for example, defines *disinvestment* as a "lower net indebtedness" to the parent company. This could include the repayment of various kinds of credit and the remittance of profits. It is, therefore, dangerous to use these data as indicators of closures or sales. See the Department of Industry, *Business Monitor: Overseas Transactions* (London: HMSO, 1971), p. 5.

2. My request for access to the special surveys conducted by the Department of Industry elicited the response that information on divestments was buried in the original responses and was not easily accessible, and in any case it was strictly confidential. I also contacted the Department of Employment in the United Kingdom that, since 1975, has collected data on significant redundancies or layoffs (which may indicate a closure). However, they informed me that they did not record the nationality of companies and that their names were confidential. The contacts were made in 1977.

3. Jagdish C. Sachdev, "A Framework for the Planning of Divestment Policies for Multinational Companies" (Ph.D. diss., University of Manchester, 1976), pp. 118-25.

4. Roger L. Torneden, *Foreign Divestments by U.S. Multinationals: With Eight Case Studies* (New York: Praeger, 1975), p. 114.

5. Sachdev, "Framework for Planning of Divestment Policies," p. 125.

6. Torneden, *Foreign Divestments,* p. 39.

7. Sachdev, "Framework for Planning of Divestment Policies," p. 125.

8. Ibid.

9. Ibid., p. 121.

10. For a good discussion of field methods, which are similar to case-study methods, see W. Richard Scott, "Field Methods in the Study of Organizations,"

in *Handbook of Organizations*, ed. James G. March (Chicago: Rand-McNally, 1965), pp. 261–304.

11. In Western Europe, union pressure has largely been responsible for publicizing the issue of divestments. Factory occupations, representation to governments, and complaints to bodies such as the OECD have raised public awareness. In the United States, some unions and progressive research and community groups are in the process of trying to get plant-closure legislation passed at the state and federal levels. A survey of some of the work being done can be found in Ed Kelly and Lee Webb, *Plant Closings: Resources for Public Officials, Trade Unionists and Community Leaders* (Washington, D.C.: Conference on Alternative State and Local Policies, 1979).

12. Business International, *International Divestments: A Survey of Corporate Experience* (New York, 1976), p. 84.

13. Ibid., p. 87.

14. For example, both the Chrysler and Imperial work forces had to prepare their cases over a weekend. In fact, the Chrysler workers informed me that they were still working on the document presenting their case for survival on the train to London, where they hoped to meet members of the government.

15. I have to point out also that both the media and the government rely heavily on company and, to a lesser extent, union sources for their information. The media and official sources tend to reproduce the information and positions in the original sources, and given the unequal control of information, it is not surprising that they are dominated by company-generated data. In particular, I think it unfortunate that the development of close, almost clientlike relations tends to inhibit journalists from probing and confronting publicly stated positions.

4 Leyland Innocenti

The original Innocenti company was family owned and composed of three divisions: (1) machine tools, (2) motor scooters, and (3) cars. Its spacious production site is located in the northeast suburb of Milan at Lambrate. By the late 1960s the car division had become increasingly crucial to the viability of the whole company. For personal reasons the Innocenti family decided to terminate its involvement in the company. The machine-tool division was sold to the Italian government's holding company (IRI), and the equipment of the scooter division was sold to India.[1] In 1972 the car division was sold to British Leyland,[2] thereby altering the concessionary agreement that had existed between the two companies for several years into an ownership relationship.

The new parent, British Leyland, was one of the most investigated and analyzed companies in Britain. As the only indigenous motor manufacturer of any consequence, it attracted considerable government and press attention. In 1975, as the crisis at Innocenti was coming to a head, British Leyland was nationalized as a desperate measure to avert the bankruptcy of a company with a work force numbering 200,000 and a sales revenue of just under £1.9 billion. It is, therefore, of passing but not insignificant interest that the multinational that liquidated Innocenti was itself half dead and legally owned by the state on behalf of the British people.

The relationship between British Leyland and Innocenti culminated in a prolonged crisis in 1975 that resulted in the eventual liquidation of Innocenti in November 1975. During 1975 the case spawned massive demonstrations by Italian workers protesting the demand by British Leyland for a one-third cut in the work force (1,700 layoffs) and the threat and act of liquidation. The case was responsible for not a little violence, as when the personnel director of Innocenti was shot in the legs and a British Leyland showroom in Rome was bombed, allegedly by the Red Brigades. It led to the occupation of the Lambrate factory by the workers, and it compelled the Italian government to set up a financial holding company, IPO GEPI, to take over dying concerns. As of 1978, Innocenti was still producing minis, on a reduced scale, under a licensing arrangement with British Leyland that was to come up for renewal in 1979. The plan was for Innocenti, using government money, to gradually convert to the production of specialist cars (for example, Maserati) and motor cycles. At the time of writing, Innocenti's future still looks uncertain.

Much of the data in this chapter come from interviews with people who participated in the major events described. All the interviews were conducted between August 1977 and January 1978 in London and Milan. Invaluable information came from ex-executives of Innocenti and British Leyland who were intimately involved in most of the major decisions concerning Innocenti's fate. Other useful information was obtained from top executives employed at Innocenti and British Leyland. Members of the Innocenti factory council and a leader of the regional office of the Federazione Lavoratori Metalmeccanicci (FLM) also provided relevant information. Unfortunately, because of the delicate nature of the information obtained and for legal reasons, it is not possible to identify the names of the interviewees. Various documentary sources were also used. Of particular importance was a document produced by the Innocenti factory council, the FLM, and sympathizers in the Milan area entitled *Alternativa Produttiva.*

Reasons for Investment

The merger of Leyland and the British Motor Corporation in 1968 created an international giant. However, it was a giant with several weaknesses. For example, it lacked a rational, integrated manufacturing and model policy at home and suffered from a chaotic distribution system in Europe. Nevertheless, it was the single most important contributor to the export side of the balance of payments and as such occupied a pivotal position in the British industrial scene.

Plans were made in the ensuing years to increase sales in Europe, particularly in the European Economic Community (EEC), the most dynamic large market in the world. At that time Britain was not a member of the EEC but was making determined efforts to gain entry. British Leyland planned to increase sales in Europe by 80 percent from 1971 to 1975. It hoped to achieve a 5 percent market share in each individual European market.[3] One of the top executives at British Leyland's head office recalled that the aim was to go from a 1 percent overall share to a 4 percent share of the European market in three or four years. However, the EEC was a trading block with tariff barriers. British Leyland hoped to circumvent some of the barriers with assembly facilities located inside the EEC. It had acquired a facility at Seneffe, Belgium in the 1960s. The Authi plants in Spain, though not inside the EEC, were acquired in order to increase the assembly capacity on, and exports to, the continent.[4] Innocenti was inside the EEC and would, with Seneffe, offer the possibility of expanding output to meet the projected increase in sales. In fact, the continental assembly facilities would supply about 300,000 of the projected 450,000 unit sales.[5] Thus, we have the scenario.

In the early 1970s British Leyland's total continental sales—that is, the whole of Europe excluding Britain and Ireland—were about 200,000 units. Of that, well over 55,000 were accounted for in Italy. That figure represented

4 percent of the third-largest market in Europe. Italy was therefore the crucial market. It represented a solid base from which to build, and the purchase of Innocenti was a necessary step to safeguard and, if possible, expand that market share.

Specific Reasons

The car-assembly division of Innocenti was developed around a concessionary agreement with British Leyland. The latter supplied kits of the mini model that Innocenti then assembled and sold on the Italian market. The arrangement had proved satisfactory to both parties. In May 1972, possibly for tax reasons, a newly created legal entity, Innocenti Autoveicoli SpA, was sold to British Leyland for L2 billion (lire) (£1.2 million sterling).[6] The newly born company had no earnings record, the basis on which most purchase prices are agreed. Instead, it was bought on a net-assets basis (often called an assets deal), and the balance sheet made very pleasant reading. The acquisition was enthusiastically promoted by the press and the executives of British Leyland. It was a "bargain," a "knock-down" deal, British Leyland's "European success story."[7]

For the L2 billion British Leyland acquired some very substantial tangible and intangible assets.[8] Some of the tangibles included ninety acres of land, the plant, and equipment. In addition, it acquired 115 Innocenti dealers throughout Italy. Less tangible but of extreme importance, the Innocenti mini came with marketing advantages. For example, it possessed a superb quality image and outsold every other car in Italy except Fiats. The Innocenti mini had a chic, glamorous image that allowed it to carry a premium. These marketing advantages, largely built up by the efforts of Innocenti, gave British Leyland a fairly exclusive niche in a market that supported an aggressive pricing policy and therefore the extraction of large profits.

That was not all, however. British Leyland paid the L2 billion with money borrowed locally. Also, as the result of a clause in the purchase agreement, British Leyland was entitled to a share of the trading profits from January to May 1972. By 30 September 1972, British Leyland was able to repay the loan, and have something left over, from the earnings of Innocenti itself. To brighten the cash-flow side of the deal even more, L5 billion in hire-purchase repayments (personal-credit repayments) was due to flow into the company. Although the terms of the deal seem surprising, a variety of personal and special situations could prompt a seller to offer a firm for sale at a price less than the present value of the expected stream of profits warrants. These situations would include the desire for immediate cash, the undervaluation of the shares by the market, and tax considerations.[9]

In hard money terms, therefore, British Leyland bought a company not by reaching into its own pockets but by using the money of others and simultaneously finding its own pockets full.

On the other side, British Leyland's being a huge multinational seemed to offer advantages to Innocenti. Innocenti could tap the research-and-development facilities, the pool of managerial talent, the European network of dealers, and the financial muscle of the parent. These are the primary benefits associated with being part of a multinational. To what extent Innocenti benefited from the turbulent association will be manifested in the following pages. Certainly in 1972 the overall feeling was that Innocenti was set for expansion. A document presented to the workers and signed by the British and Italian management of Innocenti explicitly set out the intentions of the new owners to introduce a new model in the shortest possible time, increase production by the most efficient use of labor and machines, and export a share of production.[10] Interestingly, one prescient voice of alarm was raised at the time. A shop steward at Innocenti pointed to the dangers inherent in Innocenti's status as an assembly operation reliant on only one model and warned that the new management planned to take everything it could get from the subsidiary to push production to its limit without any prearranged replacement solution to use in the case of a production stagnation or market crisis. He added, "The day when the foreign master wants to pack up his bags, wild horses could not stop him, especially when he has factories in various other countries."[11]

Summary

The major strategic reasons for the acquisition were the need for British Leyland, first, to defend its largest European market and, second, by using the facilities at Innocenti, to increase production and sales in Europe from within the EEC and therefore to eliminate the tariff disadvantage. Innocenti's image and dealership network counterbalanced the dismal reputation of British Leyland in Europe for inconsistent and irregular delivery, inadequate quality, and a chaotic dealership network. To cap it all, Innocenti was acquired for nothing and promised to generate substantial sums of cash.

British Leyland's acquisition of a foreign subsidiary was not the result of a careful and systematic selection among the alternatives. It was merely the grasping of an immediate opportunity that was pragmatically fitted into the multinational's European strategy. As with Chrysler, British Leyland's entry into Europe was late and followed by many years the entry of the international leaders (Ford and General Motors). Moreover, it contrasted sharply with the orderly and systematic expansion of the Ford Europe empire. Again, as with Chrysler, as we shall see in the next chapter, its entry was not based on oligopolistic advantages in such things as management technique, production technology, and marketing skills.

Factors Affecting the Development and Performance of the Subsidiary

Competition

The motor industry conforms to the main characteristics of oligopolistic industries. Production is concentrated in a few companies in each national industry. Gradually, but with an increasing tempo, the force of competition and the imperatives of mass-production techniques have reduced the number of companies in each national industry. The United States has three dominant manufacturers; some European countries have one or two manufacturers, often supported or owned by the state; and others have no domestically owned motor-manufacturing company. The spread of the three American giants, and the fantastic export assault of the Japanese motor companies, has produced in the international arena a situation of intense competition. However, it should be noted that the export-penetration success of Japanese vehicles has been uneven. For example, in the United Kingdom total sales rose from 5,160 vehicles in 1970 to 107,922 in 1975 (a 9 percent share of the market). In Italy, due to import quotas, only 1,000 cars from Japan were allowed in, and in France and Germany, as of 1975, the Japanese only attained 1.5 percent of the market.[12] A sorting-out process is under way in the form of mergers or substantial cooperative agreements across national boundaries that could lead to an internationally stable oligopolistic pattern. Some recent examples of mergers and collaborative agreements are the takeover of Audi-NSU by Volkswagen, of Daf by Volvo, the merger of Citroen and Peugeot and their recent takeover of Chrysler Europe, and the marketing agreements between American Motors and Renault and the manufacturing agreements between British Leyland and Honda.

In addition to the success of Japanese companies in export markets, particularly in weak, unprotected ones such as the United Kingdom, the downturn in the Western economies has had particularly serious consequences. A depression tends to have a significant effect on vehicle purchases since the demand for vehicles is highly sensitive to the rate of growth of real personal disposable income—that is, it is a purchase the consumer can put off.[13] Faced with a stagnant or slowly growing market for vehicles and severe jostling for market share, companies are forced to be cost competitive.

In the motor industry, a fairly capital-intensive industry, the most common way to depress costs is to produce in large volumes and to operate as close as possible to full capacity. An alternative but partial method (partial because it only accounts for a part of the production process) is for a company to buy parts from large manufacturers. In the first case the economies of scale are taken directly; in the second, indirectly.

Although the unit profit margin (price minus cost) is determined by oligopolistic pricing standards and by the control of costs achieved in production and purchasing, it is the whole marketing effort that will realize those potential profits. Product policy and the marketing effort assume central importance. Motor manufacturers must be able to provide the public with a full range of models that are changed regularly (even if only cosmetically—for example, the chassis and engine remain essentially the same but changes are made in body style and interior finish) if they wish to compete in the big league. The product must then be sold to the public. Advertising must differentiate the product and build up its special image. A comprehensive dealer network must be established and satisfied because one of the ways to increase market share is to win over the dealers of a competing company.

British Leyland, formed from the merger of two companies in 1968, entered the international arena full of disadvantages. One of the companies that was merged, British Motor Holdings Ltd., was itself a sprawling conglomeration of smaller plants. In fact, as late as 1975, there were still 55 manufacturing plants.[14] In such circumstances it becomes impossible to achieve the economies of scale of, say, the Japanese manufacturers. Although British Leyland managed to cover the full range of market segments, it tended to have a more-dated set of models. In particular, the mini, introduced in 1959, was many years older than its rivals [for example, Renault R5 (1972) and Fiat 127 (1971)]. Also, though some sections of British Leyland did well in some overseas markets (for example, Bus and Truck), in the more-competitive car markets the company "had a poor reputation . . . for not keeping delivery promises, for shortage of parts, and for inadequate after-sales service."[15]

British Leyland suffered several effects from its weaknesses. Its domestic market share dropped from 40.6 percent in 1968 to 30.9 percent in 1975. In the same period the percentage of its output that it exported declined from 48.6 percent to 42.4 percent.[16] Its share of the European market increased, but only from 1 percent to under 3 percent for cars.

Nevertheless, in the period from 1968 to 1973 when the car market was expanding, British Leyland managed to earn a profit, albeit a small one. The profits earned were certainly insufficient to finance the massive investments that all commentators concluded was vital if British Leyland hoped to match the quality, cost, and productivity of its major rivals. With the depression of 1974-1975, the frailty of British Leyland's situation was exposed, and the company scurried to the government for aid to avert bankruptcy. However, British Leyland, as a fledgling multinational, was composed of several subsidiaries that were themselves engaged in a competitive battle with other manufacturers. It just so happens that the parent, British Leyland, was a weak and vulnerable multinational. Therefore, we must consider the extent to which the weakness of the multinational contributed to the weakness of the subsidiaries.

Innocenti was a small company in the Italian motor industry, accounting for about 3.5 percent of production as compared to Fiat's 75 percent in the 1970s. Innocenti was therefore compelled to rely on the economies of scale and resources of its supplier and then owner, British Leyland, and on its ability to "Innocentify"—that is, differentiate—the basic model with respect to performance and interior finish. The product had a high-quality image and carved out a niche for itself in the Italian market. This niche allowed Innocenti to adopt an aggressive pricing policy since the product and the market could bear it. By 1972, the year when British Leyland acquired Innocenti, the latter had achieved a market share of over 4 percent. Innocenti had a proved, successful record in the marketplace. By way of contrast, we should note that British Leyland products exported to Italy up to 1972 were bringing in a sales revenue equivalent to about 3 percent of the amount that Innocenti products were bringing.[17]

In 1973 and 1974, under increasing pressure from competitors entering rival models into Innocenti's exclusive niche, the company began to export more of its production and to produce another of British Leyland's models, the Allegro, so as to compensate for some of the lost sales of the mini. In other words, selling the mini on the Italian market became more difficult, and exports became increasingly important to the survival of Innocenti—they rose from under 1 percent of the sales revenue in 1972 to over 25 percent in 1974.[18] The Allegro model proved to be a disaster and just was not acceptable to the Italian market. Thus, according to executives at British Leyland, the fate of Innocenti was increasingly tied to the new model, the Bertone mini, that was to be launched toward the end of 1974.

However, at the very time that Innocenti was confronted with increased competition caused by the entrance of rival models produced by Auto Bianci and Renault, and at the moment it was to launch its new model, the car markets in Europe dwindled. Of particular damage to Innocenti was the drop in Italian car production to below 1968 levels in 1975. The demand for cars had contracted in response to the restrictive monetary policies and increased taxation the Italian government had instituted to reduce the deficit on the balance of payments in the wake of the quadrupling of the price of oil in 1973.[19]

When competition stiffens and markets contract, managers invariable become highly cost conscious. Unit labor costs were estimated to have increased by 20 percent in the private sector in 1974 as a result of stable employment levels, increases in wages, and decreases in production.[20] A classic squeeze occurred on profits, and the cash position of many companies was closely monitored. One of the reputed benefits of being part of a huge multinational is that the fate that befalls many small companies in a depression (bankruptcy) is avoided due to the cash reserves or the borrowing capacity of the whole group. British Leyland was unable to afford that protection to its subsidiaries and in late 1974 was itself on the verge of bankruptcy. If the story had ended there, with the closure of Innocenti and other plants and perhaps the whole group, then the case would require a different analysis. As it turned out, the government intervened in December 1974 and provided British Leyland an

estimated £95 million, partly in loans and partly in equity, to prevent bankruptcy. The government also ordered a comprehensive review of the company
to be undertaken by Lord Ryder, a respected industrialist. His task was to conduct an overall assessment of the company's present situation and future
prospects, covering corporate strategy, investment, markets, employment,
finance, and profitability.[21]

The government's actions clearly indicated its serious concern over British
Leyland, and it was common knowledge in late 1974 and early 1975 that the
company would be saved. In April 1975 the government announced its plans to
inject £2.8 billion into the company over the next seven years. With the access-
ibility of so much cash, it could not have been a cash crisis that caused the
liquidation of Innocenti.

There is little doubt that the combination of increasing competition and
depressed market conditions affected Innocenti. However, these conditions
of course affected all motor manufacturers. Costs were rising and sales were
down for all car companies. Given such universal conditions, we must ask if
any special factors at Innocenti singled it out as particularly vulnerable from
other companies in Italy and Europe. One executive insisted that high labor
costs put the product at a disadvantage in the markets of Europe. Another added
that Innocenti was operating at too low a level of output to break even—it had
to produce something like 100,000 cars a year rather than 60,000. Yet the
unions and an Innocenti manager knowledgeable about personnel issues
responded that Innocenti's wages and fringe benefits made it an average industrial employer in Italy. Moreover, a low utilization of capacity was common in
the depressed 1974-1975 years, although Innocenti truly had exacerbated the
problem when it hired an extra 800 men in anticipation of an increase in output that never materialized. That Innocenti faced problems is clear, but the
issues are whether these problems were of Innocenti's own making and so
serious as to require drastic action.

Innocenti assembled and sold one car: the mini (the Allegro had proved
unsalable). It depended totally for its survival on the mini's success. By 1974-
1975 its future rested on the new Bertone mini. If the car succeeded against
fierce competition in the markets of Italy and Europe, then Innocenti was
secured a future. It was entering the competitive battle in depressed times
with one weapon, and one weapon only. It was vital, therefore, that as much
engineering, marketing, and overall management effort go into making the
Bertone-mini project a success.

Abundantly clear is that a subsidiary as small and as dependent as Innocenti, competing against the likes of Renault, Fiat, and Volkswagen, is but a
front-line division in the battle, and without cover, support, and encourage-
ment it is doomed to fail. A subsidiary that is given a role that fits in the
overall strategy of the group and that suits the group's purposes and interests
cannot all of a sudden be cast alone to the forture of the marketplace. The

critical question becomes: How much of Innocenti's fate was determined by market forces and how much by administered decisions?

Product Strategy

The major criticism leveled at British Leyland by many commentators was that for many years it had underinvested in comparison to its rivals. The underinvestment was a crucial factor in explaining the company's low profitability, and its low profitability meant it was unable to undertake the massive investment it required to bring it into line with its competitors. To make matters worse, it paid out some £70 million in dividends out of the £74 million in profits it made between 1968 and 1974.[22]

One of the areas that suffered from a lack of investment was product development. By 1972 the mini, one of the revolutionary cars in Europe, was over twelve years old. It was, as I have pointed out, the most successful of British Leyland's models in Europe. Nevertheless, in the late 1960s and early 1970s, serious talk about a replacement for the mini was going on. In car-marketing terms, "novelty is an important factor in determining market share," although some executives doubted the wisdom of replacing a still-successful model.[23] In any case the decision was deferred, primarily because British Leyland could not afford the development costs. Then Innocenti presented British Leyland with the possibility of developing a modified mini at a fairly low cost. The idea was pressed hard by one of the first executives at Leyland Innocenti. A top executive at British Leyland's head office recalled:

> He said he could develop a new mini from the chassis upwards that might become *the* new mini. It was a sort of test. In a way, then, the mini project fitted into the European strategy, and since we couldn't afford it here at British Leyland, Innocenti did it because it could afford it.

Little doubt exists in my mind that the fate of Innocenti and of the relationship between Innocenti and the parent rested on the new-mini project. Virtually the whole of the investment undertaken at Innocenti went into the mini project. Lines were changed and extended to cope with the projected increase in output from 60,000 to 110,000 units, the press shop was largely rebuilt so that more of the body could be stamped at Innocenti, and all this was done with great haste. The new model was completed in eighteen months, a remarkable feat. Some people claim that it was done too fast and that under the timing pressure, problems were ignored or papered over. For example, although the presses were designed to turn out 80,000 or more bodies annually, the paint shop was inadequate for the flow so bottlenecks developed. All the detailed aspects of the project cannot adequately be assessed by an outsider. However, one essential issue concerned the controversy over modifications to the new mini, more-commonly known as the Bertone mini. The development program spanned 1973, the year of the oil crisis. The Bertone mini, designed as an up-market, premium small car, all of a sudden seemed a fragile conception in the price-conscious marketplace. Management had to decide whether to modify the car to make it more acceptable in the altered market conditions (for example, lengthen it and cheapen it by stripping out parts) or to press ahead to avoid a delay that could incur extra costs. Quite a battle took place on this question inside the multinational. Local management at Innocenti had gone so far as to prepare three mock-up versions of a modified Bertone mini and had estimated the cost of alteration to be £1 million sterling. That figure proved to be £1 million more than top management at central headquarters was willing to spend.

The unmodified Bertone mini was launched at the worst possible moment: in the trough of the depression in 1974. It was well received by the trade press, but for several reasons, which I discuss later, the new model never succeeded in the marketplace. It was not so much that consumers refused to buy it but that the central staff at British Leyland contrived so many obstacles and bungled so many possibilities that it virtually ensured the collapse of Innocenti. Even at this stage in the project, parent management had grave doubts over the car's viability and refused to give it a fair test in the marketplace.

One source of difficulty was the persistence of top-level-management conflicts. Innocenti suffered from personality and management-philosophy differences. Much of the impetus for the conflicts stemmed from the character of the first head of Innocenti. He chose to operate Innocenti in an independent, forthright manner, often avoiding the organizational staff stations in the line to the top. He was, as they said, "the chairman's man," picked and encouraged from the very top. He and Innocenti struck out on an expansionary, optimistic course at fast speed. He and Innocenti were thus seen as threats and rivals by the executives who headed the international division and by those in the central staff who monitored and planned the strategy and performance of overseas subsidiaries. I include now several comments made by present and former executives, not to dwell on the personal side of the squabbles but to vividly illustrate the climate and lack of managerial clarity in which the Bertone-mini project came to an aborted end:

> There were plenty of management jealousies over the mini project. British Leyland took the view that it was only them that could develop a new mini and not some foreign subsidiary with the chairman's man at the helm. They found every objection to the car: It was too long, it was too short, and so on. They argued they wanted a completely new car and not a compromise on the old mini. Its launch was squashed deliber-ately by British Leyland. It was never shown in many of the shows. They didn't show it to journalists. They didn't push it at all. You see,

the chairman and managing director before 1975 were for Innocenti and its head. He was their man—the Whiz Kid. He created lots of jealousy. The knives came out for him. He took terrible risks. He bulldozed the new mini through against lots of opposition from central staff at Longbridge. He was a very strong-minded person, and he trod on a lot of toes. He wanted Innocenti to be responsible to him only, and he wanted to bypass everyone and report back to the chairman and managing director directly. He and the financial director, who became managing director in 1975 when there was a major management reshuffle, were really incompatible.

The new top executives had it in for Innocenti. They stuck the knife in by refusing to let us sell in the U.K. They prevented the export of the mini. They really wanted to get out.

The new mini was introduced at a time when people were saying, in the press and in the company, that there were too many models and that it was necessary to reduce the range. Given that climate at management level, the launch of a new mini was upsetting too many people. Don't forget the first head of Innocenti had designed a new car with a good image, in eighteen months. There was the jealousy of the sales director over the competition it presented against his old mini. The central staff were against because it was another model. So, psychologically, there was a prejudice against the whole scheme but we pushed on with it. British Leyland, though, adopted a "you're on your own" philosophy which was ludicrous given we were an interdependent company and couldn't survive on our own within such a network.

Indirect lines of communication had been set up. The first head of Innocenti liked to be king, and a dichotomy situation arose. In the eyes of the managing director, the first head of Innocenti was still responsible for the launch of the new model, even though he had moved to head another division in the company. It's somewhere in print that he was responsible for its implementation. The project was understood to be his baby. The rest of operations came under the head of Europe and from him to International and then to the managing director. Clearly there was a conflict—dichotomy situation."

Given the distortions that inevitably arise in remembering such issues, a remarkable consensus exists among all the interviewees on several critical matters. For example, the new mini model never received enthusiastic and practical support, either in conception, production, or sales. It developed in a corner of the multinational in splendid isolation. As it entered the rather difficult world of 1974, however, it required the active support of the parent and all its facilities. At that time the policy and personal differences combined to thwart the launch, the export drive, and finally the very life of Innocenti. One top executive at British Leyland very forthrightly set out the main areas of controversy as they affected practical matters:

On the engineering side, the Austin-Morris-Leyland cars division didn't have any sympathy at all with the mini project and only helped in the modifications of the engines after intense pressure. Innocenti needed priority from Austin-Morris for the project and they just didn't get it. Remember, he was very arrogant and provoked lots of resentment and jealousy. It was reluctant cooperation at best.

On the sales side, the U.K. sales director vehemently opposed the entry of the Innocenti mini into the U.K. The arguments presented were a bit silly. Ironically, we are at this moment reconsidering whether to allow 3,000 to 4,000 Innocenti minis in.

On export marketing, the twelve or so national sales companies had individualistic views on whether to take the model or not. They were pressurized by the first and second heads of Innocenti to take the model, even though there wasn't central authority for this. So grand confusion reigned.

The export launch got confused at the end of 1974 so that it really occurred in dribs and drabs. The launch was half-baked. At the Turin Motor Show the reaction was quite good except for the headroom problem at the back. We didn't alter the headroom area because we felt the time for that decision had passed and we were onto another direction. By then we had decided it was no go. The Frankfurt Motor Show a few months later was also a disaster. There were debates within the company on whether we should show it there or not.

We also decided to exclude it from certain export markets because of its cost. The general problem was that costs were so much higher than in the U.K. that we could only put it into and encourage it in high-value markets such as France and Germany. Everywhere else it just wasn't economic.

Under probing he added:

Central staff didn't believe the 115,000 volume projected by Innocenti. Maybe 30,000 or 40,000 at home and 10,000 or 20,000 for export. In other words, they simply didn't believe he could do it. There were two opposed views on market size, and they simply did not support him. In addition, his car was too expensive. There was a premium of 15 to 20 percent on the Bertone mini against a U.K.-sourced mini. We needed 15 to 20 percent cost improvement in Italy to make it worthwhile.

This quotation and the ones before it forcefully bring into relief the ambiguities buried in the case. It is extremely difficult to disentangle causes and effects. Were the pessimists or the optimists correct? Could Innocenti have sold 100,000 Bertone minis, and would it have made a profit? Did the catalogue of obstacles pinpointed in the quotations inhibit and finally assure the destruction of Innocenti, or were they merely the expressions of justified doubts on the viability of the project?

What is clear in retrospect is that the acquisition of Innocenti enabled British Leyland to have a model-program tryout on the cheap. Innocenti would develop a new mini using funds largely raised on the local capital markets and would act as a front-line division bearing the costs and risks. If the attempt proved successful, then British Leyland, and probably Innocenti, would benefit. If it did not, then British Leyland would cut its losses at an early stage by sacrificing one of its parts.

In reality, however, the management of Innocenti took itself more seriously and posed more threats than much of the management in the parent company could tolerate. The front-line division went further than was anticipated. It demanded more money, time, and other resources than the parent was willing and, for a period, able to provide. Slowly but surely British Leyland withdrew its support systems and Innocenti was sacrificed. Moreover, throughout the period, the policy of British Leyland toward Innocenti was confused and occasionally contradictory. On the one hand, there was investment and a policy to develop the facilities and the output capacity, as well as a liberal attitude toward Innocenti's attempts to export. On the other hand, there was, if not a policy, certainly an attitude in some quarters that impeded the development of Innocenti. At best, British Leyland provided grudging support and showed a degree of tolerance. By 1975 the attitude had turned into a policy of contraction and/or liquidation of Innocenti.

I will explore the reasons for the change of policy in the coming pages. However, we must remember that, though a rational basis existed for the change, nonrational factors also existed. As a commentator on the case observed, "If the same financial criteria were applied to the volume car operations in the U.K., they too, would be for the shop."[24] Clearly, acrimonious personal conflicts were involved, as the following comment by one of the top executives at central headquarters once again confirms:

> I know that the new chief executive was against Innocenti. As finance director he felt it was out of control, and he raised the question of its survival. The chairman before 1975 supported Innocenti and its head. Clearly the bloodbath, with the many changes in top management and the elevation of the finance director to the top position, changed everything.

Looking at the marketing aspect in more detail, we note that the problems over the Bertone mini evolved out of the sharp contrasts that existed between the marketing performances of British Leyland and Innocenti. British Leyland suffered from a very weak distribution system in Europe, and much of its product range was not acceptable in the competitive markets of France, Germany, and Italy.[25] Indeed, the only successful model in its range in Europe was the long-established mini that in 1971 accounted for a remarkable 70 percent of the group's sales on the continent of Europe.[26] Against this rather dismal background the marketing policy of British Leyland toward Innocenti developed. The Innocenti mini had earned an excellent reputation in terms of its design, quality, and performance, but as it began to sell in several European markets, it came into competition with U.K.-produced minis. Thus, when the Bertone mini was launched at the end of 1974, it presented a potentially formidable threat to the U.K. sales company. Since Europe was a hard enough market to penetrate, and since 70 percent of sales there were accounted for by the mini, it is understandable that the U.K. sales director would not want added problems and competition from a little subsidiary in Italy.

Vehement opposition from the U.K. sales director also succeeded in excluding Innocenti products from the British market. Innocenti had wanted to export 3,000 to 5,000 minis to help it cope with the depressed market in Europe. Although technical arguments were presented (for example, a substitution effect would occur rather than additional sales), the consensus among the persons interviewed in this study was that management rivalry and jealousy had sustained the opposition.

In addition to preventing some Innocenti exports, the launch of the Bertone mini occurred in dribs and drabs. The car had problems of design and cost, which central staff continually pointed out. However, a company with serious intentions should have reacted by making changes to the car and by stepping up the marketing effort. British Leyland did neither. The central-staff view was that the model was too expensive, that the model would not sell well in Europe—certainly not as well as Innocenti argued—and that the marketing effort should not be strong. In fact, British Leyland went as far as using biased advertising slogans such as "Beware of Imitations" in advertisements for U.K. minis in a clear reference to the Bertone mini, exhibiting at only one foreign show and then only showing the most expensive model (two were produced), and finally, prohibiting all exports from July to September 1975. According to a top executive at Innocenti, orders for the Bertone mini from European sales companies were placed that could not be filled because British Leyland had instructed Innocenti not to export. Several views are available on the reasons for such a remarkable step. For example an executive at central headquarters explained that the cecision was "a way to put pressure on the Italian government, telling them in effect that we wouldn't export until the problem (i.e., the demand for 1,700 layoffs) was solved." A former Innocenti executive considers that this step was taken more to force the unions to agree to the 1,700 redundancies:

My view is that it was done to put strong pressure on the unions, to show them that British Leyland meant business and that if they couldn't sell abroad then Innocenti was dead. It was really the end of Innocenti if they couldn't export.

However, another Innocenti ex-executive believes that it was designed to add the final blow to a reeling Innocenti:

> In 1975 with the Ryder Report, there was a management change which led to a change in philosophy. This was really the crucial turning point. The new management was dedicated to the export of cars. And with Innocenti selling a mini largely made in Italy and invading markets in the south of France, Switzerland, etc., then that was a threat to the U.K.-built minis, which had less of a good image. British Leyland categorically stopped Innocenti exporting. It actually instructed the sales offices in Paris, Switzerland, etc. not, on any conditions, to buy the Innocenti mini. Now the loss of about one-third of sales meant losses were inevitable. A cynical view with which I agree is that they knew it would mean tremendous difficulties for Innocenti, but they said, "Tough, make it in Italy or die."

The executive at headquarters acknowledged that the U.K. car division feared the prospect of competition from Innocenti minis but insisted that the cost premiums attached to the Innocenti model priced it out of the market anyway.

Thus, while Innocenti had control over the marketing in Italy, in Europe it was at the mercy of decisions made in Britain. For two years British Leyland's policy toward Innocenti exports was neutral, and according to Innocenti executives, any advances that were made in that period were the results of the efforts of Innocenti. With the launch of the Bertone mini in late 1974, the policy of British Leyland became contradictory and finally destructive. The blocking of all exports was part and parcel of the coup de grace. It was, one executive commented, like "feeding a sick patient strychnine."

Industrial Relations

British Leyland accompanied its demands for 1,700 layoffs in early 1975 with several accusations leveled at the workers: too much absenteeism; low productivity; and high labor costs, particularly that part accounted for by social benefits. These factors combined to inflate costs some 35 percent over budgeted figures, according to an executive at headquarters, and were important contributory factors in British Leyland's final decision to withdraw.

The workers carefully countered every charge, to the point of drawing attention to the similarity between divisions in Britain and Innocenti in these problem areas. In the process, they undermined British Leyland's case. For example, they provided the following comparative facts and figures.

Strike Hours. Comparing the strike hours per employee of Innocenti and

British Leyland (England) they showed that whereas the latter's record was 54, 50, and 81 hours in 1970, 1971, and 1972 respectively, Innocenti's was 39, 28, and 78 hours respectively in the same years.[27] In fact, only in contract-negotiating years, which is every third year, do any significant number of strikes occur in Italy. Otherwise, as both unions and management agreed, relations on the shop floor are quiet with few, if any, job-control disputes. Workers tend to follow central union direction, and demands for improved working conditions are linked to pay in the three-yearly negotiations, which are comprehensive. The provisions reached in the agreement are usually adhered to. This contrasts with the continuous shop-floor negotiations in British plants.

Absenteeism. Absenteeism was a problem at Innocenti. It was higher than at British Leyland and, according to the Innocenti personnel director, higher than at other medium-sized firms in Italy. Many reasons account for this (for example, some workers have two jobs), but the workers argued that absenteeism tends to be higher on the continent of Europe and that the low incidence of disputes more than helps redress the balance.

Duration of Production-Line Work. The workers calculated that six hours and fifteen minutes of an eight-hour day were worked on average at the main English plants as against six hours and seventeen minutes at Innocenti. The duration of work was longer at other Italian motor manufacturers (for example, Fiat and Autobianchi), but this was due to different technological conditions.

Labor Costs. The workers calculated that the average hourly salary of Innocenti and Longbridge (one of the main British Leyland assembly plants in England) workers was L2,635.25 and L2,673.25 respectively—that is, 38 lire an hour less at Innocenti. However, an additional L1,166.17 must be added to the Innocenti salary for contributions to family allowance; pension fund; workers' housing; and insurance against tuberculosis, unemployment, accidents, and so on. These compulsory payments increased Innocenti labor costs over English labor costs by about 44 percent.

It is important to grasp the different nature of remuneration in Italy. What is called the "social wage" is of extreme significance and represents a norm in Italy. In an Innocenti manager's words, "When you work you have everything; if you don't work you have nothing—no health benefits, assistance, and so on. Therefore, in reality, it is impossible to dismiss workers in Italy." So, although Innocenti's labor costs were higher than English ones, they were average for a medium-sized Italian manufacturer.

From this discussion, and from comments made by most of the interviewees, there is little doubt that Innocenti was an Italian company characterized by average (for its size and industry) industrial-relations conditions. The one truly serious problem centered on the 800 workers recruited in late 1973 in preparation for the planned increase in production that never took place. The workers, at any rate, could not be blamed for that.

The averageness of Innocenti in the Italian context ceased to be important when British Leyland decided to reduce overseas capacity as we shall see in the section on the reasons for the withdrawal. At that point Innocenti was thrust into the international arena, and its costs and productivity were compared to another British Leyland subsidiary, Seneffe, in Belgium.

Transfer Pricing

Given the state of our knowledge of transfer pricing, particularly illuminating is a look at firsthand reports on the practice and attitude of executives of multi-nationals toward transfer pricing. To penetrate the secrecy that surrounds a multinational's intracompany pricing policy is no easy task, so a legitimate question is: How was it done in this case? In effect, I used two tactics whose success owed as much to chance as to design. First, I was fortunate enough to interview ex-executives of Innocenti who were willing to divulge a fair amount of information, and second, by asking a series of questions framed in such a way that they appeared more knowing than in fact they were, several executives (ex- and current) revealed collectively more than each intended individually.[28]

Once it was established that I knew that British Leyland had manipulated transfer prices, the consensus was that such manipulation is part and parcel of the management of multinational companies. One former financial executive commented on the pricing policy of British Leyland to Innocenti:

> It was certainly not an arms-length transaction because the subsidiary did not have alternative suppliers—they were locked into British Leyland. Of course, though the pricing was totally unfair, ultimately it should not make a great deal of difference to an integrated company where and how profits are taken.

It is only necessary to add that it does matter to the tax authorities, as we shall see shortly.

Like all good multinationals, British Leyland, in the flush of its serious entry into Europe in the late 1960s and early 1970s, set up a subsidiary in Lausanne, Switzerland. British Leyland International Services (BLIS) was to become the focal point of many international financial transactions. A top Innocenti executive observed:

> Switzerland was used as an invoicing office as it had lower tax rates than the U.K. But, of course, that was all set up in the expectation that British Leyland would make profits. Mostly they didn't so they didn't have to pay tax in the U.K. anyway.

Nevertheless, the pricing policy that applied to the supply of kits from the car division of the company at Longbridge, England for assembly at Innocenti became a matter of considerable debate and conflict between the managers of Innocenti, Longbridge, and central staff in London.

Forty-eight to 58 percent of the value of total purchases by Innocenti were accounted for by purchases from British Leyland itself.[29] Several former executives of Innocenti claimed categorically that British Leyland's pricing policy to Innocenti was either patently unfair or irrational or both. Some typical comments made by former executives on the transfer-pricing policy are given to illustrate the extent and nature of the conflicts and the unequal position that a subsidiary often finds itself in vis à vis the parent:

> I felt that British Leyland [was unfair to] Innocenti on price. For a start, the warranty charges were too high. They simply pulled rank on us and overcharged us. They made an accounted profit at Longbridge, and it kept going up on both the mini and the Allegro models. They actually increased their margins as time went on; right till I left the company in 1976 they were still doing that. They didn't make such a profit elsewhere but looked for it at Innocenti.

> Whenever we pushed up our prices within the bounds of competition, British Leyland took our margin away.

Here are some responses to the question of the extent of profit or over-charging that Longbridge made on the supply of kits to Innocenti.

> I don't know the exact figures, but we had several arguments over it. In fact, over the mini and the Allegro we went to internal arbitration at central staff. We lost each time, partly because the arbitrator was a Longbridge man. We had less weight than them.

> They made a £1.4 million profit on the sale of the kits, in addition, of course, to the trading profit that was shown in the first year. I'm sure it went up after that.

It is important to be as specific as possible here and to examine in some detail the amounts involved and the methods used. All the interviewees agreed that the way British Leyland chose to manipulate the transfer price was through royalties. The total kit price was around £330 in late 1974. Of that, £30 was designated royalties and engineering fees. If one takes an average of 60,000 kits supplied to Innocenti each year from 1972-1974, then the sum taken via royalties and engineering fees is about £1.8 million or between L2 and 3 billion a year. A conservative estimate (if one assumes the margin remained constant) is that in the years 1972-1974, British Leyland made £5.4 million or about L8 billion in addition to the profits Innocenti made on trading (which I will examine shortly). British Leyland took royalties and engineering fees even in the crisis year of 1975.[30]

The simple reason why British Leyland chose to take its share of the profits via royalties and engineering fees rather than via the repatriation of profits can be found in the bilateral agreement between Italy and the United Kingdom, which excludes royalties and engineering fees from any withholding-tax liability.[31] Ironically, the Italian tax authorities chose to carry out one of their sudden, unannounced raids on Innocenti in October 1974. Apparently the raids have a theatrical quality—a group of men swoops down on all exists and seals all doors and file cabinets. Two sets of books were discovered—this, I was informed, is normal practice in Italy. Not surprisingly, the tax authorities queried the royalties and engineering fees, but for some reason only for the 1973 year. One of the executives involved in the investigations summarized the situation in this way:

> The Italian authorities argued it shouldn't be more than 2 percent of the value of the materials, and British Leyland was charging us 10 percent to 12 percent of the value. Probably it should have been £6 per kit and we were charged £30 per kit.

The issue was finally settled in October 1977, according to a top parent executive, with the company paying the tax authorities £100,000 or L170 million. The authorities had wanted L1 billion or 40 percent of the L2.5 billion charged in the 1972-1973 year. British Leyland claimed the engineering fees as warranty charges for the parts it was shipping to Innocenti. Innocenti and presumably the tax authorities disagreed, arguing that Innocenti should not be liable for the costs of replacement and repair due to faults arising on parts made at Longbridge. The response of an executive at the head office to questions on transfer prices was not to deny any of the allegations:

> Innocenti was constantly arguing over kit prices—on whether, for example, the prices should be gross or net of warranty charges. There were continuous changes in the policy on this as a result of arguments and compromises. They, of course, don't know the prices Longbridge charged to New Zealand and other subsidiaries on similar kits.

The last comment is meant to indicate that Innocenti had no way of conclusively proving unfair treatment.

Two distinct issues, in fact, intertwine and are subsumed under the transfer-pricing relation. First is the question of tax avoidance. Clearly, British Leyland carefully arranged its intracompany pricing in such a way as to avoid tax in Italy by using royalties and engineering fees, and it planned further to reduce its tax liability in Britain by routing the invoices through Switzerland. Second are the issues of a fair price and a fair split of the profit margin between different parts of the multinational. These issues need not always coincide with tax considerations. Internal considerations may determine intracompany prices or the split of the margin. For example, such considerations include political factors such as the heavier weight a part of the group carries in the headquarters, attempts to bolster the performance of certain subsidiaries or divisions of the company by nonmarket success, and the desire to understate profits to avoid trade-union pressure for higher wages. In the case of British Leyland, three former executives claimed Innocenti was unfairly treated because of the influence the Longbridge division exerted at central headquarters. It is also possible to conjecture that as British Leyland's divisions and subsidiaries operated as profit centers, there may have been some wish to bolster the performance of the ailing central division by overcharging more-successful subsidiaries that could bear the overcharging.

There is no doubt that for several years Innocenti's privileged position in the super-small-car segment of the market enabled Innocenti to make a trading profit and British Leyland to make an additional profit on the supply of kits. A former upper-level executive at Innocenti, in answer to a question on whether British Leyland had been using Innocenti as a cash cow (that is, as a subsidiary that is profitable and whose profits are used elsewhere in the company with minimal reinvestment in the subsidiary), responded:

> No, I don't agree with that assessment at all. Look, British Leyland was milking Innocenti for years before anyway. While the market could take it and everyone was making money it was fine. But when sales began to disappear, then Innocenti began to worry about the pack price.

So why did British Leyland not change its pricing policy toward Innocenti in the difficult period of 1974-1975 when the latter was facing a multitude of severe problems? One possible explanation is that British Leyland had made the decision to snap the ownership link with the subsidiary because the trading position was becoming highly unprofitable and was preparing itself for a restoration of a licensing and supply contract with new owners. A former upper-level executive suggested:

> British Leyland wanted to sell. Therefore, they didn't lower the kit price because they were thinking ahead to the arrangements with the new buyer and the licensing agreement. The real buyer shouldn't know the real price because they wanted to keep shafting Innocenti.

Perhaps this view of British Leyland's motivation assigns too much foresight and calculation to the actions of this multinational. An alternative explanation could well be rooted in what another former executive called "British Leyland's disease—its irrational pricing policy."

Although several former executives thought the transfer-pricing issue sufficiently important to mention and often to voluntarily expatiate on, most of them declined to assign it critical weight in the constellation of reasons that led to the liquidation. They viewed the transfer-pricing squabbles as part and parcel of the shenanigans that underlie all multinational financial transactions. It may have deprived Innocenti of bigger margins, or led to internecine conflict that debilitated management confidence, but it was not instrumental in the demise of Innocenti. It is not the stuff of life and death of subsidiaries.

I have to concur with these views. The manipulation of transfer prices does not directly affect the creation or the realization of profit. It affects the distribution of the profit between countries and subsidiaries. Although Innocenti operated with two sets of books, multinationals, no matter what is or is not shown on the books of the subsidiary, clearly know or have a record of the total contribution of each subsidiary to the group's performance. Thus, if the transfer prices whittle away the trading profits of the subsidiary, the multinational will or should know what part of the total profits originated from the subsidiary. This shift in the distribution of profits is, as has been shown, motivated by the desire to minimize tax, to bolster the performance of ailing divisions for managerial reasons, and to manipulate the public face of performance for strategic reasons or for other financial reasons such as being able to take advantage of movements in the exchange rate. Certainly several union representatives in each of the three cases covered in this book had grave doubts about the publicly stated performance figures, sometimes to the point of suspecting the multinational of manipulating the profit/loss figures via the transfer-pricing mechanism to facilitate a closure or running down of the company. However, the shenanigans contained in the transfer-pricing relation and, more generally, in the international financial relations between subsidiaries and entities of the multinational illustrate, in striking fashion, the weakness fashioned out of the ignorance of tax authorities, local management, and working communities. The true picture exists in the shadowy world of the minds of tax accountants and financial directors where one can find a set of figures for the public, the Italian tax authorities, and the British tax authorities. These paper machinations are sources of power. They have the quality of business magic and are controlled by latter-day financial priests. The mystification and secrecy that envelops such international book transactions will have to be exploded if workers and governments are to have sufficient and reliable information on which to base their policies. Several solutions to the problem have been proposed, the most effective but least likely being that all host governments cooperate and jointly tax multinationals, thereby rendering the whole process of profit transfer irrelevant.[32] A recurrent theme in this book is the way that multinationals, according to calculable criteria, can maintain and exploit the differences and divisions that exist among various parts of the world in, for example, tax and wage rates, at the same time that they are unifying much of the world in, for example, marketing, products, and laws concerning capital mobility.

Profitability

Innocenti operated as a profit center. Although no certified published data exist on the financial performance of Innocenti, I was able to obtain sufficient inside information to piece together the following picture. As table 4-1 shows, Innocenti made a profit in fiscal years 1972-1973 (September to September), made a small profit or broke even in 1974, and made a sizable but unknown loss in 1975.

The return-on-investment measure is really meaningless in this case, at least in the early years, as Innocenti was bought, in book terms, for so little (L2 billion) and in cash terms for nothing. In fact, in the first year of British Leyland's ownership of Innocenti, the rate of return on investment was about 200 percent, assuming the investment was L2 billion. Assuming the investment in Innocenti was between L15 and 20 billion until late 1974 (figures cited by former executives) and that trading profits for the same period were L10.9 billion, then the rate of return on investment for the period was at least 50 percent. Some confusion existed on the rate of return on sales. On a turnover or total-sales value of about L70 billion, the rate for Innocenti was about 6 percent in 1972, declining thereafter. In contrast, according to the annual reports, British Leyland, in the same years, averaged a rate of return on sales of between 2 and 3 percent. If one remembers that British Leyland was also making over £1 million per year in accounting profits on the sale of kits to Innocenti, then the latter's contribution to the group's profits as expressed in the consolidated accounts was well beyond expectations based on its proportion of sales and capital employed.

Two clear conclusions can be drawn from the limited financial data. First, Innocenti's performance outshone that of the group's. Second, until late 1974,

Table 4-1
Pretax Profit and Loss: A Comparison of Innocenti and British Leyland

	Innocenti		British Leyland
Year	Lira (billion)	Pounds (millions)[a]	Pounds (millions)
January-September 1972	4.5	3.0	31.9
September 1972-September 1973	3.9	2.6	51.3
September 1973-September 1974	2.5	1.67	2.3
September 1974-September 1975	(unknown)[b]		(76.1)

Source: Interviews with former executives of Innocenti and British Leyland annual reports 1975, 1976.

[a]Converted at an exchange rate of 1,500 lire to the pound.

[b]Figures in parentheses indicate losses.

as indeed no one denied, Innocenti was in good financial health. The controversy centers on the reasons for, and the extent of the problem in 1975.

The press, probably reflecting British Leyland press releases, made a great play of the loss that Innocenti made in 1975 and the injection of L15 billion, or £10 million, by British Leyland to cover the losses. The *Wall Street Journal* actually reported that this sum ($21.4 million) had gone "down the drain."[33] Not one of the ex-executives accepted the L15-billion figure. Their estimates varied between L9 and 12 billion. Moreover, an unusual consensus existed on the purpose of the transfer and injection of funds. One former executive can speak for the rest:

> It is completely impossible that British Leyland put in 10 million pounds or 15 billion lire in July 1975. Probably what happened was that an amount was put in and taken out. So real, net put-in was nothing. They diverted money to Italy to pay the group creditors, which was essentially Longbridge. So in essence it was a book transaction with British Leyland paying themselves.

I dwell on the the 1975 figures because the £10 million was uniformly quoted in the press and was used in the propaganda battle over the period of 1975, when redundancy and liquidation were at issue, as evidence of the hopelessness of the situation at Innocenti. The facts of the matter are less clear than much of the press would have had us believe. The press, therefore, joins the government and the unions in its heavy dependence on large companies for information on vital matters.

A slight paradox exists in the financial relationship between British Leyland and Innocenti. On the one hand, British Leyland agreed to a substantial capital-investment program at Innocenti even though much of the funding was financed from Italian sources—for example, the trading profits of Innocenti and loans from Italian banks. Nevertheless, the parent contributed by issuing more shares in Innocenti to itself and by extending credit to the subsidiary by delaying the payment terms for kits supplied from England. On the other hand, British Leyland manipulated the transfer price against Innocenti and in the latter period of the relationship delayed and frustrated the launch of the new model, the fruit of the investment program. The paradox is partly resolved when technical factors such as taxation rates are considered. The remainder of the paradox is explained by the confused, almost contradictory policy that various management enclaves pursued. At the very least, the claim could not be made that Innocenti had been liquidated because of a poor financial record.

Reasons for the Decision to Withdraw

Nearly all the material necessary to work out a plausible explanation of the closure is contained in the previous sections, and in a sense, all of it is relevant to the outcome of the case. However, in this section I select out and pull together the most important factors leading to the closure decision.

The depression of 1974-1975 was a familiar enough phenomenon in many ways, but what was unusual was the severity of the depression. Throughout the capitalist world it was a time for retrenchment. Business failure was widespread, unemployment rose, costs were paired, and strategies reexamined. That is the big picture, the context in which the Innocenti case came to a head. But the very universality of the economic depression forces the question: Why British Leyland and why, of all British Leyland's parts, Innocenti? The specific and general meet here.

British Leyland was a large but sick company. Faced with companies as large or larger than itself, companies that had a more-modern plant and equipment and a more-rationalized structure, it suffered in competition from low productivity and high overheads. Investment per man was abominably low. The social relations of production were characterized by a high frequency of conflict and a chaotic bargaining structure. Working at low levels of capacity utilization, its cost curves often diminished its margins to zero. Abroad it had mixed fortunes. Though some divisions did well (Truck and Bus, Special Products), its car division had dismal export performances. Its overseas subsidiaries were almost always the smallest in whatever market they were located. For example, looking at the 1973 figures, in Italy Innocenti produced 63,000 cars as against 205,000 by Alfa and 1.5 million by Fiat. In Spain Authi produced 40,000 cars as against 358,000 by Seat, 166,000 by Renault, and 63,000 by Chrysler.

By early 1975 British Leyland was approaching bankruptcy. Its cash-flow position was acute, and it had exhausted its ability to borrow money. In these conditions a discussion of the reasons for the liquidation of Innocenti becomes straightforward. However, no one in the company, the press, or the government believed that a temporary cash-flow problem would lead to the death of British Leyland and the loss of 200,000 jobs and hundreds of millions of pounds of export revenue. So, although its weakness conditioned much of British Leyland's actions, this weakness was not a decisive element in the decision to liquidate Innocenti. By December 1974 the government had initiated a review of British Leyland, and by April 1975 the Ryder Report had been published. It recommended the injection of £2.8 billion in the course of seven years—a massive transfusion—and the nationalization of the company. British Leyland had a new lease on life.

Indeed, by 1975 when Innocenti was under review, the pressing need to act out of desperation and weakness no longer existed. The Ryder Report envisaged an invigorated and competitive British Leyland challenging its rivals in all parts of Europe. The strategic questions thus became: What would be the estimated market size? What level of production would be needed to supply the markets? Where and how could the production and sales targets be met? British Leyland took a pessimistic view of the future demand as did many other specialists in the field. For example, one study estimated that sales of cars in Western European markets would only reach the high 1972-1973 levels by 1980, and they projected a 25 percent over capacity in the area until 1985.[34] With a reduced or stagnant market, British Leyland must have decided that it had spare capacity. From that conclusion followed the one that some of that spare capacity had to be removed. The following is how a top executive described the strategy:

> The aim as described in the Ryder Report was expansion, and money was to be spent on marketing. Ryder aimed to go from 2 percent to 4 percent of the European market in three or four years via exports using the United Kingdom and Seneffe. We planned to supply Europe by increasing the capacity at Seneffe (Belgium) and the United Kingdom. *Innocenti seemed like excess capacity, at least until the post-1979 era. We felt we didn't need it for four to five years* [emphasis added].

This statement is most crucial. It drives home the point that in the multinational headquarters, forecasts and plans determined a cut in production capacity. The next question is: Which part of the multinational should be run down or closed? From an economic point of view, an assembly operation is more dispensable than a full manufacturing facility. It is more marginal to the company's operations and therefore causes less disruption when liquidated. It is, in the words of an FLM leader, an "empty box." Clearly, since the Ryder Report envisaged massive changes in the company that would require both the cooperation of the British work force and government money, a dramatic closure and large layoffs had, as far as possible, to be avoided in Britain. That left Seneffe and Innocenti.

Several interviewees reported that a direct life-and-death comparison of Innocenti and Seneffe was made with studies comparing costs and productivity. By 1975 Seneffe won hands down on nearly all points in the comparison. It is very hard to find any reference to Seneffe in the press, and the executives said very little about it. By all accounts, the subsidiary had not had a strike for as long as people could remember, it consistently churned out cars close to its programmed targets, and it had low absenteeism. In response to the question why, a British Leyland executive could only say: "They work harder." Also, of course, Belgium's political climate was far less volatile and violent than Italy's. Several interviewees mentioned that the shooting of the Innocenti personnel director, Valerie di Marco, in 1975 acted as a catalyst and confirmed everyone's belief that Italy was just too dangerous a place in which to stay to do business. Seneffe, closer to Britain geographically, with a good, quiet, almost humble record as a subsidiary, would be saved and perhaps expanded. Innocenti would have to go.

In chapter 2 I mentioned the possession of alternatives and the ability to compare as crucial and distinguishing features of multinationals. In this case and in the case of Imperial, the availability of alternative production facilities able to supply markets previously supplied by the divested subsidiary was vital. No company will lightly terminate its involvement in a country if that also means losing important markets. The multinational carefully and meticulously prepares for the closure and the supply of the closed subsidiary's markets. Also, as much as the multinationals publicly profess that they adapt and fit into the local environment, particularly the local labor market, in critical situations they adopt a comparative international perspective and set of standards.

The workers and unions at Innocenti took great pains to rebut the arguments of British Leyland on the cost, productivity, absenteeism, and strike record of Innocenti compared to factories in Britain. They and a personnel director of Innocenti repeatedly emphasized the conformity of Innocenti to the Italian industrial context. It was not an oddity; it was a fairly typical employer. A top executive at the head office responded: "Look, that is not our concern. We compared it to Seneffe and it was far more expensive to make cars at Innocenti."

The comments of former Innocenti executives on the main reasons for the closure reinforce the conclusion that the decision to liquidate was a fundamentally strategic one and had little to do with conditions at Innocenti. For example:

> Wage costs were higher at Innocenti than at Seneffe, though it's true they weren't higher than at other Italian car companies. Fringe benefits were very high in Italy, especially compared to Seneffe. For example, the indemnity-fund provisions were very generous. The market was depressed and the car wasn't right post-oil crisis, but I agree with the unions that everyone was suffering and that a serious way out was to redesign the car. One can make a fair case for the labor-cost argument, absenteeism, and so on, but the decision was a fundamental one, taken well in advance at a high level.

and what was the fundamental decision?

> They reviewed the group strategy for ten years ahead. They decided that given the crisis in the car market following the oil crisis that the group had too much capacity. They looked at the whole of their European operations, compared Seneffe and Innocenti and chose Seneffe. They took the view: Let's cut our losses today. They certainly didn't make much effort to make a go of the company.

> All that stuff about labor costs, poor productivity is rubbish. There was no more difficulty at Innocenti than there was at British Leyland U.K. There were no special, distinguishing, harmful features at Innocenti. We ran it as it had been done, in a very Italian spirit. The decision has little to do with such issues. It was a very fundamental decision.

To repeat, that Innocenti was chosen for closure is a result of a constellation of factors. For example, Seneffe came out better in comparisons, the new-
mini project was seen as a threat and as requiring money and effort to become
successful, and in any case British Leyland was heading in another direction with
public money to develop its own far-grander-mini project.

Innocenti was used by British Leyland in a way that hardly corresponded to
the interests of its work force or of Italy. For three years as British Leyland
benefited, so did Innocenti in spin-off terms. However, as things got difficult,
British Leyland withdrew. An ex-chief executive pinpointed the danger that is
always inherent in a multinational dependency relationship:

> Innocenti could never have contemplated the new-mini project without
> the support of British Leyland—a big boy behind it. It would have been
> folly for a company like Innocenti to have put all its eggs in one basket
> like we did. I would never have done it if British Leyland hadn't been
> behind us.

Process of Withdrawal

British Leyland's Tactics

By late 1974 and early 1975 major reviews and reconsiderations of Innocenti's
position clearly had been undertaken. I was unable to obtain the precise dates,
but one executive at central headquarters recalled that early in 1975, perhaps
in February or March, "a shock-troop team was sent out to check over the whole
company" because:

> The cash flows that Innocenti was sending us just did not look believ-
> able at all. We considered them suspicious forecasts. In particular, we
> thought them too optimistic on the sales side. The company was show-
> ing signs of absorbing enormous amounts of cash.

The report of the task force indicated that the company was in bad shape, and
a top executive was sent out to resolve some of the problems.

Many of the interviewees suspected that this executive went to Italy to
liquidate. British Leyland offered the government and unions this choice:
If the latter accepted 1,700 redundancies out of the work force of 4,700 and
reduced production to 40,000 from 60,000, and if British Leyland were lent
about L14 billion (£9 million) by the government at low interest rates, then
British Leyland would guarantee to stay for another two years. If those conditions were not accepted, then Innocenti would be liquidated. We should note
that these demands were made public in July 1975, a couple of months after
major changes had been made on the board of directors of Innocenti.[35] These
changes clearly presaged a new and different policy toward Innocenti.

The suspicion that British Leyland really intended to liquidate is supported by the position the company took. Many of the interviewees stressed that 1,700 redundancies in one go is unheard of in Italy—that it is unacceptable to ask for them and even more fantastic to expect to get them. A union leader commented that 1,700 redundancies would amount to the "biggest redundancies in a single Italian company for twenty years."[36] A top executive at headquarters acknowledged this view in answer to several questions. He accepted that it was highly unlikely that 1,700 redundancies would be acceptable and commented that their negotiating position was "totally rigid. We wouldn't negotiate on it. We didn't move," and he added, "A strong healthy company can afford to play around. British Leyland couldn't afford to ride it out." However, I have already discounted the basis of the weakness thesis for the closure in the immediate post-Ryder Report period in 1975.

The discussions and negotiations continued throughout the summer, and a temporary solution was agreed in late August, to last for three months, whereby the 1,700 reduction in the labor force would be rotated among the whole work force with the government supplying 80 percent of the salaries of those laid off. Throughout this period British Leyland presented its case publicly. Innocenti was losing huge sums of money, each car sold was losing the firm L400,000 (£270),[37] productivity was disastrously low, and fringe benefits such as canteen subsidies were far too high. Also, according to British Leyland, the company had to be slimmed down to meet the tighter markets, and labor costs and productivity had to improve. To nudge the negotiations along and perhaps to further aggravate the financial position of Innocenti, British Leyland stopped all exports from July to September. It was a show of strength, a signal to unions and government telling them in effect, "We control the markets."

In October, British Leyland publicly threatened to liquidate Innocenti unless the redundancies were accepted, and it specified the date when the ultimatum would expire. Throughout the month of November, British Leyland extended the date of liquidation in response to pleas from the government. In mid-November, Valerie di Marco, the personnel director of Innocenti, was shot. Finally, on 26 November, British Leyland put Innocenti into liquidation. Negotiations continued into 1976 on a rescue plan for the company, and in May 1976 "Nuova Innocenti" was created from the remnants of the old concern. British Leyland was still legally and economically involved, though in a reduced capacity, as a supplier of kits for the mini and as the controller of distribution for Innocenti products in Europe.

Workers' Response and Tactics

Most of the decisions affecting Innocenti were made by the management of British Leyland in Britain. Other than in the discussion of production relations, the workers and their representatives have lurked in the background of this presentation. In a sense they have been given the role of passive elements, a sort of blank slate on which the multinational script is written. Things get done to workers, sometimes for reasons that are known to them and sometimes for unknown ones. Their reactions, for rarely do they take the initiative, are determined and conditioned by the level of consciousness and organization that exists among them. The fate of the workers was not considered in the calculations that led to the decision to liquidate. In fact, not once in the interviews with executives did they mention the fate of the workers as a factor in the decision-making process.[38] The workers' reactions, however, were taken into account in the formulation of the tactics.

The Innocenti workers, therefore, had to organize their own defense and strategy. In each phase of the process they attempted to counter the moves of British Leyland and also developed their own lines of attack. The workers' response to the demand for redundancies was unequivocal. They rejected the demand totally and undermined British Leyland's either/or tactics. They argued publicly and to the government that British Leyland had no intention to stay on any permanent basis and that its demands were designed "to weaken and divide the workers, preparing the ground for their defeat."[39] British Leyland, they claimed, was proposing a gradual and less-dramatic pullout that would involve the reduction of the company's size for two main reasons. First, if the whole of Innocenti as it then stood was bought by, say, Fiat (which had in fact bought Authi plants from British Leyland in Spain), that would represent the aggrandizement of a British Leyland competitor in European markets. Second, British Leyland was hoping to reduce the economic and publicity impact of closure by spreading it out while obtaining cheap loans from the government, again thereby maintaining some of Innocenti's market shares while other supply arrangements were being made, and not appearing to be socially irresponsible.[40]

Whatever the validity of these arguments, apparently the Italian government accepted them. An executive involved in the negotiations attests to the tactical success of the workers in destroying the credibility of British Leyland's avowed intentions: "The government and unions worked together. The government didn't take us seriously. It did not believe our intentions were to stay. In this respect they followed the union's view." In addition to that countermove, the Innocenti workers aimed to secure a strong commitment on the part of the government to save or support the work force in its entirety and as a working unit.

To that end the workers organized conferences, marches, and meetings; distributed pamphlets; and propagated the image of British Leyland as the arrogant colonial master threatening to disrupt the lives of Italians. They organized, with the FLM of Milan, a half-day strike of some 300,000 metalworkers.[41] A conference was held in late September and was attended by several unions. They obtained the help of academics to rebut, point by point, the charges of low productivity, high labor costs, and the efficiency of operating at 40,000 output, and they accused British Leyland of neglecting Innocenti, of managing badly, and of manipulating the launch of the new mini.[42] They referred to one of the executives from London derisively as "Sir" and accused him of acting "like a viceroy in India" or like a "grand liquidator." One union leader, in England to drum up support from British shop stewards and unions, is quoted in a major newspaper as saying:

> The working class does not bow down to threats. The hands of the clock cannot be turned back, and nor can we be. Workers are not pieces to be added or removed from the productive machinery according to whether that machinery is going well or not.[43]

The unions referred to the threats made by British Leyland as "typically colonialist and humiliating for Italy."[44] All in all, whereas British Leyland hoped to deal with the matter quietly, the workers ensured that the Innocenti case remained constantly in the full glare of public and media attention. Sympathy was invariably tilted toward Innocenti. One executive, now out of the group, castigated the behavior of British Leyland in an article in a conservative weekly periodical. Commenting on the appointment of an executive who had recently liquidated Authi as the British Leyland special negotiator in Italy and on the demand for redundancies, he observed:

> As the Italians saw it, one might as well appoint a hangman to negotiate for a condemned man . . . The plain fact is that it is simply not on in Italy, with the highest level of unemployment in Europe at present, for any group of union representatives to accept and get accepted by their members an enforced redundancy of one-third of a company's work force. In attempting to force through the impossible, Leyland has succeeded in projecting for itself the unacceptable face of international capitalism and in embarking on a battle which the unions could not afford to lose.[45]

The Economist headlined an article on the case, "The Innocenti Suffer with the Guilty as the Foreigners Leave."[46] Indeed, as the article points out, throughout 1975 there were cases of multinational companies' considering or carrying out redundancies and closures. A union leader commented: "The Innocenti case occurred at the same time as other union struggles with multinational companies in Italy. Therefore, the struggle of Innocenti symbolized a struggle against multinational colonialism."

Following the liquidation announcement, the Innocenti workers occupied the factory. Although several other instances of factory occupations occurred in Italy in the 1970s, a member of the factor council claimed in an interview that this was "the first case to involve and mobilize the local community and population." The purpose of the occupation was "to maintain the factory as a unit and to pressure the government and other parties to find a solution," and the most important aspect of the struggle was "to involve the population, the political forces, and the unions. We were together and there was no doubt about it."

Workers from Innocenti visited schools and factories everyday to publicize their case. They were able to reach a high level of sustained mobilization of their resources, and their success in this area was an important factor in pressing the government to find a solution. The occupation did not cease until April 1976 when a solid agreement to continue production was reached. In addition to being effective mobilizing tools, occupations also tie up large amounts of inventories. Reports indicated that 5,000 finished vehicles worth £7.5 million on the market were blocked in the factory compound. Indeed, British Leyland took out an injunction to free the cars and refused to pay the workers indemnity pay until the cars were released.[47]

Although the major thrust of the workers' campaign was to mobilize the Italian workers' movement to pressure the government to intervene, they also pursued the tactic of international union cooperation. This tactic proved very disappointing from the workers' point of view. Innocenti workers, from the very beginning in 1972, had assiduously worked to develop strong bonds and a flow of information with the shop stewards of British Leyland in Britain. Several meetings had occurred and delegations had exchanged visits.[48] However, at the critical time the Italian workers felt they had been let down. A union leader voiced the disappointment for the others.

> We didn't expect that the British workers would go on strike all over the place, but we thought we could build a movement of solidarity and that the problem of British Leyland U.K. was similar to ours and this would unite us. The only concrete result was a telegram.

In response to some skeptical questioning on the reality of their expectations of international cooperation, two workers' representatives firmly maintained that if the situation had been reversed, they and their colleagues would have voted for strike action. As it was, the situation was not reversed, and unfortunately, though I tried, I was unable to obtain the point of view of the British shop stewards on this matter. The Innocenti case does demonstrate the gap between establishing links and information flows and organizing effective internatonal action around concrete issues. Whether this was due to the parochialism of the British workers or the impracticality of effective action is impossible to say with certainty. However, the fragmenting and divisive nature of such crises that induce a "save-our-own-skin" attitude certainly plays a part.

One of the interesting aspects of the workers' campaigns in all three cases was the nature of the solutions they pressed their governments to adopt. The Innocenti workers' representatives argued forcibly for a rational and comprehensive solution. They acknowledged the depressed state of the car market and the new economic and ecological situation in the post-oil crisis world. They therefore pressed on the government the need to grasp the opportunity to restructure the whole transport section and alter the balance between private and public transport. They did not want the government to simply and indiscriminately pour money into dying concerns merely to save them at public expense. Innocenti, they suggested, could be converted to the production of socially useful products such as school buses and other light vehicles.[49] In effect, they were arguing for positive action rather than for the adoption of a defeatist attitude. For Innocenti to be closed, for the workers to be made redundant, for the community to experience higher unemployment was, in their view, wasteful of human and physical resources. If the product was no longer socially useful or salable, then they advocated the production of other products; if British Leyland could not or did not continue to own and run the concern, then some other owner would have to be found. However, unlike many other cases involving workers' resistance to closure, they did not press strongly for nationalization or for workers' control and management. Their demands, therefore, represented an attempt to limit, but not transcend, the established rights of capital to determine a whole series of production-related issues, including closure. The demands were progressive in that they called for publicly planned restructuring of industrial sectors to respond to changes in socioeconomic conditions without neglecting the needs of workers and consumers, and realistic in that they reflected the local nature of the movement.

Government's Response

The Italian government is reported to have adopted a friendly and supportive attitude to the workers' and union's position. A member of the factory council commented that "the government was in solidarity with the workers" but that it was for a long period too weak to provide a long-term solution. Instead it chose the politically less-controversial option of paying the workers a part of their earnings under a scheme called *casa d'integrazione guadagni*, which was designed to cushion the financial impact on workers that may result from a loss of job because of crisis conditions or industrial restructuring. Throughout the months from July 1975 to April 1976, the government sought to find a buyer for Innocenti or at least a company that would enter into a joint-venture type of operation such that the government would supply the finance, and the other party would undertake the management of the company. Several alternatives were considered, though how seriously is impossible to tell as the negotiations were kept secret. It was reported that Honda was interested in acquiring the facility. It seems fairly clear that Fiat, with a virtual monopoly in the Italian market, objected strongly on the grounds that the Japanese would penetrate the EEC's tariff barriers and then proceed to compete unfairly with European manufacturers. Simply put, Fiat feared the competitive threat posed by Honda.[50] The workers also rejected the Honda solution because, according to a member of the factory council, it was another multinational that could again imperil Innocenti's future, and the know-how and technology would stay in Japan with the factory remaining an assembly operation. Fiat, or course, as the leading motor manufacturer in Italy, figured in the negotiations. By all accounts it was willing to take over the factory and reconvert it to produce light commercial vehicles provided some very stringent conditions were met. It estimated the cost of reconversion at the very high amount of at least £80 million, and it wanted the government to finance a large part of that cost.[51] In addition, Fiat insisted on the freedom to renounce the commitment to build a bus factory in the depressed south of Italy, thereby in effect seeking to trade off the gain in employment in a favored region with a loss in a depressed region.[52] The high cost of the proposal coupled with the either/or nature of the conditions did not recommend this solution to the government or to the unions.

An agreement was finally concluded in March 1976 between A. de Tomaso, an Argentinian entrepreneur involved in the production of motor cycles, and British Leyland and IPO GEPI. IPO GEPI was a state-owned finance corporation formed in early 1976 to take over endangered industrial concerns and, more specifically, to pay the salaries of workers at Innocenti, Singer, Angus, and Ducati, all foreign-owned firms in serious trouble. Essentially, its role was to cover wage payments and to support private capital. The agreement led to the creation of Nuova Innocenti, to be owned jointly by IPO GEPI, de Tomaso, and British Leyland. The major proportion of the funds was to be supplied by the state through IPO GEPI. A. de Tomaso would organize the management of the factory, gradually introducing the production of Maserati cars, then Guzzi motorcycles. For three years, from 1976 to 1979, Nuova Innocenti would continue to assemble cars from kits supplied by British Leyland at a minimum rate of 40,000 a year. British Leyland also undertook to export about 10,000 cars a year for the new company. The workers would be rehired gradually over an unspecified time period, and those that had to wait would have their salaries paid by the government through the *casa d'integrazione* scheme (as of late 1977, 2,000 worked at Innocenti and about 1,500 were still on *casa d'integrazione*). Also, a whole series of detailed clauses in the agreement altered labor practices. In essence, the workers gave up some of their rest pauses because, as a union leader said, "We have accepted the need to produce more because now the situation is different and conditions are harder. So whereas we worked six hours and fifteen minutes in 1975, now we work six hours and fifty-five minutes."

The government therefore, like the unions, was a reactor to situations. For a whole set of complex reasons it was a weak government with a precarious hold on the political-economic situation in Italy. Under intense pressure, public money was used to pay workers on *casa d'integrazione* and to fund the re-development plans of de Tomaso. Without the pressure from the workers, it is less likely that any concrete action would have been taken.

Consequences of Withdrawal

The long-term strategy of the new top executives of British Leyland in 1975 required, among other things, a shift to supplying European markets primarily by exports from Britain. Tactically, the withdrawal from Innocenti had to be arranged in such a way as to preserve as much of its market share in Italy and Europe at the lowest cost possible. To that end the new executives opened their negotiating strategy by offering to maintain a reduced Innocenti work force that produced a smaller output for two or three years, provided the Italian government supplied Innocenti with cheap loans. This would ensure an orderly transition to other marketing arrangements. If that was not accept-able, as British Leyland probably suspected, then it wanted to convert the relationship with a reduced Innocenti into a licensing and supply contract, as in pre-1972 days. Again some British Leyland presence in the old Innocenti markets would be maintained. British Leyland bet on the belief that the Italian government would not let a company employing 4,500 workers disappear and that it would rescue Innocenti in some fashion. The multinational also calculated that any reconversion of the factory to make other products would take time and large sums of money. In that intervening period at least, British Leyland controlled some very strong cards. As it turned out, the agreement between the workers, the Italian government, and British Leyland met most of British Leyland's objectives. British Leyland was to supply kits to Nuova Inno-centi while the government supplied the funds for reconversion, covered any losses, and paid the 1,500 workers on *casa d'integrazione* 80 percent of their salary. In addition, British Leyland secured a 20 percent ownership share in Nuova Innocenti's Italian distribution company for three years. In return it gave Nuova Innocenti a 20 percent share in the distribution company that was to market British Leyland imports. Again, as it turned out, this was a more-favorable arrangement for British Leyland given that its imports were to account for only 0.5 percent of the Italian market as against 1.6 percent for Innocenti products.

British Leyland tried to paint a rather different picture of the consequences. A top executive claimed that the liquidation had been very costly with an exposure on the balance sheet of around £68 million, implying a potential book loss of some magnitude. It is always difficult to adequately assess the actual cost involved in liquidations because of the accounting conventions and taxation rules that are used. In the case of an internal liquidation—that is, of a subsidiary or division of a multi-unit company—the difficulties are compounded by the unavailability of published figures. The best we can do when confronted with the £68-million figure is to note several points. First, the figure could be a gross exaggeration. Second, some of the amount represented claims on Innocenti by suppliers, creditors, and workers through the indemnity fund. However, as several interviewees admitted, a large part of the claims of suppliers were of British Leyland on Innocenti. In other words, from the group perspective, this was a book transaction that involved no cash outlay. According to some of the interviewees, only the monies owed to workers under the indemnity-fund provisions represented cash outlays by the parent, and these were supposed to have been accumulated by charging them against earnings from earlier years. Third, losses sustained because of liquidation and that could be written off against taxes on profits in later years might encourage a parent to inflate the losses, especially if the parent was also the major creditor. Finally and ironically, such a financially unhealthy company was sold for between £17 and 18 million to IPO GEPI, the government-owned holding company. I think it worth stressing that a company bought for £2 million, which paid for itself in nine months and was profitable for two years, was one year later labeled a failure and sold in depressed times for about £17 million. It is hard to believe that such a sum could have been collected on the open market. All this discussion is not to suggest that the liquidation was costless for British Leyland but rather that it emerged from the affair with many of its interests protected.

Despite its tactically clever withdrawal, the three former executives of Innocenti and British Leyland believed that the parent had made a mistake. They criticized the liquidation as misguided. They argued that Innocenti was "on a good site with good machinery and excellent facilities," that British Leyland should have "taken it on the chin for a while, lengthened the car, and then had 50,000 extra vehicles competing against the Renault 5, the Ford Fiesta, and VW Polo." They all acknowledged the problems posed by the new mini in the new conditions of the market in which competition had intensified and whittled away margins. They accepted that some problems of labor cost existed, but they all expressed the view that the car could have been modified and that, in the post-1975 years, Innocenti could have been made profitable again. One former executive, writing at the height of the crisis, concluded, "Leyland has achieved the singular distinction of turning a limited short-term problem in to a total and probably long-term disaster."[53]

The consequences for the workers has to be seen in the context of the overall industrial and employment situation in Italy in 1975. Italy in that year, like many other capitalist countries, was in the deepest recession since the early 1950s, with industrial output down by nearly 10 percent.[54] Yet the official unemployment rate remained at the decade's average because of the strong economic and social inhibitions to dismissals.[55] In these depressed times, and faced with the threat of massive layoffs, the workers pressed not only for unemployment compensation but also for work that would maintain the Innocenti work force as a body engaged in socially useful production. In this, despite valiant efforts, the workers were only partially successful. The government refused to consider the workers' demands for the restructuring of the transportation sector and the production of socially useful products. Two years after the liquidation, the fate of the work force was still in doubt as the government repeatedly delayed supplying the promised funds for the reconversion of the factory.

One of the disheartening consequences for workers is that the sense of insecurity engendered by withdrawal situations tends to make workers more amenable to management demands for fewer safety and health regulations, fringe benefits, and less pay. As we saw in the previous section, the Innocenti workers were no exception. Nevertheless, their strong campaign, allied to that of other workers in similar situations, pressured the government to increase benefits to laid-off workers to 80 percent of foregone gross earnings and to form IPO GEPI. These advances are significant in that they were generalized beyond Innocenti to other threatened or closed factories. Not least, the Innocenti workers, by their refusal to accept the decisions of the multinational passively, became an example to other workers faced with similar difficulties of how to mount an effective and progressive resistance movement.

The government, using public money, managed to socialize much of the cost of withdrawal ("externalities" in the language of conventional economics), while allowing past and any future gains to remain largely private. For example, they paid L25 billion for the reconversion of the factory and paid out several billion lire in wages to workers on *casa d'integrazione.* They also lost various tax revenues. All these substantial actual and promised expenditures could perhaps have been better used to reorganize the transportation sector, as the workers had demanded. At least some lasting benefits may have resulted.

Conclusion

The details of this case provide a fascinating inside view of a large, ultimately unsuccessful multinational coping with recession in conditions of intensified competition.[56] Innocenti was subjected to recession and increased competition twice over. Directly, these forces reduced its markets. Indirectly, they were again experienced through the intermediary of the parent. The parent's strength or weakness could modify or exacerbate the direct effects on the subsidiary. Unfortunately for Innocenti, the parent was weak in production, marketing, and until early 1975, cash terms. In fact, Innocenti contributed more in marketing and finance to the group than could be expected from its size and the funds invested in it by the parent. This element has led one writer on the case to argue that British Leyland "exported" its crisis to the subsidiary, thereby producing the conditions that led to Innocenti's liquidation. Moreover, he contends that British Leyland, under government direction, chose to place the burden of the recession on Innocenti, not because it was the weakest part of the group but because it was politically more expedient.[57] This analysis is certainly congruent with the information presented in this chapter.

The Innocenti case also brings to the surface the importance of internal relations between various parts of a multinational company. Multi-unit companies are prone to internal conflict. The sources of this conflict are structural and occasionally personal. The personal conflicts and jealousies of some of the executives in the British Leyland group were particularly severe and acrimonious, and they damaged both parent and subsidiary.[58] Innocenti was unfortunate in that the management enclave that was its voice in group headquarters was outgunned when a rival and hostile enclave was elevated to the top positions. No doubt the management battles and their outcomes influenced the tasks and resources that Innocenti was assigned. Nevertheless, the persistence of internal conflict is rooted in the structural features of multi-unit companies.

The centralization of the power to decide on the allocation and distribution of resources within an organizational form in which many units are competing for favorable decisions becomes a key source of internal conflict. In the Innocenti case the subsidiary was able, for a period, to avoid being overdependent on central allocations. Its trading profits, which it largely retained and reinvested, and its aggressive leadership, which pushed it into European markets without formal approval from headquarters, enabled it to operate in relative independence. Above all, the protective umbrella thrown up by its friends in high places shielded it from competing units. The new-model-development program and the worsening economic conditions increased its dependence on group resources for engineering services, funds for investment and marketing, and greater access to export markets. At this time the competition between the units intensified as each unit tried to protect itself. When the protective umbrella was removed, Innocenti lost the battle.

Notes

1. For more on the history of Innocenti see Marino Gamba, *Innocenti* (Milan: Gabriele Mazzotta, 1976).

2. Although the name "British Leyland" was not adopted by the company until 1975, I refer to the company as British Leyland throughout. From 1968-1975 it was known as British Leyland Motor Corporation Ltd.

3. *Investors Chronicle,* 13 December 1971.

4. British Leyland bought an initial 49 percent share in Authi, which

was increased to 97.2 percent in 1973. By 1974 British Leyland was looking to get out of Spain completely, ostensibly because it could not afford the expansion plans the Spanish government insisted it undertake.

5. *Financial Times,* 21 April 1971.

6. I use the exchange rate of £1 sterling for L1,500 throughout the chapter. This was in fact the official rate between 1972 and 1974.

7. See, for example, Ray Dafter, "Innocenti Purchase to Cost Leyland about £3M," *Financial Times,* 8 May 1972, p. 36; *Sunday Times,* 7 May 1972; and *Daily Telegraph,* 8 May 1972. Different amounts are quoted in the newspapers for the purchase price. The price cited in the text is the one used in the original contract transferring ownership.

8. The ensuing account is based on interviews with ex-executives and the newspaper sources listed in the previous note.

9. See Edith Tilton Penrose, *The Theory of the Growth of the Firm* (New York: Wiley & Sons, 1959), pp. 158-61.

10. Innocenti Leyland, *Note Per La Presentazione Alle Rappresentanze Aziendali* (Private document, Milan, 1972).

11. Quoted in Enzo Pontarollo, "The Truth about the 1,700 Sackings," *Alternativa Produttiva* (Milan: FLM, 29 September 1975).

12. See Gene Gregory, "From Nissan with Love," *MSU Business Topics* 24 (1976):47-59.

13. Neil Young and Stephen Hood, *Chrysler UK: A Corporation in Transition* (New York: Praeger, 1977), pp. 250-52.

14. See Graham Turner, *The Leyland Papers* (London: Eyres & Spottiswood, 1971); and House of Commons, *British Leyland the Next Decade* (known as the Ryder Report) (London: HMSO, 1976).

15. Central Policy Review Staff, *The Future of the British Car Industry* (London: HMSO, 1975), p. 67.

16. Society of Motor Manufacturers and Traders, *The Motor Industry of Great Britain* (London: SMMT, various years).

17. Mariot Villiam, "Come Una Multinazionale puo Esportare La Crisi: Il Caso Leyland Innocenti" (Ph.D. diss., University of Milan, 1975), tables 7 and 11.

18. Ibid., table 11.

19. OECD, *Economic Survey: Italy* (Paris, March 1977).

20. Ibid.

21. The Ryder Report, p. v.

22. Ibid., p. 19.

23. Central Policy Review Staff, *Future of British Car Industry,* p. 67.

24. Geoffrey Robinson, "Italian Fiasco," *Spectator,* 6 December 1975, p. 721.

25. See the comments in the Central Policy Review Staff *Future of British Car Industry,* pp. 70-75.

26. *Investors Cronicle,* 13 December, 1971.

27. This and other data in this section are taken from Pontarollo, "Truth about 1,700 Sackings."

28. It is important to constantly bear in mind that both government and workers, but especially workers, while they often have strong suspicions, have no legal way to gain access to such crucial information.

29. Villiam, "Come Una Multinazionale puo Esportare La Crisi" table 11.

30. Ibid., table 10.

31. W.B. Deadman and G.G. Wells, *Taxation in Europe* (London: Farrington, 1975).

32. S. Lall, "Transfer Pricing by Multinational Manufacturing Firms," *Oxford Bulletin of Economics and Statistics* 35 (1973):181-184.

33. "British Leyland Ltd. Says It Will Liquidate Its Italian Subsidiary," *Wall Street Journal,* 28 November 1975, p. 14. The £10 million figure is cited in Terry Dodsworth, "Fiat May Step in and Rescue Innocenti," *Financial Times,* 27 November 1975, p. 34; and in John Fryer and George Armstrong, "The Cars Run Out of Road," *Sunday Times,* 2 November 1975, p. 53.

34. Central Policy Review Staff, *Future of British Car Industry,* p. ix.

35. Anthony Robinson, "Rome Approves Innocenti Deal," *Financial Times,* 28 May 1975, p. 1.

36. Fryer and Armstrong, "Cars Run Out of Road," p. 53.

37. Rupert Cromwell, "Innocenti Compromise Formula," *Financial Times,* 2 November 1975, p. 17.

38. This lack of consideration is confirmed in a study on divestments wherein the authors comment that social responsibility did not "rank high in the company's frame of mind regarding divestments." Business International, SA Research Report, *International Divestment: A Survey of Corporate Experience* (New York, 1976), p. 49.

39. See Pontarollo, "Truth about 1,700 Sackings."

40. Ibid.

41. "Innocenti Protest by Milan Workers," *Times,* 30 October 1975, p. 20.

42. Pontarollo, "Truth about 1,700 Sackings."

43. Cited in Fryer and Armstrong, "Cars Run Out of Road," p. 53.

44. Ibid.

45. Robinson, "Italian Fiasco," p. 721.

46. *The Economist,* "The Innocenti Suffer with the Guilty as Foreigners Leave," 29 November 1975.

47. *Financial Times,* 4 and 5 February 1976.

48. Villiam, "Come Una Multinazionale puo Esportare La Crisi."

49. Pontarollo, "Truth about 1,700 Sackings." One member of the factory council told me in an interview that the plan to alter production was a serious and realistic one based on the capacities and capabilities available at Innocenti. The plan was developed by the factory council and academics from the local polytechnic.

50. "The Leyland Innocenti Saga: Learning Some Hard Lessons in Italy," *Business Europe Weekly Reports*, 5 December 1975, p. 386.

51. "Fiat Says Converting Innocenti Will Cost 81.5 Million Pounds," *Times*, 20 January 1976, p. 16.

52. "Leyland Innocenti Saga." p. 386.

53. Robinson, "Italian Fiasco."

54. OECD, *Economic Survey: Italy* (Paris, January 1976).

55. OECD, *Main Economic Indicators* (Paris, December 1976). One disincentive to companies contemplating layoffs is the very strong indemnity-payment provisions. Nevertheless, the unemployment rate in Italy has been attacked as misleading and as understating the true figure.

56. British Leyland, despite several changes in top management, continued to make losses after 1976, despite the infusion of large sums of public money. In the process it has been systematically rationalized or, to use a less-formal term, dismembered. There can be little hope for its continued existence, except perhaps in merged form.

57. This is one of the central theses in Villiam, "Come Una Multinazionale puo Esportare la Crisi."

58. For a brief discussion on various aspects of individual political behavior in organizations see Virginia E. Schein, "Individual Power and Political Behaviors in Organizations: An Inadequately Explored Reality," *Academy of Management Review* 2 (i):64-72.

5 Chrysler U.K.

This case study differs from the other two in an important regard—that is, Chrysler U.K. Ltd. was not divested in 1975, the focal point of my investigation. Rather, the parent, Chrysler Corporation (Chrysler), *threatened* to withdraw from Britain, but actually stayed and continued to produce and sell. However, three years later in mid-1978, Chrysler did sell its three European subsidiaries to the French company, P.S.A. Peugeot-Citroen. Even this dramatic method of raising funds could not overcome the severe cash shortage at Chrysler. A year later the company was close to bankruptcy. It took an unprecedented rescue operation mounted by the federal government and grudgingly supported by hundreds of banks, suppliers, dealers, and workers to prevent, or at least delay, the collapse. These latter events are not investigated in depth in this study, although I consider their essential significance in the final sections of the chapter.

Before Rootes Motor Company Ltd. became Chrysler U.K. it was a long-established family-owned and run motor manufacturer. From the 1920s to the 1950s, Rootes expanded by the acquisition of other small British companies and by internal growth in order to match the growth of the car market. By the early 1960s it was an important but rather precarious member of the British motor industry, accounting for around 10 percent of total production but recording the only losses in the industry.

In 1964 Chrysler acquired 30 percent of the voting shares and 50 percent of the nonvoting shares in Rootes. Rootes continued to record losses, and in 1967, after much hand wringing by the British government, Chrysler took a majority shareholding in Rootes that was made total in 1973.

The multinational that acquired Rootes is paradoxically one of the largest industrial companies in the world and yet surprisingly vulnerable on its home turf, the United States.[1] Its share of the U.S. market shows a consistent tendency to fluctuate in correspondence to movements in the business cycle. For example, during one of the upswings in the company's fortune, Chrysler began its move into Europe by acquiring Simca in France and Barreiros in Spain. During a downswing in 1975, it threatened to withdraw from Britian. Since those years Chrysler has slid perilously close to bankruptcy.

The relationship between the parent and the British subsidiary over the nine or so years covered here is particularly difficult to unravel. Chrysler U.K., in contrast to the subsidiaries in our other two cases,was a large company in its own right, employing 25,000 workers and comprising several plants. We are, therefore, tempted to view the company as a largely autonomous entity with crucial authority resting at the national headquarters. However, this assumption would be a mistake as the evidence to be presented indicates.[2]

Over the period from 1967 to 1975, Chrysler U.K.'s financial performance was uneven and, on the whole, poor. It made small profits in five of those years and large losses in four of them. The trough of the depression in 1974–1975 saw Chrysler U.K. record a particularly serious loss. With severe financial problems of its own, Chrysler announced in October 1975 the possibility of some form of divestment. Within a matter of days, the British prime minister and other senior ministers began a series of secret meetings with top executives from Chrysler. The content of those meetings is a matter of some controversy. There is considerable doubt as to whether Chrysler seriously meant to divest or whether the threat was a bargaining ploy designed to extract concessions and government aid.

While the secret negotiations were in progress, the workers directed their efforts at the British government, arguing forcefully for some form of government intervention. In January 1976, the British government and Chrysler signed an agreement whereby Chrysler would remain and introduce new models in return for government grants and loans and the acceptance by the workers of some 8,000 layoffs.

The agreement was to run for three years and was expected to put Chrysler U.K. on the road to profitability. However, 1976 and 1977 were loss-making years. In the United States, Chrysler recovered from the losses of 1975 but faced a massive investment program of some $7.5 billion into the early 1980s. Unexpectedly, in August 1978, and in the search for cash, Chrysler announced the sale of Chrysler U.K. and its two other European subsidiaries to Peugeot-Citroen. At the time of this writing, Chrysler is undergoing massive restructuring, and the old Rootes-Chrysler U.K. Company, now known as Peugeot S.A. Talbot, is shedding workers in response to another depression in the motor industry. The future existence of both companies is in considerable doubt.

I have relied heavily on two documentary sources throughout the chapter. The publication of a book on Chrysler U.K. by two British economists in 1977 coincided with the beginning of my data collection on the case.[3] I therefore decided not to duplicate their research efforts and made use of their data, in particular the statistics they had gathered. However, I undertook original research in areas that arose out of the focus of this study and that were somewhat underrepresented in their book. In particular, I concentrated on the overall strategic policy of the parent toward its European subsidiaries. I was also fortunate that the Expenditure Committee of the House of Commons had conducted extensive hearings on the government-funded rescue and had issued the minutes of evidence and a report.[4] Other helpful sources were a document prepared by workers and their sympathizers, that I shall refer to as "The Workers' Document,"[5] and various newspapers.

Several interviews were conducted between June 1977 and March 1979. The interviewees included a top executive of Chrysler who was intimately concerned with the company's overseas operations and who had a good knowledge of the British subsidiary, a manager of international personnel, two middle managers at Chrysler U.K. and one at Chrysler France, and three shop stewards at one of Chrysler U.K.'s plants.

Reasons for Investment

Chrysler was a latecomer to the European motor industry, trailing Ford and General Motors by many years.[6] In fact, not until the 1960s did it establish majority control of Simca (1963), Rootes (1967), and Barreiros (1969) and could it face its European competitors as a substantial manufacturer.

We need to consider two aspects of its overseas expansion: (1) why it embarked on the large-scale entry into Europe in the 1960s and (2) why it acquired the companies it did. On the face of it, it is hard to attribute the move into Europe as an outgrowth of the possession of monopoly-type advantages. By industry standards, Chrysler neither possessed any particular advantage in production technology, since the technology was fairly standard by the 1960s, nor in product, since Europeans were accustomed to a very different type of car than was made in the United States. Additionally, whatever special skills it might have had in marketing and management were not sufficient to outweight the advantages possessed by local manufacturers. In fact, both Ford and General Motors possessed more advantages in these areas, at the least because of their longer experience in Europe and the bigger European companies such as Volkswagen, Renault, and Fiat were sufficiently advanced to compete with Americans in Europe on almost any terms. Of course, these aspects do not indicate that Chrysler could not improve the performance of the companies it took over. They do stress the fact, however, that Chrysler was entering a competitive environment with fairly standard weapons.

A more-compelling explanation can be forged out of two other factors—oligopolistic competition and the attraction of a rapidly expanding European market. A top executive of Chrysler commented that the two main reasons for the corporation's entry into Europe were "to participate in the second-largest market in the world and because Lyn Townsend, the former chairman of Chrysler Corporation, strongly believed in expansion to match Chrsyler's rivals." Chrysler's main rivals, Ford and General Motors, were well placed in Europe to take advantage of the boom in the car market in the 1950s and 1960s, which at its height in the 1959-1964 period saw the market for new cars grow by over 10 percent a year.[7] Not to move into Europe and win a share of that market was a risk with incalculable consequences, not only in terms of foregone profits but also in terms of other benefits Chrysler's rivals might be able to extract from the European connection and then use in the American market.[8] The pull of the market and the fear of forfeiting potential benefits to the advantage of its competitors combined to draw Chrysler into Europe, even though the obstacles to successful operations must have seemed formidable.

The timing of the entry coincided with a very successful period for Chrysler. Between 1962 and 1968 Chrysler recovered from one of its periodic downturns by increasing its share of production from 10.3 percent in 1962 to 17.9 percent in 1968 and by substantially improving profitability. It was thus able to move into Europe from a position of relative financial strength. The form of entry Chrysler chose was acquisition. As a latecomer it would, if it decided to establish new manufacturing facilities, have to build up from scratch its capacity, experience, and reputation within an industry and market framework in which many other companies had staked a powerful claim.[9] Without overwhelming advantages, the frailty of such a conception must have been obvious. Acquisition, however, would immediately give Chrysler expertise, facilities, and a market share in Europe.

The selection of the companies for acquisition was determined by a combination of design and availability. According to a top executive, Chrysler's policy was to "locate in the largest markets where the opportunities were greatest and the risk minimized." It attempted to locate in Germany but no companies were available. Therefore, Chrysler acquired companies in the second- and third-largest markets in Europe at the time—the United Kingdom and France. Spain was viewed as a market that "would grow and which would provide an opportunity to get into a growth market before other U.S. competitors." In other words, the entry into Spain enabled Chrysler to build an element of competitive initiative into an otherwise defensive strategy. Additional advantages of that pattern of location were that Chrysler obtained a foothold in the two major European trading blocs—the EEC and the European Free Trading Association (EFTA) (although the company always expected the United Kingdom to become a member of the EEC)—and could benefit from the relatively cheap labor in Spain.[10]

Turning to the specific question of why it chose Simca, Rootes, and Barreiros, little doubt exists that, in the best of all possible worlds, Chrysler would have wished to acquire healthier companies. It had to settle, however, for second-rank companies in terms of size and performance, partly because that was all that was available and partly because it could not afford to buy first-rank companies.[11] It is also doubtful whether European governments would have permitted the acquisition of large and healthy automobile companies.[12]

A brief discussion of the advantages and disadvantages of the acquisition of Rootes from the perspective of the parent and the subsidiary provides a useful background for the examination of the development of the relationship between the two.[13] The main advantages to Chrysler were Rootes's share of the British market that fluctuated around 10 percent; its unused capacity so that expansion could be undertaken quickly and cheaply; its good dealer network; and its products, in particular, brand names with a good-quality image.[14] The image associated with the brand names enabled Chrysler, if it wished, to aim upmarket. However, Rootes also had a foot in the mass market by virtue of the Imp model in the small-car segment and the Avenger model (which was still in the development stage) in the mid-size segement.

The disadvantages, viewed with hindsight, add up to a weightier list. Perhaps the most serious problem was the size of Rootes. It was fundamentally too small to compete effectively in the large European market, partly because it could not offer a full range of models but, more importantly, because its size did not enable it to gain the economies of scale of its larger rivals.[15] At the very minimum, therefore, it needed to operate as close to full capacity as possible to spread the high fixed costs associated with motor manufacturing so as to attain competitive until costs. Even then it would still be at a cost disadvantage with the likes of Fiat and Renault. Rootes could have avoided the disadvantages of small size if it had pursued only an upmarket policy. However, in the early 1960s, Rootes chose to spread its relatively meager resources by aiming at both the upmarket and the mass market. The expansion of capacity with the opening of new facilities at Linwood, Scotland in 1963 and the production of the Imp model committed it to the "big league." Rootes thus undermined its position as a quality producer of upmarket cars without being able to establish itself as a full-blown motor manufacturer.

Additional problems included the wide spread of manufacturing facilities, which raised logistics costs; the low sales of the Imp model, which meant low levels of utilization of capacity at Linwood (an average of around 40 percent from 1963-1967); and the old age of several models, which made increasing or even holding market shares more difficult. As a result, Rootes's profit performance after 1960 worsened dramatically, tumbling from earnings of £6.8 million and a rate of return on investment of 25.5 percent in 1960 to losses of £10.8 million in 1967.[16]

The expectation was that the takeover by Chrysler would eliminate some of these problems or at least alleviate their impact. From Chrysler's multinational perspective, the problem of small size could be overcome by integration with other European subsidiaries. The three subsidiaries combined had the potential capacity to produce engines, bodies, and components in sufficiently large numbers to match the unit costs of some of the large automobile companies.[17] Integration could also help solve the marketing handicap of a restricted and aging model range by complementarity and the pooling of resources for the development of new models. Moreover, multinationals are allegedly superior in such areas as finance and management. All in all, the deficiencies of Rootes seemingly could be turned into opportunities.

From the perspective of the workers employed at Rootes, the Chrysler takeover (although workers were given no say in the matter) was probably the best thing they could have hoped for once Wedgwood Benn, minister of industry in the Labour government, had rejected the nationalization option claiming Rootes was not by itself a "viable organization with or without government money, owned or not owned by a British company."[18] As small- and medium-sized companies, particularly in some industries, lose their viability, their only hope is to become part of a larger group. However, membership in large groups, particularly multinational ones, brings with it new problems, as we shall see.

Factors Affecting the Development and Performance of the Subsidiary

Competition

Although Chrysler had worldwide operations, conditions in two areas significantly affected the group's overall performance. About two-thirds of its total production and unit sales took place in the United States, and of the remaining one-third, 80 percent was in Europe. It is necessary, therefore, to briefly explore the competitive conditions in those two areas.

The U.S. motor industry is a classic example of an oligopolistic industry. The top three companies accounted for well over 80 percent of the market until 1979. Among the "big three," Chrysler sometimes found (and still finds) itself in a precarious position, particularly in recessionary periods. Direct price competition, however, it not what damages Chrysler. Its precariousness lies in the lower margins it earns that it cannot unilaterally increase given the pricing interdependence of the big three. The primary reason for its lower margins is a cost structure that is higher than the one at General Motors and Ford.[19] Comparing the cost of goods sold as a percentage of net sales revenue across the big three, we can clearly see Chrysler's historic handicap. Whereas the figures for General Motors ranged between 71 percent in 1963 to a peak of 88 percent in 1974, and those for Ford ranged between 83 percent in 1969 to 91 percent in 1975, Chrysler's figures ranged from 87 percent in 1969 to 95 percent in 1975. Three important reasons exist for these lower margins. First, because Chrysler is smaller than its two main rivals, it has had to spread largely fixed design, engineering, and production costs over lower volumes, thereby forfeiting some scale economies. Second, it bought a higher proportion of its components from outside suppliers, which tended to inflict a cost penalty on Chrysler since it had to pay the suppliers' profit margin. Third, the lower margins were due to Chrysler's heavier concentration in the small and sub-compact end of the U.S. market, where margins are traditionally smaller. To overcome these relative disadvantages, Chrysler needed to either increase its market share, which would improve its relative costs, or to develop some particular product advantage, which would enable it to price its models at a premium.

Chrysler has been unable to do either with any consistency. In fact, its problems have been exacerbated by the recurring downswings in the economy. Although sales decline for all companies, they do so more for Chrysler because it has a higher proportion of low-income customers who are more likely to defer purchase when their income is squeezed.[20] In the words of a Chysler executive: "We are the company that goes up fast when the market goes up and goes down fast when the market goes down."[21] Thus, although the whole industry's performance has fluctuated in line with the cyclical ups and downs in the economy, the fluctuations in Chrysler's profit performance have been more pronounced, taking it into the red on several occasions. For example, the 1975 recession produced a drop in profit for the big three but still found General Motors and Ford earning $1.3 billion and $323 million respectively, while Chrysler had a loss of $259.5 million.

However, taking the whole of the 1966-1976 period, Chrysler made profits in eight out of the eleven years and bounced back from the doldrums of 1975 with record profits of $422.6 million in 1976. Throughout that period the company was a going, if precarious, concern. It generated enough profit to stay in business but was cash short, particularly after 1973. To sustain, as it did, a capital-spending program that was of similar proportions to that of the big two, Chrysler was forced to carry a much-higher debt-to-equity ratio.[22] The company found itself heavily in debt and with low or nonexistent profits to service the debt. What is significant in terms of the attempted withdrawal from Chrysler U.K. in 1975 is that the parent suffered a cash squeeze and was unable to raise finance on the private-capital markets. The same combination of circumstances hit Chrysler again in 1979. The implications of this problem is investigated in later sections.

In Europe, Chrysler's operations experienced mixed fortunes, with Chrylser France outperforming the British subsidiary. Above and beyond any company-specific characteristics, the nationality of the subsidiaries had much to do with the unevenness of their performance. In the boom period of 1964-1973, for example, when car production in Western Europe increased by 66 percent from 7.7 million units to 11.5 million units, French and Spanish companies were able to increase their output by 80 and 130 percent respectively. In contrast, British companies increased output by only 11 percent,[23] reflecting both the slower growth of the market for automobiles in Britain and the steadily increasing penetration of Japanese models.

The Chrysler subsidiaries successfully participated in what turned out to be the final period of the long post-war boom. Both the French and Spanish subsidiaries doubled their output in the 1967-1973 period, and Chrysler U.K. did better than the national industry average by increasing output by 40 percent.[24]

However, their success in building up production was marred by their inability to increase domestic market shares. Rather, to make use of the available production capacity, the French and British subsidiaries in particular had to establish sizable export markets. Although winning export markets can be a sign of competitive strength (for example, the Japanese companies), in the case of Chrysler France and Chrysler U.K. the indications were that it was more a sign of weakness. Chrysler France consistently had to export over 60 percent of total output to compensate for its inability to win more than 10 percent of the French market, while Chrysler U.K.'s exports fluctuated between 40 and 60 percent of output.[25] Car-industry analysts report that sales in the domestic market are more profitable than are those in export markets, and they estimate that to reach a break-even point (no profits/no losses) a company should export no more than 40 percent of output at a production level of about 70 percent of capacity.[26] We can reasonably assume, then, that both subsidiaries would have preferred to be less dependent on exports. The destination of the exports also indicates competitive weakness. Chrysler France was only able to penetrate easier markets such as the Danish and Austrian ones, where no large indigenous manufacturers existed, and the bulk of Chrysler U.K.'s exports went to essentially captive markets. For example, a long-term fixed contract between Chrysler U.K. and an Iranian company ensured an expanding volume of sales to a largely protected and captive market. Even Chrysler U.K.'s brief penetration into the U.S. market in 1971 was determined by the decision of the parent to supply its dealers with a U.K.-produced car. I return to these important issues in the next section.

The picture that emerges is of three subsidiaries hugging the bottom rungs in their respective industries. Each of them is handicapped by the problem of small size relative to their main domestic competitors, and each has relied more heavily than rivals have on overseas sales to remain viable. There the parallels end, however. Throughout the period, Chrysler France was a healthy and successful producer. It made up for its relatively small size as a company by achieving excellent production economies at its massive, integrated facilities at Poissy, near Paris. By operating at the full capacity of around 500,000 units in all but recession years, it was cost competitive and able to compensate for the handicap of exporting so much of its output. Moreover, it was the recipient of new models designed at Chrsyler's European design center in England.

Chrysler Spain, in contrast, was a small producer with an ancillary role in Chrysler's European strategy. Although it had a production capacity of 100,000 units, which it almost reached in 1973, thereafter, and against the trend in the Spanish industry, production declined steadily and reached a 30 percent level of unused capacity in 1976. Never allocated new models, its main function was to augment the assembly capacity for the French subsidiary's successful models and to manufacture parts for Chrysler's Latin American subsidiaries.[27]

Chrysler U.K. turned out to be the most marginal subsidiary in Chrysler's

overseas empire. It was beset by several serious problems that were not significantly alleviated when it was absorbed into the multinational structure. Chrysler
U.K., even operating at maximum capacity, was estimated to be 30 percent
below the optimum size necessary to achieve competitive unit costs in production.[28] Since it often operated at less-than-full capacity and suffered from low
labor productivity, its cost structure put it at a severe disadvantage.[29] On the
marketing side, it was weakened by the absence of new models and by a record
of inconsistent delivery of products to dealers. These marketing problems,
coupled with increased import penetration into the U.K. market, caused an
erosion of Chrysler U.K.'s market share from 12 percent in 1967 to 9.5 percent
in 1973, which was a good year for auto sales. By 1975 its share had collapsed
to 6.6 percent.[30] Its export performance, as we have seen, also was unconvinc-
ing, with only a handful of cars pentrating European markets. It is not surprising, therefore, that Chrysler U.K. without new products, with low productivity
and high costs, and with an unbalanced overseas sales effort, hugged failure
throughout the period but, in particular, in 1974 and 1975. Thus, we must ask:
Why did the parent not pursue integration, the one policy that might have
corrected many of these problems? Why did Chrysler U.K. not produce more
than one new model in nine years? Why did it not export more to European
markets? Why did it have lower productivity and a worse financial performance
than Chrysler France? I now turn to these questions.

Product Strategy

By late 1975 and early 1976, when Chrysler U.K. was making huge losses and
the parent was threatening withdrawal, agreement seemed to be unanimous
that the subsidiary's salvation had all along lain in integration.[31] The argument
for integration was indeed powerful. The three subsidiaries taken together
could benefit from increased economies of scale by producing common components (engines, gearboxes, and so on) for a common range of models to be
sold through a common marketing effort. Although such an entity would still
be the smallest of the European mass producers, it would achieve significant
cost reductions. However, if the argument for integration was conceptually
compelling, the parent had only taken partial and hesitant steps along that
strategic road up to 1976.

Management at headquarters apparently had accepted the strategy of
integration for the European subsidiaries as long ago as 1969. The executive
I interviewed put it this way:

> In 1969 we developed the first planning stage of how the companies
> would merge together. It began with product planning. As the product
> cycle leads by at least three years, it meant that it wouldn't be till
> 1972 at the earliest date that the fruits of that planning would emerge.

We took a car—the 180/2 liter—and planned to make it a car to be sold by all dealers in Europe. This car had been styled at Rootes and was part of the Rootes product plan. We took it and formed the Chrysler product plan for Europe. It was a modest beginning towards integration. The car was to be manufactured in France and Britain. We also had Chrysler International in Switzerland, a sales company which in 1969 was expanded to sell Chrysler Europe cars outside Europe. The overall responsibility for selling in Europe, however, was still national.

In addition, Chrysler transformed the Rootes design center, located at Whitley in Conventry, England, into the European design center with the task of designing and styling products for the three European subsidiaries. Set in place, then, around the product plan were the three central elements of an integrated European operation. First, the design centers would be unified and would develop models for the subsidiaries. Second, the distribution outlets and marketing efforts would be gradually integrated. Third, common products would be produced at the three subsidiaries, which logically paved the way for full manufacturing integration in the production of components. In the words of the executive, the aim was "to minimize country aspects and maximize product aspects." Chrylser, like Ford and, more recently, other large automobile manufacturers, conceptualized Europe as one geographic area scattered with plants and dealers. If that was the plan, however, Chrysler, unlike Ford, was unable to implement this grand strategy. Chrysler U.K. remained effectively isolated until 1976, with only the Spanish and French subsidiaries' achieving any measure of integration. The integration strategy was eventually scuttled when the parent reversed its decision to allocate common products to both the British and French subsidiaries. The two new models, designed at Whitley and destined for production at the two subsidiaries, were assigned exclusively to the French subsidiary.

Apparently, general and operational reasons existed for the isolation of Chrysler U.K. and the policy reversals. The general reasons revolved around a reluctance from some areas within the company to accept the concept of integration. One source of early resistance was the French subsidiary. A manager at Chrysler headquarters remarked:

When we had minority shareholders of any size in France, the French were the major impediments to integration and even common sourcing. We were worried that the French could have used integration as a public relations line, claiming, for example, that we were trying to tie them to the U.K., which was an inconsistent supplier.

The top executive of Chrysler's international operations also pointed to this aspect:

It was very difficult, given the difficult labor scene in the U.K. to convince others to integrate with the U.K. Within the corporation it is difficult to marry a losing proposition with a winning proposition. I was arguing [while he was in a top position at Chrysler U.K.] that the U.K. was underutilized in terms of capacity and that given Poissy's full capacity, the U.K. could really be of help. But the greatest concern was reliance on a supply base that wasn't very good.

The successful French subsidiary, less in need of integration because of its large size, with established access to European markets and an excellent industrial-relations record, lobbied effectively against integration with the troubled Chrysler U.K. Underlying this parochialism on the part of the subsidiaries was their legal status as separate profit centers. According to the top executive, until Chrysler Europe became a reality in the mid-1970s, each subsidiary attempted to maximize its profit opportunities and engaged in special pleading with the European-product planning committee. Discussions on integration were characterized by haggling over such things as the guidelines to be used to determine each subsidiary's contribution to the development costs of common products. The executive attributed this in part to "their not having been involved in the formulation of the overall plans" and their not being able to "see the whole picture," adding, "It's tough for people to forget nationality." However, beyond these attitudinal impediments were the structural sources of internal conflict. As companies with long traditions of independence now operating as profit centers within the organization, they were bound to come into conflict as they fought for a share of the limited resources. That Chrysler France was often victorious in this battle was due to its successful record and its obvious strengths. Of course, its victories in these internal battles also helped to assure its continued success and the reinforcement of its strength. Chrysler U.K. experienced the reverse cycle. Its poor record and equally obvious weaknesses persuaded others not to join with it. This reinforced its problems and rendered it unable to win resources (for example, new models) in the internal battle, which aggravated its downward spiral. Chrysler never confronted this problem directly but chose to hedge its bets, dallying with the promises of integration without wholeheartedly supporting the strategy with resources.

A further fundamental constraint on Chrysler's ability to pursue integration was the shortage of funds throughout the multinational. Chrysler U.K., consistently earning small profits or making losses, could not contribute funds to cover some of the cost of integration. The parent, rarely blessed with abundant funds, also was unable, or unwilling, given the demands of other important capital-spending programs, to do so.[32] It was not until 1976, with money supplied by the British government, that Chrysler "shoved integration no matter what."[33]

As one would expect, more-prosaic and technical factors inhibited a move toward integration. Since the French and British subsidiaries produced different types of cars, they complemented each other in the marketplace by attracting customers who wanted both front-wheel- and rear-wheel-drive cars. A switch to common products would eliminate some sales, at least in the short run. The top executive observed that "the marketing and product-selection people took an anticommon-product position in order to maintain the sales of all distribution outlets and in that way achieve maximum sales." However, this position need not have prevented common products with different engineering designs being produced at both subsidiaries. After all, the 180 model, a conventionally engineered car, was assigned to Chrysler France, a company that was more experienced at producing front-wheel-drive cars. Other factors mentioned by the executive were the difficulties of establishing mechanisms to facilitate the flow and exchange of various currencies within the European organization. However, these operational start-up problems are encountered by all truly multinational companies and would not, or at least should not, have prevented integration.

If Chrysler, for various reasons, deferred integration, we must still consider why Chrysler U.K. produced only one new model in the nine years after Chrysler had become the majority shareholder.[34] By 1975, Chrysler U.K. was competing with the Imp, the Hunter/Arrow, and the Avenger models, which were thirteen, ten, and six years old respectively.[35] In contrast, Chrysler France introduced three new models in the same period: the 1100, the 180, and the C6/Alpine. The managing director of Chrysler U.K., in an address to union leaders in 1974, tried to assuage the concerns of the work force by praising the existing range as "competitive" and "classic" and asserted that "the public does not want newness for newness' sake."[36] A middle manager at Chrysler U.K. found this defense "strange given the emphasis on new models in the car industry—it is like a death knell," and the Chrysler International executive attributed Chrysler France's better performance to, among other things, this newness of its products. In reality, Chrysler France was allocated new models because it could afford to pay for their development and production, and Chrysler U.K. lost out because it could not.

In the absence of integration, Chrysler instituted a policy on investment that insisted that after an initial large injection of capital by the parent into the subsidiary, each was expected to be self-sustaining. Any investment in new-model programs, plants, and machinery had to be financed without recourse to the parent. The former vice-president of European operations claimed that the parent "never loaned or invested a penny in Chysler France directly" but that Chrysler U.K.'s position was such that it could continue operating only because the parent "invested money or made guarantees or had loans or did certain things that assisted Chrysler U.K."[37] However, while the parent deviated from its stated policy sufficiently to prevent the collapse of the British subsidiary, it was unwilling to finance new-model programs, which it acknowledged Chrysler U.K. desperately needed.[38]

Here we can detect that Chrysler was trapped within a policy that perpetuated a downward spiral. Chrysler U.K. performed poorly. Many people saw that the root cause of its poor performance lay in its small size. Chrysler realized this as early as 1969 and developed a plan for integration to overcome the deficiencies associated with small size. However, integration still was not pursued, and Chrysler U.K. remained isolated. These problems worsened its financial position and starved it of funds for investment in new models that, at least, may have cushioned the decline. Chrysler thus failed to break the downward spiral. Rather, it ended up simply tinkering with the fundamental problems at the British subsidiary and, ultimately, in its European empire.[39] I think that Chrysler clearly hesitated on integration because, operating with comparatively meager resources, it could not accept the risks involved in spending large amounts of money to integrate a healthy subsidiary with a sick and very unreliable one. And yet, the imperatives of international competition were such that Chrysler could not aspire to be a credible European competitor with only one operation of the size of Chrysler France. Having sunk large amounts of money into Chrysler U.K. in the 1960s, the parent was stuck with nursing its subsidiary along in the 1970s.

The pattern of overseas sales also highlights the differences between the British and French subsidiaries. Chrysler France sold well over 80 percent of its exports and 50 percent of its total production in Western Europe. In contrast, Chrysler U.K. sold only 4 percent of its total output in that market. To add salt to the wounds of the British subsidiary, Chrsyler France increased its sales in the United Kingdom from 3,738 units in 1969 to 32,917 in 1972, a peak year.[40] Rather than a mutual sharing of each other's distribution outlets, as envisaged in the integration plan, we find Chrysler U.K.'s doing the sharing and Chrysler France's reaping the rewards. Clearly, Chrysler France had products that were acceptable in the markets of Europe, including Britain.

Why were Chrysler U.K.'s sales in Europe so low? The executive attributed the low sales in Europe to two reasons. One was to avoid competition between French and British models in the same range, such as the Hunter and the Simca 1500. Second, and more important, he pointed to the refusal of European dealers to accept Chrysler U.K. products because of their poor quality and because their delivery was highly erratic. An additional factor favoring Chrysler France may have been the fact that France was a member of the EEC long before the U.K. The first and third points, however, are not convincing explanations for the differences in export sales. As Young and Hood point out, some models were not competitors but rather complemented each other, and Chrysler France outsold Chrysler U.K. in all the non-EEC countries as well. Noting that Ford and General Motors seem to operate market-sharing policies among their subsidiaries in Europe such that each is assigned certain markets and restricted from others, Yong and Hood conclude:

While no such restrictions apparently apply to Chrysler U.K., the small numbers of cars that the company sold in all the EEC countries suggests a complete lack of commitment. With an acceptable car such as the Avenger, the sales potential foregone in the community is undoubtedly very substantial. In 1975, indeed, registrations of Chrysler U.K. cars in the main markets of France and West Germany were so low (663 and 698 respectively) as to suggest mere window dressing.[41]

However, it is hard to attribute the consistent pattern of trivially low sales (for example, 700 units in Italy and 2,424 in Belgium and Luxembourg) merely to a lack of commitment. One is left to conclude either that U.K. products were totally unacceptable to dealers in Europe or that a deliberate policy was the exclusion of these products from Europe. The workers on the Chrysler Action Committee claimed, for example, that they had evidence that Chrysler dealers in Belgium were "required to sell seven Simcas for each Chrysler U.K. model they are allowed, in spite of a waiting list of customers for the U.K. cars."[42] I was unable to corroborate this accusation, but conceivably the Chrysler France lobby prevailed and managed to preserve Europe for itself, persuading Chrysler to use Chrysler U.K. as a supply base for its traditional markets in Commonwealth countries. This would not have made much economic sense, however, given that Chrysler U.K. had unused capacity with which it could have supplied Europe.

Another episode in Chrysler U.K.'s export performance can be used to underline either the unacceptability of U.K. products in overseas markets or the shabby way the subsidiary was treated by the parent. In 1970 Chrysler decided to import the Avenger model into the United States to be sold as the Plymouth Cricket. Imports increased from 3,160 units in 1970 to 29,038 in 1971. In the very next year, though, the decision was rescinded, and Mitsubishi (a Japanese manufacturer) models were imported and marketed under the Colt name. The top executive attributed the reversal to the "poor continuity of supply from the U.K." and added, "The dealers were fed up. They didn't like it." Whatever the truth of this factor, a test of only one year seems unfair. Perhaps as significant was the fact that in 1971 Chrysler had bought a 15 percent share, with an option to increase it to 35 percent, in Mitsubishi.[43] Possibly as part of the Chrysler-Mitsubishi deal, Chrysler agreed to import a number of cars that happened to be in the same size range as the Avenger. Again, we see the tentativeness in Chrysler's attempt to integrate the British subsidiary into its worldwide operations.

The Iranian contract in the end saved Chrysler U.K. from being saddled with massive unused capacity. In 1970, Chrysler U.K. signed an agreement with the Iran National Manufacturing Company (INIM) that provided that Chrysler U.K. supply INIM with completely knocked down (CKD) kits of the Hunter model for assembly and sale in Iran up to 1980, at which time the contract could be renewed or terminated at one year's notice. The fixed nature of the contract and the protected nature of the market insured a guaranteed level of sales, even of aging products. By 1974 about 30 percent of total output and 55 percent of exports were accounted for by the Iran contract.[44] On the positive side the contract insured a certain number of sales, even in depressed times as in 1974-1975. However, its profitability was unclear. The executive I interviewed thought it covered the overhead costs, and the Chrysler Action Committee alleged that management had reported to them that "it always covered its fixed costs but not necessarily its variable costs." If it was not a very profitable contract, it was all that Chrysler U.K. achieved or was allowed to achieve.

In this section I have identified the lack of integration as the critical factor in Chrysler U.K.'s downward spiral as a competitor, and I have attributed the failure to integrate to vacillation at parent headquarters and to resistance from certain parts in the company. The resistance and the hesitancy were, in large part, attributable to the problems at the British subsidiary and to the financial weakness of the parent. In the next section I consider in some detail the extent to which the problems at Chrysler U.K. were caused by the state of industrial relations and in later sections return to the significance of the cash problems of the parent.

Industrial Relations

One of the reasons repeatedly cited for Chrysler U.K.'s pariah status was its poor "labor climate."[45] What this meant essentially was that management at the British subsidiary had great difficulty in controlling the work force. Concretely, this lack of control manifested itself in a high frequency of disputes and low productivity. In sharp contrast, Chrysler France had never experienced a strike for over thirty years and had much higher productivity. Before I explore the reasons for the differences between the two subsidiaries, I examine the state of industrial relations at Chrysler U.K. and how it affected performance.

Many of the difficulties Chrysler U.K. had in controlling the work force stemmed from the industrial-relations conditions that were, by the 1960s, entrenched in the U.K. auto industry. The power of labor on the shop floor had grown with the increasing strength of the shop-steward movement. In particular, under the piece-rate system of payment, stewards had acquired the right to bargain over the rate for the job. This tended to dilute management and union power and to concentrate a considerable amount of influence in the hands of shop stewards. When Chrysler took over Rootes it found as many as eighty employment agreements covering various plants and occupational groupings. Many of the contracts had different termination dates and embodied different pay and conditions-of-work provisions that enabled these groups to repeatedly leapfrog each other.[46] This meant that the company was in almost continuous negotiation throughout the year with various shop-steward committees.

Chrysler, as an American multinational used to centralized and ordered relations with labor, attempted simultaneously to centralize control and to reduce the power of shop stewards. However, the workers and their representatives resisted these efforts. The long process to centralize negotiations and achieve a common contract-termination date was not successful until the mid-1970s. The introduction of measured-day work (MDW), designed to remove control from shop stewards and relocate it in the hands of management, merely shifted the arena of struggle.[47] Instead of bargaining over the rate for the job, shop stewards turned to bargining over the labor loadings or manning levels, the fairness of time standards and job evaluations, and the conditions of work. Moreover, management had to compensate for the removal of the self-disciplining effects of piecework by increasing the ratio of foremen to shop-floor workers from about 1 to 100 to 1 to 20.[48] Management also discovered that workers now had an incentive to slow down the pace of work to try to get more overtime, as this became the only way for them to increase their earnings between the yearly pay negotiations.

Chrysler U.K., operating within the parameters of the downward spiral identified in the previous section, tried desperately to improve its performance, and hopefully its image, within the multinational by acting to establish firm control over the labor force. In this attempt it used a mixture of incentives and threats. It was, in fact, an innovator of sorts, conceding, after strike action, staff status first to the toolmakers and then to the electricians and accepting, again under pressure, the principle of pay parity between workers in different regions of the country—a dangerous precedent in the view of many industrialists as it connected previously segregated labor markets with different costs of living. Also, in desperation, in May 1975 the subsidiary floated an employee-participation scheme that offered workers two seats on the board of directors of Chrysler U.K. and comprehensive consultation in return for central negotiations and compulsory arbitration. When the workers refused, it went so far as to offer £50 to each employee if they would simply agree to discuss the principles in the scheme. These innovations must, however, be seen as a response to the weakness of the company and the strength of the workers rather than of some grand design.

In addition to these sweeteners, the company made use of what Young and Hood call the "investment weapon." Its repeated linking of industrial peace to investment, new products, and access to export markets played upon the job insecurity of workers and sustained a pervasive atmosphere of uncertainty about the future of the company. As early as 1969 a Chrysler spokesman in Geneva is quoted as saying, "Labor troubles at Coventry and Linwood could jeopardize the long-term program."[49] A letter from a member of Parliament to the managing director at Chrysler U.K., written in 1970, expressed concern over the future status of the Stoke plant and received the reply that the company had "no intention of closing the Stoke factory."[50] A strike in 1973 led the company to announce that capital investment and expansion were to stop until an agreement was reached and "until we have demonstrated over a reasonable period of time that we can work out our problems in a constitutional manner, while production is maintained."[51] The company also announced at this time that "the planned investment to produce the Alpine in the United Kingdom was halted and investment switched to France."[52] A series of small disputes in early 1974 prompted the company to warn shop stewards not to embark on a long strike over pay differentials for it could not be "sustained for long if we are to stand on our two feet" and might therefore lead to "voluntary liquidation."[53] In October 1974, after another strike by toolmakers, the company also announced it might shelve plans and allocate export markets to other subsidiaries.[54] The insecurity fostered by the use of such threats began to emerge in late 1974 and in 1975. In November 1974, a staff union reacted to the sacking of several hundred white-collar workers by expressing a widely shared fear:

> The climate is one of increasing doubt about Chrysler management's desire or intention to maintain an effective U.K. subsidiary and their inability or unwillingness to disclose long-term plans.[55]

In January 1975, the U.K. secretary of state for industry wrote to Chrysler Corporation asking it to clarify its intentions for the U.K. subsidiary. Chrysler's chairman replied that the subsidiary had "substantial excess average-annual capacity for the assembly of built-up vehicles," but with the support of labor and government Chrysler intended to "remain a strong competitor in the British market."[56] Finally, in May 1975, a strike at the Stoke plant in Coventry, ostensibly about pay, is widely believed to have been an attempt by the workers to resolve the insecurity surrounding their situation once and for all. The workers' representative challenged: "Let Chrysler withdraw from England if they cannot pay a living wage," and added, "We are not going to be used by a multinational company as cheap labor and the poor relations in our district."[57]

The cynical and repeated use of the threat to reduce investment or withdraw did little to bolster management efforts to control the work force. In fact, only after the dramatic and harrowing crisis in late 1975, at the height of the recession, did management report an improvement in labor discipline, with the head of industrial relations at Chrysler U.K. reporting, "The change in attitude by our unions has been a complete revelation." In the callous words of another executive, the "threat of the plughole" finally worked.[58]

Despite management's attempts to link the actions of workers to all the serious difficulties at Chrysler U.K., however, we must carefully examine the disputes and labor-productivity records and their impact on the overall performance of the subsidiary. The most fruitful way to arrive at some conclusions on this matter is to compare Chrysler U.K.'s performance against some potential standard and against other competitors.

Assuming a standard of uninterrupted production, Chrysler U.K. performed poorly. Indeed, some 212,000 units were lost—that is, not produced when they could have been—in the four years to 1975. However, it is more difficult to calculate the impact of this lost production on the financial performance of the company because lost production does not automatically imply lost sales. Young and Hood estimate that out of the 212,000 lost units, at best 90 percent might have been sold (based on continued high sales in the U.S. market) and at worst only 30 percent.[59] Moreover, not all lost units can be attributed to industrial disputes. The workers forcefully rejected charges that they were a major contributing factor to the poor production performance at Chrysler U.K. Using national data they pointed out that in the U.K. motor industry "twice as much time was lost through sickness, injury, and absenteeism (5-7 percent of total working days) than through industrial disputes (2.5 percent)" and referred to a study that indicated "that industrial disputes accounted for only about *one-half* of lost production, the rest being due to breakdowns, supply difficulties, repairs, and maintenance. These causes of lost production are the sole responsibility of *management*."[60] Figures taken from internal Chrysler U.K. documents substantiate these points. For example, in 1973, 3,282,184 hours were lost due to all causes. Of that loss, 1,750,403 hours, or 53 percent, were the result of strikes. In 1974, only 18.7 percent of the total hours lost were due to strikes. And, in 1976, of 40,496 vehicles lost to all causes, only 10,338 were lost because of disputes and the "aftereffects of disputes," while most of the others were lost because of material shortages, the launch of new models, and breakdowns.[61]

If a high proportion of the vehicles and hours lost were not directly due to disputes, however, a feature of the disputes record at Chrysler U.K. may have had a disproportionate impact on company profitability. Chrysler U.K. was characterized by frequent minor work stoppages of short duration (under four hours) that involved a handful of workers (see table 5-1). These short stoppages are considered to be often more damaging to profitability than are long major strikes involving the whole work force.[62] A major study of the car industry has argued in this context that "the loss of one hour's production in an eight-hour shift reduces a plant's profitability by at least 40 percent." The study went on to say that only "uninterrupted production on a daily basis" can ensure an "adequate profit."[63] Assuming a work year of 250 days, Chrysler U.K. averaged two or more stoppages a day, These stoppages, added to the major disputes and machinery breakdowns, meant both lost vehicles and revenue and the persistence of fixed overhead and variable costs. Moreover, additional costs were imposed on the company as overtime working attempted to meet daily or weekly targets. The interrupted production probably also contributed to a reluctance of the dealers to market Chrysler U.K. products. The high incidence of these minor disputes also points to the already mentioned difficulty management had in controlling the work force. As table 5-1 shows, management was constantly challenged in areas normally considered their preserve. This has implications for productivity as we shall presently see.

Table 5-1
Chrysler U.K.'s Disputes Record—Minor Stoppages

Cause	Percentage of Hours Lost[a]		Frequency of Stoppages	
	1973	1974	1973	1974
Manning and work allocation	15.5	42	124	183
Working conditions and supervision	14.7	14.2	151	131
Trade-union matters	17.9	17.2	65	101
Discipline and dismissal	19.5	6.8	47	38
Duration and pattern of hours	15.7	5.6	32	70
Pay—rates and extra earnings	16.2	13.1	36	58
Pay—extra wage and fringe benefits	3.6	0.4	24	5
Miscellaneous	6.8	0.7	21	14
Total	100	100	500	600

Source: Chrysler U.K. internal records prepared by Motivation and Productivity Department.

[a]Represents 125,078 hours out of a total of 1,750,403 hours in 1973 and 194,069 hours out of 581,259 in 1974.

Comparing Chrysler U.K.'s disputes record to British competitors, we do not find differences of sufficient significance to make an impact on profitability. The most germane comparison is with Vauxhall, the General Motors subsidiary. Vauxhall, roughly of similar size to Chrysler U.K., had a better disputes record but also had a poor record of profitability.[64] However, all British motor companies tended to have worse dispute records than their overseas competitors— one reason, among others, for their worse trading and profit performances. Further, as repeatedly becomes apparent in this study, subsidiaries are engaged in two competitive battles—one external and one internal. In comparison to its major internal rival, Chrysler France, Chrysler U.K.'s disputes record was damnable.

The management of Chrysler France and Chrysler claimed with some pride that not a single dispute had occurred at Chrysler France since 1947.[65] This fact is remarkable given the nature of the industry and its history of industrial relations. Not only was Chrysler France free of major disputes but also a manager there claimed that no problems were encountered along the job-control frontier on issues such as manning, line speed, discipline, and conditions of work. Workers could easily be moved from one job to another, negotiations rarely occurred over man assignments, disciplinary action met little union resistance, and management was free to alter the line speed. Before I present an explanation for this state of affairs and for the superior productivity performance of Chrysler France, I shall present the data on labor productivity.

A rigorous comparison of the labor productivity between the Ryton assembly plant in Coventry and the assembly plant at Poissy was completed by the industrial-engineering staff of Chrysler U.K. in 1976. The comparison was facilitated because both plants were assembling the same car, the Alpine model.[66] The study showed that Chrysler U.K. was targeted to produce a car in 32.11 man hours, whereas they in fact produced one in 36.42 man hours. In contrast, Chrysler France produced the same car in 28.98 hours. The actual differences was therefore 7.44 man hours per car and was accounted for by more hours taken for repair and relief (5.41 man hours) and by a poorer line balance at Chrysler U.K.[67] Looking at relief allowances per man (see table 5-2), we note that Chrysler U.K. workers have two-and-a-half times as much relief per week as do Chrysler France workers. Chrysler U.K. workers get more relief than is formally recognized in the contract, whereas Chrysler France workers get less. The Chrysler France workers have time (on average 70 minutes per man per week) spent idle during breakdowns counted as relief and subtracted from their recognized allowances. At Chrysler U.K., breakdown time counts as extra nonworking time for workers. They still insist on their recognized allowances. Very simply, Chrysler U.K. workers spend less time working.

The intensity of work is also greater at Chrysler France. The line speed is faster and the rhythm of work is faster because the flow of work is longer (due to the longer production runs). At Chrysler U.K. more interruptions to production take place, which breaks up the flow and rhythm of work. Management at Chrysler France is also able to make up for breakdown losses by increasing the speed of the line.

An industrial engineer who participated in the productivity study also cited several examples of restrictive practices by workers at Chrysler U.K.:

> If we need ten men out of a section of twenty-five for overtime, the men respond we have to take all twenty-five or none. If we want a weekend shift, they will ask for a long-term guarantee for weekend work before they will agree. If an industrial engineer calculates five men are needed to do a job, the union will say six, and they often win. In nearly every case where the work process is being changed, the British unions demand negotiations; at Chrysler France they are just told what to do.

Table 5-2
A Comparison of Relief Allowances between Chrysler U.K. and Chrysler France, 1976

Relief per Man	Ryton	Poissy
Working minutes per week	2,400	2,400
Recognized allowances	226	177.7
Actual relief	246.6 to 257.7	107.7
Relief taken during breakdowns	–	70

Source: Adapted from Chrysler U.K. records. Prepared by industrial engineering staff.

However, if workers at Chrysler U.K. spend less time working and appear more intractable from management's point of view than do workers at Chrysler France, they also get injured less often. Taking 1977, a year in which Chrysler U.K. adopted the groupwide system of recording accidents, we find that the severity rate (which refers to the numbers of days lost due to recordable injuries per 200,000 hours worked) is 4.5 for Chrysler U.K., 72 for the whole Chrysler Corporation (sixteen times higher), and 280 for Chrysler France (fifty-eight times higher).[68] Concretely that translates into 1,400 lost days per million hours worked at Chrylser France due to accidents and only 23 lost days per million hours worked at Chrysler U.K.[69] The pattern seems to be consistent for the 1970s. This is the neglected but relevant underside of productivity comparisons that focus specifically on labor effort or on how hard people work. Although only a multivariate analysis (controlling for many other factors) could establish the soundness of the relationship between labor effort and accident rates in factory work, sound commonsensical grounds exist for expecting the association to be real. At Chrysler France, risks were apparently taken on the factory floor in the drive for maximum production.[70] As the industrial engineer noted in this context, "In Chrysler France they get away with much more."

What is the explanation for such differences between two subsidiaries that operate under the control of one parent in the same part of Europe? Why does Chrysler France have a superior productivity record, an unblemished disputes record, few hindrances to management actions on the job-control frontier, and a worse accident record?

The answer takes us into a fascinating area that can be only touched upon here. Chrysler France is dominated by the Confederation Francaise du Travail (CFT), an allegedly right-wing company union.[71] The union has a small national membership but figures strongly at Chrysler France, Peugeot, and Citroen.[72] CFT is accused of voting irregularities and fraud in factory elections, of receiving instruction and money from the companies, of using physical intimidation by commandos to quash any opposition among the workers, of dismissing workers on improper grounds and using threats of dismissal to pressure workers to increase productivity, and essentially of protecting the interests of management rather than that of workers.[73] A manager at Chrysler France agreed that the favorable industrial-relations climate was due to the CFT, which adopts an "attitude of cooperation. They participate and don't contest every day."

Within this unusual structure of worker/management relations, another aspect has to be considered. Some 50 percent of the hourly workers at the Poissy complex are foreigners, a pattern of employment that can be traced back at least to the early 1960s.[74] The foreign workers at Chrysler France supply 80 percent of the assembly-line force, while skilled work is reserved for the French workers. According to a manager at Chrysler France, personnel managers are sent to North Africa to recruit workers:

This is the best way because we can find people who have never worked

in industry and who have never used social-security facilities. They are
recruited on special one- or two-year contracts. We can extend their visa
by applying to the government for extension. There are few problems
in their work attitudes as they want to earn a lot of money. They were
less worried about conditions of work, but this is changing due to union
and government pressure.

Again, this is a fascinating but tangential area that I cannot fully explore
here. What is relevant is the combination of sanctions and incentives—via the
extension of the visa—and the attitude of the foreign workers—that is, to earn
as much money as possible in the short time they are there—that reinforces
the production fever at Chrysler France. As a bonus, having a large foreign
work force enabled the subsidiary to cope with the many workers rendered
superfluous in the 1974 crisis period, when sales dropped, in a fairly costless
manner. In 1973, total manpower was 39,872. In 1974 it dropped to 35,244
only to rise to 38,107 in 1975 with the end of the immediate crisis and the
launch of the Alpine model. Chrysler France was able, in 1974, to make some
4,000 North African employees fully redundant. The workers returned to
Morocco and most were rehired in 1975—costless not only for the company
but also for France.[75]

The brief look at industrial relations at Chrysler France goes part way
in explaining its better performance and, when taken together with its larger
size, provides a sound rationale for the preferential treatment it received vis à
vis Chrysler U.K. A question still remains, though: What is the significance
of the multinational connection to the industrial relations of the two main
European subsidiaries? In the first place we note that the parent intervened
in the industrial relations of Chrysler U.K. but left the French subsidiary un-
touched. Second, the parent considered, but rejected, plans to integrate the
two subsidiaries, to some extent for the reasons mentioned in earlier sections
but possibly also because of the fear of contamination. Integration would have
probably increased the frequency and intensity of contact between the two
sets of workers, thus increasing the likelihood that the organization and power
of the British workers would be picked up by the French workers and, from
the other side, also give impetus to demands for pay parity from the lower-
paid British workers.[76] In other words, whereas several rational factors were
in favor of consolidating the multinational connection, the differences in the
industrial relations between the two subsidiaries encouraged the parent to
maintain the segregation of the work forces.

Transfer Pricing

Unfortunately, I was not able to penetrate the veil of secrecy that surrounds
the subject of transfer pricing in this case. However, I can lay out the various

opportunities available for transfer-price manipulation and review what various interested parties had to say on the matter.

In keeping with common multinational practice, Chrysler had set up a sales subsidiary, Chrysler International SA, in Switzerland, a country with lower taxes. Manufacturing subsidiaries such as Chrysler France and Chrysler U.K. would direct their overseas sales through the Swiss subsidiary. Therefore, given the high volume of exports of each subsidiary, the opportunity is available for the manipulation of transfer prices. However, one high-level executive for Europe, categorically stated that the sale of kits to Iran from Chrysler U.K. was a direct one and did not go via any intermediary.[77] As regards Chrysler U.K., therefore, that only leaves intracompany trade (for example, the sale of Avengers to the United States) and other exports amenable to manipulation.

Chrysler management denied tampering with transfer prices and claimed under repeated questioning by the Expenditure Committee that transfer prices were set on "a competitive basis" and at "arms length."[78] The Expenditure Committee was obviously skeptical, dryly commenting that "CC did not follow a pricing policy which was to the greatest advantage of the corporation."[79] The Workers' Document cited accusations by the Labour Research Department that "artificially low export prices were charged to other Chrysler subsidiaries, particularly in Switzerland where taxes and profits are lower than in the UK," and that if this were so, then "in the last three years alone Chrysler U.K. had, in effect, given away £93 million to the Swiss subsidiary." Chrysler management's position was that not only did they not unfairly tamper with transfer prices but also that if they did tamper, "the best thing to do would be to put all the profits into Chrysler U.K. which pays no tax at all" because it has frequently been a loss maker.[80]

Other accusations and denials have also been made. For example, a private research group, the Economist Intelligence Unit, did find that kits of Hunters were being exported FOB to Iran at an average value of £531 each, "compared with £660 for all other exports of cars CKD by the industry in the same range of engine size (mainly Cortinas)."[81] However, if the assertion that sales to Iran are direct is true, then all we can conclude is that Chrysler negotiated a poor deal with INIM. Some doubt also exists on the fairness of the allocation of costs incurred on the design of models that were not produced, with worker representatives' suggesting that Chrysler U.K. carried a disproportionate share of the cost.[82] Finally, the government charged the Swiss subsidiary, CISA, with not filing accounts with the Registrar of Companies, as was legally required for a company trading in the United Kingdom. Chrysler responded by filing accounts for the years 1970-1974 in 1975, but these did not include group accounts as required by law. For unknown reasons the British government did not prosecute the case. The absence of hard evidence renders a discussion of these accusations rather pointless. It does seem fair to conclude, however, that such issues probably did not critically affect the profitability of the subsidiary.

Profitability

Although Chrysler U.K. made profits in five of the nine years in the 1967 to 1975 period, they amounted to only £8.4 million as contrasted with losses totalling £74.5 million (see table 5-3). The rate of return on investment was correspondingly meager, ranging from a high of 6.3 percent in 1973, its best year, to substantial negative rates in 1974 and 1975.[83] Thus, although Chrysler invested around £50 million in Chrysler U.K., most of it in the period to 1970, the investment program did not yield the corporation any dividends in the following five years. The Expenditure Committee, however, felt that this investment program did little more than replace aging plants and equipment and was not sufficient to improve Chrysler U.K.'s performance.[84]

The multinational connection, therefore, prolonged the life of the British company but did little to make it viable. Clearly, one cannot lay all the blame for this on Chrysler. The British subsidiary had severe inherited weakenesses, and country-specific factors such as the low growth in demand for cars and the high inflation rate aggravated its financial position. Nevertheless, on balance, one has to conclude that Chrysler did little to improve the condition of the company it acquired in 1967. Many of the touted benefits of absorption into multinationals, such as access to technology and manufacturing integration, failed to materialize for Chrysler U.K.

By early 1975, in the middle of recession, Chrysler U.K.'s marginal financial position was exposed, and the parent, on an emergency basis, injected $38 million into Chrysler U.K. in a three-month period to enable it to meet the cost of operations.[85] Moreover, its debt structure was heavily tilted toward short-

Table 5-3
Profit and Loss: A Comparison between Chrysler U.K., Chrysler France, and Chrysler

Year	Chrysler U.K. (pounds)	Chrysler France (francs)	Chrsyler (dollars)
1967	(10.5)[a]	11.9	203
1968	3.5	31.8	303
1969	0.6	36.6	99
1970	(10.9)	10.8	(8)
1971	0.5	91.1	84
1972	1.6	98.3	220
1973	3.7	154.0	225
1974	(17.7)	(71.8)	(52.1)
1975	(35.4)	(110.6)	(259.5)

Source: Chrysler U.K., Chrysler France, and Chrysler annual reports, various years.
[a]Figures in parentheses indicate losses.

term loans that did not give it very much financial stability. In early 1975 it tried to replace these short-term loans with medium-term loans. Its British bankers refused and so, in effect, did a government-supported consortium of banks known as Finance for Industry (FFI).[86] Unable to trade at a profit and to raise finance in the U.K. capital markets, Chrysler U.K. could not fund new-model programs or its share of the costs of integration. Without new models and integration, it could not point to the future for an improvement in profitability. Worse, the parent was saddled with a subsidiary that promised to be a continued drain on group funds, a situation that would, according to a top Chrysler executive, "jeopardize the rest of the European operations." These facts alone provide a compelling case for withdrawal and give some credence to the comment made by this same top executive that, "When you have an infected part of a body, it's better to cut it off."

Reasons for the Decision to Withdraw

Why, then, did Chrysler not amputate its infected British subsidiary? Why did it threaten to withdraw and then reach an agreement with the British government that ensured its continued presence in the United Kingdom for a least another three years? Had it, in fact, wanted to withdraw and stayed only after the government had applied intense political pressure and guaranteed it massive financial aid, or had it all along wanted to stay and skillfully used the threat merely as a ploy to extract cash from the government and concessions from the workers? In other words, what was its strategy in mid- and late 1975? I was unable to uncover corroborated information on Chrysler's real intentions in order to answer these questions conclusively. However, it is possible to piece together Chrysler's strategy and position at that time by examining circumstantial evidence. My conclusion is that Chrysler's strategy was to remain in Europe as a full manufacturing operation and that to do that it required the marketing facilities of Chrysler U.K. and at least some of its manufacturing capacity. Chrysler, at least in the short run, wanted to stay in Britain. But it is also clear that without substantial aid from the government, the severity of its cash shortage would have forced it to withdraw from Britian. In that sense the threat was neither idle nor a ploy.

Several pieces of evidence can substantiate this conclusion. First, Chrysler's behavior prior to the announcement of possible divestment did not indicate a company preparing to withdraw. Throughout 1975, Chrysler frantically tried to raise money for Chrysler U.K. The top executive I interviewed described these attempts in the following way:

> Prior to the government agreement we [Chrysler] were reluctant to put money into the UK because CUK bankers themselves said go to

hell. So we went to the government. We looked at the Industry Act and its provisions for aid, we went to the Finance for Industry consortium of banks and asked for £35 million. We worked our butts off within the UK to generate money for Chrysler U.K. They all said no.

In fact, the discussions with the Department of Industry were about government aid for the development of new models and began as late as July 1975, only three months before the announcement of possible withdrawal, and continued through August and September.[87] This certainly indicated a willingness to continue operations in Britain, provided funds could be generated within the country. We should also note here that Chrysler, as late as May 1975, was desperately trying to improve industrial relations by offering workers seats on the board of directors. Only with the massive drop in Chrysler U.K.'s market share for cars from 8.5 percent in July to 4.3 percent in September did Chrysler reconsider its position in Britian and threaten withdrawal.[88] The issue as perceived by Chrysler was a massive and immediate shortage of cash and not a need to change strategy.

Parallelling the cash problem at Chrysler U.K. was a cash squeeze at parent headquarters. In mid-1975, Chrysler announced half-yearly losses of $153 million, and the speculation was that its bankers, who had recently extended it a $410-million revolving-credit facility and who were represented on the board of directors, pressured Chrysler to stem the financial drain.[89] This is an additional indication that the paramount preoccupation throughout Chrysler was a severe cash squeeze and not a change of strategy.

Finally, we have to examine the effect withdrawal would have had on the Iranian contract, on Chrysler's share of the U.K. market, and how important these effects were to Chrysler's overseas presence. The executive I interviewed was convinced that Chrysler could have saved the Iranian contract and fulfilled its legal obligation by "employing the technical support from a worldwide corporate base" and by using non-European subsidiaries to supply Iran. Whether Chrysler could have overcome the problems associated with such a changeover rapidly enough to preserve the contract is a matter of conjecture. What is clear is that most of Chrysler's U.K. market share would have been lost. Chrysler France, the most realistic alternative source of supply, was in the process of launching a new model and was working at full capacity. As a Chrysler France middle manager admitted in an interview, "We can't pretend to have the capacity to produce all the cars for Chrysler in Europe. It would have been a problem for Chrysler if Chrylser U.K. had ceased to exist." Depsite Chrysler U.K.'s actual isolation within the European empire, it seems to me that Chrysler viewed its operations there as a piece. If it was to withdraw, it would do so from the whole of Europe in an orderly manner because it could not lose a sizable presence in one of the largest markets in Europe and still pretend to be a credible European competitor.

One should neither overstress the desire of Chrysler to stay in Britain for strategic reasons nor underestimate the depth of its financial problems, which may have been pulling it in the other direction. Chrysler did have a preference, as I argued previously, but it would only stay if the financial terms were right. If not, it would withdraw. This flexibility or relative indifference between the options greatly strengthened its bargaining position with the British government.

Process of the Withdrawal Attempt

Although the negotiations that went on about the future of Chrysler U.K. were secret, enough information emerged to enable us to piece together the following tentative picture. The drama was set in motion when the chairman of Chrysler announced on 29 October 1975 the possibility of the disposal of loss-making operations.[90] Both workers and the British government learned of this decision from press reports.

Immediately the prime minister and other top officials of the government began negotiations with top executives of Chrysler. Apparently from the way Chrysler framed its opening position, it was both prepared for a long process of bargaining and had a certain flexibility built into its position.

At the first meetings with government in early November, Chrysler presented three options: (1) it could give the subsidiary to the government; (2) it could transfer over 80 percent of the interest to the government, keeping the rest for itself; or (3) it could consider and discuss other options. If no acceptable solution was arrived at, the parent would close Chrysler U.K. by February 1976.[91] The Expenditure Committee's report makes much of Chrysler's inflexible bargaining position, but an analysis of Chrysler's problems and its actions prior to October seems to indicate not a desire to withdraw but a desperate need for cash. If money was put on the table, Chrysler would consider other options.

During the month of November, the government either did not see this point or avoided it. It also refused, quite rightly in my opinion, to be enticed by Chrysler's more-explicit options. Full or majority control of Chrysler U.K. would have saddled the government with £160 million of liabilities, the prospect of continued large losses, and a massive investment program of several million pounds. Moreover, nationalization of one part of a larger enterprise, even one as isolated as Chrysler U.K., would have presented major problems to the new owners in areas such as research and development, marketing, and distribution. The Imperial case (chapter 6) highlights this dilemma more clearly. The possibility of a takeover by other U.K. auto manufacturers was floated, but no one showed interest. In a time of depressed sales and surplus capacity, a rival company would have gladly taken over some of the dealers but would have probably closed most of the manufacturing plant. This solution would not have dealt with the government's primary consideration—jobs.

The government pursued a number of other options such as asking Chrysler to consider remaining in Britain in a reduced form. Chrysler continued to negotiate but categorically refused to take financial or even managerial responsibility for a reduced Chrysler U.K. In fact, on 26 November Chrysler again cleverly demonstrated its seeming resolve to leave by making the government an offer it could refuse. It offered to give Chrysler U.K. to the government with £35 million thrown in. It also offered to provide technical, marketing, and managerial services on a fee basis.[92] Again, the government rightly refused this offer. Chrysler U.K. on its own was too small to compete in Europe, and a government takeover would have done nothing to change that. On 5 December the government finally stopped skirting the central issue and asked Chrysler to state its terms.[93]

Chrysler demanded that the government share in the projected losses and arrange finance for a capital-expenditure program for new models. An agreement along these lines was signed on 16 December 1975. The principal terms of the agreement were as follows:

The agreement was to run for three years.

The government took on a contingent liability of £162.5 million.

Of this amount, £72.5 million was to be made available by government to cover, as necessary, any losses Chrysler U.K. incurred in the 1976-1979 period.

£55 million was in the form of long-term government loans to be used for capital investment in plant, equipment, and models, and £35 million was to be raised on the private-capital markets and was to be secured by the government and by Chrysler assets.

There would be 8,200 layoffs.[94]

In return, Chrysler agreed to provide £10 million if losses for 1976 exceeded £50 million and to match the commitment of public funds toward any losses in the years 1977-1979. It also volunteered to produce the very successful C6/Alpine model in the United Kingdom and to cover the costs of that program (£10-12 million), as well as to vigorously pursue integration.[95] The agreement clearly met Chrysler's objectives. The cash problem was resolved, both in terms of short-term future losses and investment needs, and the problem of insufficient capacity in Chrysler France was solved without Chrysler's having to undertake costly new development in France.

The ambiguity in the government's position during the negotiatons reflected an ideological division within the state apparatus on the question of the nature and extent of the government's role in the economy. This ideological division is a central feature of all advanced capitalist states and surfaces in each of the three cases in this book. The British state in 1975 had gone through some strange gyrations on this question. On the one hand it had, on an ad hoc basis, rescued British Leyland and put it under state control and, for a time, had actively supported several worker cooperatives formed to save jobs and output at enterprises that had been judged failures by their owners. On the other hand, by late 1975 the government tried systematically to set out an industrial strategy that promised to regenerate the economic strength of Britian by, among other things, giving aid only to companies that were "likely to be viable in the longer term."[96] At about the same time, a government-sponsored think tank published a report on the automobile industry that concluded that too many manufacturers were in the industry relative to current and projected demand.[97] Putting these new objectives and projections together, it seemed rational that many civil servants and government ministers would argue against rescuing Chrysler in any way. Apparently that is what happened, and it may have been one of the factors explaining the delay in the government's offer of aid. In the end, however, the forces favoring rescue won the day and Chrysler was given aid.

Several factors were crucial to Chrysler's victory.[98] At the forefront was an estimated direct job loss of 25,000 with an additional indirect loss of 30,000 jobs, excluding multiplier effects. The cost to the state of these 55,000 lost jobs was estimated to be around £150 million if those 55,000 workers remained unemployed for an average of a year. With a historically high national unemployment rate of 5.2 percent in September 1975, and with the prospects of regional rates' rising from 6.5 to 11.8 percent at Coventry and from 4.8 to 12.6 percent at Paisley, Scotland, a Labour government could not, for electoral reasons if no other, allow complete closure. The special significance of lost jobs in Scotland, a traditional area of Labour-Party support, was increased by the electoral switch of Labour voters to the Scottish National Party. The Iranian contract was also an important factor. The government was concerned that the loss of the contract might jeopardize the close trading and political relations that existed with the fast-developing Iranian economy. The loss of the contract would also figure in the balance-of-payments effects. An estimated adverse effect of £200 million over four years was calculated on the basis of lost exports and increased imports. All these estimates involve assumptions at each step of a series of calculations and are therefore subject to a large margin of error. Nevertheless, they are significant for they are one of the few examples of publicly available figures on the national financial cost of closure.

The workers at Chrysler U.K., the ones who would be most directly affected by the outcome of the negotiations, were excluded from them. To a degree they accepted this state of affairs because they expected a Labour government to defend their interests. Nevertheless, they were not passive. As early as January 1975, in view of the absence of new models and the short-time working, they pressured members of Parliament and government ministers to investigate the situation at Chrysler. After the announcement of possible withdrawal, they lobbied Parliament and organized meetings to publicize their point of view. Moreover, they planned to occupy the Chrysler factories in the Midlands if the government did not safeguard jobs.[99] They also hurriedly prepared a document, "Chrysler's Crisis: The Workers' Answer," in which they challenged the view that they were responsible for the crisis, made several detailed allegations against Chrysler (as regards investment, transfer pricing, exports, and so on), and proposed a three-stage plan for the rescue of the enterprise. The first stage demanded practical short-term improvements in production, marketing, and management. The second stage involved investment in plant, a new model, and the reestablishment of a toolroom at Linwood. The third stage demanded nationalization of Chrysler U.K. without compensation (an option preempted by Chrysler's offer of the company and £35 million to the government). The workers also made a progressive proposal:

> We must explore the feasibility of new kinds of product of a socially useful kind to harness the skills of the existing work force and the existing plant and machinery and to direct it away from a commodity whose usefulness is rapidly declining.[100]

The workers also pursued the possibility of international union collaboration. They wrote a letter to the United Automobile Workers (UAW) head office in Detroit, requesting that the union help by "bringing all pressure to bear on the Chrysler board" to maintain Chrysler U.K. The UAW did bring up the matter with top Chrysler management but were told that delicate negotiations were proceeding with the British government and nothing could be divulged at that stage.[101] No contact was made with the French unions.

The agreement reached between Chrysler and the British government, though preserving most of the jobs at Chrysler U.K., did set out the need for 8,000 layoffs. The workers vainly fought this clause by going on strike but accepted the layoffs after Minister of Industry Eric Varley warned the strikers that if the layoffs, productivity deals, and reorganization plans were not accepted, the whole deal would be off.

Consequences of the Withdrawal Attempt

On almost all counts, Chrysler, emerged successfully from the withdrawal attempt. It kept the Iranian contract, maintained a foothold in the U.K. market, and was able to utilize quickly some of the spare capacity in the United Kingdom to produce extra Alpines that the French subsidiary could not, which probably saved Chrysler some investment costs. The deal also improved Chrysler's stock on the New York Stock Exchange since it stemmed a financial drain. As a bonus, as I have already mentioned, the crisis produced a more-tranquil industrial-relations climate with fewer major and minor disputes and an improvement in productivity. The multinational had been able to turn its weaknesses into strengths at the bargaining table. It bargained another three years of life in which time top management believed Chrysler Europe could be made cosmetically attractive to prospective buyers.[102]

The laid-off workers did not suffer economically as much as might have been expected. Most of the layoffs were on a voluntary basis, and within a year, because of the unexpected buoyancy in the demand for cars, some 5,800 workers were recruited or rehired. The shop stewards I interviewed noted that Chrysler U.K. management became the most open management in the motor industry, holding regular meetings to discuss various forecasts and plans. However, on a more-somber note, a redundancy study conducted by the Manpower Service Commission on those volunteering for layoff found that out of the 1,050 men studied one year after layoff, some 200 had been continuously unemployed for a year and that on average an individual was out of work for 27 weeks in the 12-month period.[103]

In addition to the financial cost to the state of the agreement—that is, grants and loan facilities as well as the fiscal effects of the redundancies—there were several other national political effects. The case demonstrated once again the near impossibility of the government's allowing a large company to close. The concentration of capital had raised the political and economic stakes to a point at which closure and the "discipline of the market" became costs the government could no longer tolerate. It also rammed home the difficulties of nationalizing a manufacturing subsidiary of a multinational company. As multinationals increasingly integrate their subsidiaries, the myriad connections between them make it more-operationally difficult for governments to assert national control over industrial sectors. Less visibly, but no less importantly, it made embarrassingly clear the chronic imbalance of information between multinationals and governments (let alone in relation to workers). In the hurried negotiations at the end of 1975, the British government was heavily dependent on the information and figures provided by Chrysler.[104]

Two-and-a-half years later, in mid-1978, Chrysler did withdraw from Europe, but this time it did so en masse and quietly, having concluded a deal with P.S.A. Peugeot-Citroen after several months of secret negotiations, of which neither the British government, with all its financial interests in Chrysler U.K., nor the workers had an inkling. In the intervening period, Chrysler had modernized plant and equipment, introduced new models, and proceeded with integration, much of which was funded by government-backed loans of £35 million. Losses of £64.4 million were made in 1976 and 1977, of which government grants covered £51.5 million.[105] Despite these large losses, Chrysler U.K. was a more-salable company. So although Peugeot-Citroen likely would have preferred to acquire the Simca facilities and only the British and Spanish dealers, Chrysler could point to the modernization program, the integration, and the agreement with the government (which gave the British government veto power over the sale of Chrysler U.K. until 1979) to support its position that Peugeot-Citroen should acquire the whole European empire. In September 1978, Chrysler sold its European subsidiaries to Peugeot-Citroen for $230 million, a 15 percent share in the group, and the transfer of responsibility for the subsidiaries' liabilities of $400 million.[106] Peugeot-Citroen became the largest European motor manufacturer overnight with an 18 percent share of the market.

The reasons for Chrysler's large-scale withdrawal can again be traced to a lack of funds. However, this time it was not an immediate cash crisis that had prompted withdrawal. Chrysler had made record profits of $422 million in 1976 and profits of $163 million in 1977. However, faced with spending programs of many billions of dollars by its two main U.S. rivals, Chrysler planned an investment program of $7.5 billion into 1983 just to maintain its relative position. Chrylser was compelled to alter its strategy and concentrate all its resources in the United States. Overseas liabilities had to be eliminated, and overseas assets had to be cashed in. The postponed withdrawal was finally carried out in an orderly fashion.

The workers were once again left to ponder their future in relative darkness. A glossy company brochure was distributed among the workers that explained in highly vague terms the new fait accompli. It argued in all-too-familiar style that Chrysler U.K. needed "to be part of a large, strong, stable group" to have any chance of survival and reassured the work force that Peugeot-Citroen was "just that."[107] However, there were good grounds to suspect that the French company would gradually hive off excess manufacturing capacity in the United Kingdom and Spain, rationalize its product range by dropping several models (probably British ones), and integrate the valuable Chrysler dealer network into its distribution system.[108] This at least seems to be the most sensible medium-term strategy for little reason exists to suppose that takeover by itself would make Chrysler Europe profitable. Another source of worry for the workers was that they were now joining an empire whose rulers were well accustomed to dealing with the company union, the CFT. Given Chrysler U.K.'s highly marginal status in the new empire, the French management would not likely tolerate British industrial-relations customs for long.

Conclusion and Postscript

Chrysler's retreat from overseas markets turned out to be but a prelude to one of the most dramatic attempts to save a large company in recent history. One of the largest manufacturing companies in the world was by 1979 on the verge of bankruptcy, and only massive intervention by the federal government prevented its collapse. The causes of Chrysler's near collapse and the political maneuverings surrounding its rescue cannot adequately be treated here. It is worthwhile, however, to identify and briefly reflect on some of the salient features of this recent episode, especially as they touch on the theme of this book.

This latest closure crisis brings to the surface the nature and extent of the restructuring that has been going on in the international economy since the 1960s and that underlie many of the developments described in the three cases. The automobile industry, in particular, has experienced profound changes that are likely to lead to a further pruning of companies and cars. By the end of the century, a handful of giant multinational companies most likely will be competing with a small number of so-called world cars. The shrinkage of Chrysler represents an early sign of what is to come.

In the last few years, Chrylser has drastically reduced its involvement around the world by selling off various proportions of its ownership interests to rival companies in such areas as Europe, Argentina, Brazil, Venezuela, and Australia, and it has seen its market share in the United States tumble from 14 percent in 1975 to 8 percent in October 1979, with a consequent loss of dealers and the closure of at least five manufacturing plants.[109] In this reduced state, Chrysler has tried to put the best face possible on its new product strategy of quickly shifting to the production of small cars produced in the United States that are powered by a large number of engines supplied by rivals. For example, Mitsubishi, Volkswagen, and Peugeot all have agreements to supply Chrysler several hundred thousand engines into the 1980s.[110] However, making the best of circumstances is not a strategy that will guide Chrysler in the changed international economy. While Chrysler is shrinking, the trend is toward increased size and concentration, which will give competitors scale economies and substantial advantages in the investment race to produce more-fuel efficient and -electronically sophisticated cars. At some point Chrysler's rivals will decide to stop supplying it with advanced engines and components and will attempt to take over its declining market share.

Two important conclusions can be drawn from the retrenchment. First, it illustrates the intense nature of international competition between multinational companies in this phase of late capitalism. Even very large companies are threatened with collapse. Yet it also demonstrates the incredible resilience such multi-unit giants have because of their structual flexibility. Chrysler has delayed collapse in large part because it could restructure itself by divesting subsidiaries, plants, products, and workers.

In the end, however, Chrysler's financial position was in such a mess, with losses of $1 billion in 1979 and with worldwide debts totalling $4.4 billion, that only some form of government intervention could save it.[111] Chrysler in crisis publicly demonstrated the incredible multiplicity of interests with a stake in its health. These interests included 350 lenders across the world, ranging from small banks in the hinterland of the United States to rival multinationals such as Peugeot and Mitsubishi, the Canadian government, several state governments in the United States, dealer associations, the UAW, and the federal government.[112] All these groups, in one way or another, had to make concessions, extend loans, or provide guarantees to enable Chrysler to survive. This is some measure of the penetration multinationals make into the international political economy. Ironically, their potential failure has become their most potent political weapon.

Notes

1. Paul Blustein, "Another Chrysler Turnabout: But Is This One for Real?" *Forbes,* 15 November 1976, pp. 39-43.

2. One indication of the dependence of Chrysler U.K. on the parent is that the subsidiary could only spend up to £20,000 without reference to any other part of the multinational. See the comment by G. Gillespie, former vice-president for Europe, in House of Commons, Expenditure Committee, *Minutes of Evidence Taken before the Trade and Industry Sub-Committee in Session 1975-76, Public Expenditure on Chrysler UK Ltd.* (London: HMSO, 1976), p. 123.

3. Neil Young and Stephen Hood, *Chrysler U.K.: A Corporation in Transition* (New York: Praeger, 1977).

4. House of Commons, *Eighth Report from the Expenditure Committee, Public Expenditure on Chrysler UK Ltd., Volume 1–Report.* (London: HMSO, 1976); and *Minutes of Evidence.*

5. Chrysler Action Committee, "The Workers' Document" (Unpublished document, Coventry, 1975 and 1976).

6. Ford established manufacturing operations in Europe very early in the twentieth century, with some production in Britain in 1909. General Motors followed by acquiring Vauxhall in Britain in 1928.

7. Central Policy Review Staff, *The Future of the British Car Industry* (London: HMSO, 1975), p. 31.

8. In fact in later years, Ford, General Motors, and Chrysler relied heavily on the experience and expertise of their European subsidiaries when they were forced to switch to the production of small cars to meet the massive shift in consumer demand.

9. For example, neither Ford nor General Motors was able to increase their share of the Europe market in the 1960s. They merely kept a fairly constant proportion of an expanding market. This implied that it would be very hard for Chrysler to win market shares. Young and Hood, *Chrysler U.K.*, p. 31.

10. Ibid., p. 63. Young and Hood suggest that Spain could be used as a "base on which to extend Simca capacity."

11. The Chrysler executive informed me that the company had conducted an extensive search, contacting several companies with a view to purchase, before settling on the three bought.

12. As it was, Chrysler bought into Simca surreptitiously via the purchase of shares in Switzerland and acquired Rootes after intense but hollow political debate suggested that no other solution was available.

13. A fuller exposition can be found in Young and Hood, *Chrysler U.K.*

14. The dealer network was extensive and loyal. As to the brand names, the chairman of the Chrysler U.K. Dealers Association claimed, "Rootes had one thing they were well known for. This was the good quality of their product. The names of Humber and Hillman were synonymous with quality." House of Commons, *Minutes of Evidence,* p. 250.

15. There is virtual unanimity among those who are familiar with the Chrysler case that the critical problem was that of scale. See, for example, House of Commons, *Eighth Report,* pp. 30-31.

16. House of Commons, *Fourteenth Report from the Expenditure Committee, The Motor Vehicle Industry, Volume 1* (London: HMSO, 1975), p. 203.

17. By the 1970s Chrysler had a production capacity in Europe of around 900,000 units. A study on the car industry estimated that an annual production of at least 750,000 units is necessary if a company is to compete in volume car markets. See Central Policy Review Staff, p. 23.

18. House of Commons, *Eighth Report,* p. 28.

19. Much of the following data are taken from Department of the Treasury, *News. Statement of the Honorable G. William Miller, Secretary of the Treasury before the Subcommitttee on Economic Stabilization of the House Committee on Banking, Finance and Urban Affairs. Appendix 2.* (Washington, D.C.: Government Printing Office, 6 and 7 November 1979).

20. Blustein, "Another Chrysler Turnabout."

21. Statement by G. Gillespie in House of Commons, *Eighth Report,* p. 35.

22. For example, the ratio for Chrysler ranged between 120 and 160 in the 1969 to 1978 period, rising sharply after 1973. The ratios for General Motors ranged between 50 and 75 and for Ford between 75 and 125 in the same period. See Department of Treasury, *News. Statement of G. William Miller.*

23. Central Policy Review Staff, *Future of British Car Industry,* p. 29.

24. It thus increased its share of total U.K. production from 11.7 percent in 1967 to 15.2 percent in 1973. Young and Hood, *Chrysler U.K.,* p. 139.

25. The information for Chrysler France is from an interview with a middle manager at the subsidiary and that for Chrysler U.K. is calculated from figures in a memorandum submitted by Chrysler U.K. to House of Commons, *Fourteenth Report,* pp. 149 and 205.

26. See the submission by the Society of Motor Manufacturers Traders in ibid., p. 432.

27. See International Metalworkers' Federation, *Facts about Spain's Automobile Industry* (Geneva: IMF World Auto Councils Release, April 1977).

28. House of Commons, *Eighth Report,* p. 108.

29. In 1976, for example, the Linwood plant operated at 39.4 percent utilization of capacity and the Ryton plant at 73.4 percent. House of Commons, *Minutes of Evidence*, p. 371.

30. House of Commons, *Eighth Report,* p. 116.

31. Ibid, pp. 107-15.

32. See the statements by G. Gillespie in House of Commons, *Minutes of Evidence,* pp. 127 and 143.

33. This is how it was put to me by the top executive I interviewed.

34. Throughout this dicussion I do not consider the commercial-vehicle operations of Chrysler U.K. Although relatively successful, they only formed a small part of its total production.

35. There were, of course, several modifications of older models, in particular, new bodies placed on top of existing chassis. See Young and Hood, *Chrysler U.K.*, p. 109. Also, I should note that the Hunter model was given a new lease on life by the Iran contract.

36. From "D.H. Lander's Address to Officials and Stewards Representing the Hourly Paid Unions" (Private document, 15 January 1974).

37. House of Commons, *Minutes of Evidence*, p. 124.

38. Ibid., p. 128.

39. House of Commons, *Eighth Report*, p. 111.

40. Young and Hood, *Chrysler U.K.,* p. 138.

41. Ibid., p. 143.

42. Chrysler Action Committee, "The Workers' Document", 1975.

43. John Fayerweather and Ashok Kapoor, *Strategy and Negotiation for the International Corporation* (Cambridge, Mass.: Ballinger, 1976), pp. 133-59.

44. Young and Hood, *Chrysler U.K.,* p. 147.

45. See, for example, the comments made by a Chrysler executive to the Expenditure Committee in House of Commons, *Minutes of Evidence,* p. 536.

46. Ibid., p. 363.

47. The measured-day-work system of payment is based on fixed pay and carefully calculated work standards and labor loadings. The latter are typically determined by industrial engineers.

48. Interview with middle manager at Chrysler U.K. on 6 October 1977.

49. See Chrysler Action Committee, "The Workers' Document."

50. Letter from G. Hunt, managing director, Chrysler U.K., to William Wilson, member of Parliament, 22 May 1970.

51. Cited in Young and Hood, *Chrysler U.K.,* p. 234.

52. Ibid.

53. Peter Cartwright, "Chrysler U.K. Warns on Future if Coventry Dispute Continues," *Financial Times,* 27 June 1974, p. 40.

54. *Daily Telegraph*, 6 October 1974.

55. Terry Dodsworth, "No Give Way Sign Ahead," *Financial Times*, 11 December 1974, p. 9.

56. Letter to A. Wedgwood Benn from J. Riccardo, 8 February 1975, cited in House of Commons, *Fourteenth Report*, p. 221.

57. Terry Dodsworth, "No Give Way Sign Ahead," *Financial Times*, 11 December 1974, p. 9.

58. This phrase was apparently used by a top executive of Chrysler. It was reported to me by one of the middle managers I interviewed at Chrysler U.K.

59. Young and Hood, *Chrysler U.K.*, pp. 246-47.

60. See Chrysler Action Committee, "The Workers' Document." Emphasis in original.

61. All data in this section are from internal company records and documents unless otherwise stated.

62. A company can, to some extent, prepare for a major strike by building up inventories beforehand and will not have to incur some variable costs such as wages during the stoppage.

63. Central Policy Review Staff, *Future of British Car Industry*, p. 24.

64. Young and Hood, *Chrysler U.K.*, pp. 226-27.

65. Interview with manager at Chrysler France. The same claim was made by G. Gillespie, vice-president of Chrysler International, in evidence to the Expenditure Committee.

66. As with all productivity comparisons, this one has to be treated cautiously for, although the product was essentially the same, the researchers could not adequately check whether the same methods were used for the 20,000 or so operations involved.

67. "Line balance" refers to the distribution of workers along a line such that no bottlenecks occur to interrupt the flow or speed of work. The greater versatility and flexibility of the work force at Chrysler France means that a smaller reserve of workers is needed to cover absences and special situations. All data are from Chrysler U.K. documents (1976) entitled "C6 Comparison. CUK vs. Chrysler France" and "Relief Allowances: Ryton and Poissy Assembly Plants," 4 September and 25 November 1976.

68. Data on the severity rate at Chrysler U.K. was obtained from the company's publication "Safety News." Data for Chrysler France was obtained in an interview with a manager at Poissy, France.

69. The severity rate is calculated on a base of 200,000 manhours worked. Therefore, multiplying by five we can get the number of days lost per million hours worked.

70. A document reporting a press conference given by members of the communist union CGT claims that a former doctor at Simca had stated that the instruction medical staff received was: "Don't interfere with production." In this context the document cites examples of accidents that did not lead to the stopping of work for the injured, a refusal of a card to visit the factory clinic,

returning men to work before complete recovery, and sacking men who refused to work because work was too hard. Press conference with l'Union Departmentale des Syndicats des Yvelines, 29 October 1974.

71. See Jean Daniel Renaud, *Les syndicates en France* (Paris: Seuil, 1975), p. 117; Henri Rollin, *Militant chez Simca–Chrysler* (Paris: Editions Sociales, 1977); and Maurice Caille, *Les truands du patronat* (Paris: Editions Sociales, 1977).

72. All three are now in the same group.

73. See Caille, *Les truands*; Rollin, *Militant chez Simca*; and L'Union Departmentale, *Conference de Presse* for further details.

74. See Stephen Castles and Godula Kosack, *Immigrant Workers and the Class Structure in Western Europe* (London: Oxford University Press, 1973), pp. 263, 319-34.

75. Personal communication from Chrysler France, 10 June 1978.

76. Chrysler U.K. workers earned an average of £280 per month, which could be increased to £308 by overtime. Chrysler France workers earned a basic Fr2,822 (francs) per month (at an exchange rate of about 8.5—that is £332), which averaged about Fr4,052 per month (about £476) with premiums. On an hourly basis the comparison is of £2.20 at Chrysler U.K. versus £3.75 at Chrysler France. Data are for 1977.

77. House of Commons, *Minutes of Evidence*, p. 140.

78. Ibid.

79. House of Commons, *Eighth Report*, p. 102.

80. House of Commons, *Minutes of Evidence*, p. 141.

81. "The Multinational that Wanted to Be Nationalized: A Case History of the Chrysler Rescue," *Multinational Business*, no. 1 (1976).

82. See Chrysler Action Committee, The Workers' Document.

83. House of Commons, *Eighth Report*, p. 30.

84. Ibid., p. 29.

85. Ibid., p. 34.

86. Ibid., pp. 37-39.

87. Ibid., pp. 39-42.

88. Ibid., p. 117.

89. Securities and Exchange Commission, *Form 10-K Reports: Chrysler Corporation 1975*. Washington, D.C.

90. House of Commons, *Eighth Report*, p. 44.

91. Ibid. p. 61.

92. Ibid., pp. 68-69.

93. Ibid., pp. 70-71.

94. See House of Commons, *Minutes of Evidence*, pp. 1-7 for further details.

95. Ibid.

96. Department of Industry, *An Approach to Industrial Strategy* (London: HMSO, 1975), p. 10.

97. Central Policy Review Staff, *Chrysler U.K.*, p. v.

98. See House of Commons, *Eighth Report*, pp. 78-91 for a complete discussion of these factors.

99. Interview with Chrysler U.K. shop stewards at Chrysler U.K., Coventry, England, 15 June 1977.

100. See Chrysler Action Committee, The Workers' Document.

101. Private correspondence between G. Hawley of the Transport and General Workers Union and D. Fraser of the United Automobile Workers, 13 and 25 November 1975.

102. See the comment by J. Riccardo, chairman of Chrysler, on this matter in *Business Week*, in which he is reported as saying that the rescue "was what made it possible for Chrysler to sell off its U.K. operations." See "Is Chrysler the Prototype?" *Business Week*, 20 August 1979, p. 106.

103. Manpower Services Commission, "Chrysler (Linwood) Redundancy Study," London, 1978. I am grateful to the commission for allowing me to cite these results.

104. See the comments by the Expenditure Committee in House of Commons, *Eighth Report*, p. 59.

105. John Petty, "State Takeover is only Alternative" *Daily Telegraph*, 11 August 1978, p. 1.

106. See "Chrysler Retreats from Europe," *Time*, 21 August 1978, p. 55.

107. Chrysler U.K. Ltd., "Our Future with P.S.A. Peugeot-Citroen," December 1978. Issued by Employee Participation Department, Chrysler U.K.

108. See Terry Dodsworth, "Peugeot at the Top," *Financial Times*, 11 August 1978, p. 18, for a similar analysis of the situation.

109. *Wall Street Journal* 19 December 1979, pp. 1 and 24; and 13 May 1979, p. 10.

110. See *Wall Street Journal*, 18 July 1980, p. 22.

111. *Wall Street Journal*, 13 June 1980, p. 14.

112. *Wall Street Journal*, 16 April 1980, p. 10.

6 Imperial Typewriters

The takeover of Imperial Typewriters by Litton Industries joined two highly dissimilar companies. Imperial Typewriters, founded in 1908 in Leicester, England, was a small noninnovative producer of typewriters. Although it had increased its output and sales in the 1950s and early 1960s, it gradually found its profit margins squeezed in the fiercely competitive international marketplace.[1] In 1966, after some public debate, the last British-owned typewriter manufacturer was acquired by the U.S. conglomerate, Litton Industries.

Litton was formed in California in 1953, and it rapidly became one of the most famous of all conglomerates. It pursued a policy of growth founded on the utilization of the highest level of scientific and technological expertise and on skillful conglomeration by acquisition. By 1967 it had grown at a staggering rate to become a truly large multinational conglomerate. For example, its sales value jumped from $9 million in 1953 to $1.7 billion in 1967, it went from producing one product in 1953 to producing 300 in 1966,[2] and a $1.70 investment in 1953 was worth $900 in 1967.[3]

The acquisition of Imperial was part of Litton's large-scale entry into typewriter production. In 1965 it had bought Royal McBee, a U.S. company, and in 1968 acquired another long-established manufacturer, Germany's Triumph-Adler. Imperial's fate was continuously tied to the fortunes of Litton's other companies. In 1969 Litton began to run down two of the ex-Royal plants in the United States and transfer their production to Imperial in England. By 1972 the process was complete, the U.S. plants closed, and Imperial expanded to supply the U.S. market. A major reason for this transfer of production was the need for Litton to find cheaper-labor areas in response to fierce price competition at the lower end of the product range (that is, office manual and portable models), where no technological barriers to entry existed to protect companies.

Triumph-Adler, in contrast to Royal and Imperial, operated at the advanced end of the market, producing electric models and a diversified range of office equipment (for example, minicomputers and calculators). A more-successful company than Imperial, it was picked out to be the main base of Litton's venture into the office-equipment industry. In 1975, the middle of the recession, Imperial was closed and its markets were supplied by products made at Triumph-Adler and elsewhere. Although efforts were made by some Imperial workers to save their jobs, the necessary political support did not materialize.

Unlike the other two cases, I was not able to obtain interviews with Litton and Imperial managers who participated in the events surrounding the closure.

An Imperial executive refused to grant an interview, and I was unable to trace the Litton executive who oversaw its withdrawal. Nevertheless, I was able to obtain copies of two detailed confidential reports prepared by private consultants for the British government in early 1975 and documents prepared by Imperial Typewriters and a workers' action group for submission to the consultants. All these documents are used extensively. Other documentary sources are various company reports, newspapers, and official sources.

I conducted in-depth interviews with a Labour member of Parliament in a constituency where one of the Imperial plants was located and two members of the Hull Workers' Action Committee, one an academic, the other a leading official of the regional branch of the Transport and General Workers' Union.

Reasons for Investment

As Litton's acquisition of Imperial coincided with its entry into the typewriter industry, it is necessary to examine first some of the reasons that attracted Litton into the industry before turning to the specific reasons for its acquisition of Imperial.

Litton, as a conglomerate dedicated to continuous growth, constantly searched for opportunities to expand into new industries.[4] The typewriter industry, as part of the office-equipment industry, was a growth market with considerable potential. It has been calculated that in the period 1955–1963, typewriter production grew by 78.1 percent in West Germany, 155.1 percent in Italy, 35 percent in Great Britain, and only 3.3 percent in the United States, giving an overall increase in the Western world of 67.3 percent (an average growth of 8.4 percent per year).[5] World production of typewriters continued to expand in the following years—from 4.7 million units in 1964 to 7.2 million in 1973, the last year for which figures are available.[6] Of course, although the United States did not share in this growth of production, U.S. companies did increase their production overseas, and the United States remained the largest single market for typewriters.

The industry also was characterized by rapid technological change in product development (with moves from mechanical to electrical to automated machines). But given the unevenness of development between nations and national differences in the relative costs of labor and capital, the market was good not only for advanced products but also for older and more-standard products (for instance, manual models).

A rapidly expanding industry characterized by technological progress seemed ideal to a company with a record of extraordinary growth and boasting a scientist-to-staff ratio of better than 1:10.[7] However, the existing international pattern of production and sales and the fact that it was entering the industry many decades late clearly influenced Litton's early strategy.

Litton acquired three important and established manufacturers with production facilities and marketing outlets in several important markets: (1) Royal was the second-largest company in the U.S. industry and owned a plant in Leiden, Holland; (2) Imperial was a small but significant manufacturer in Britain with access to overseas markets, in particular ex–British colonies; and (3) Triumph-Adler, the best catch of all, was the largest producer in Germany and about to introduce new electric typewriters in the U.S. market.[8] Within the space of three years, Litton became a crucial multinational producer and marketer of typewriters. It gained access to three large industrial markets, to whatever markets these companies had developed in the rest of the world, and to a range of products that gave it a credible market presence (it also bought Willy Feiler, a small German company, to get its portable-electric design and technology).[9] Moreover, by pursuing the acquisition strategy, it eliminated competitors and furthered the process of concentration in the industry such that one source estimated it controlled some 30 percent of world typewriter production.[10]

The acquisition of Imperial was probably motivated by three reasons. First, Litton captured 27 percent of the U.K. market.[11] Second, though perhaps this factor gained in importance over time, the British plants could be used as cheap-labor facilities from which to supply the U.S. market. Third, the Imperial plant enabled Litton to rationalize the production of typewriters in Europe by specializing the production of each model in its range at one plant. So, for example, it planned to phase out production of manual portables in the United Kingdom and concentrate it all at its Dutch plant, with the Hull and Leicester plants' manufacturing a portable and office electric respectively.[12] The specific assets acquired by Litton included the best network of exclusive dealers in the United Kingdom,[13] a brand name that had accumulated a favorable image in about sixty years of trading (both the name and the distribution network figured prominently in the closure struggle), access to overseas markets, and two plants that could be expanded. Litton paid about £2 million, which some shareholders considered a low bid.[14] However, in a letter to shareholders advising them to accept the Litton offer, the chairman of Imperial argued that profits had been falling as a consequence of rising costs and severe competition from larger groups with far greater financial resources. He went on to say that, "without access to the more-advanced research facilities, manufacturing techniques, and marketing opportunities only available to a large international organization," Imperial could not long survive. Once again, the benefits of the multinational connection are invoked in the name of survival, greater efficiency, and other economic objectives.

In terms of the factors usually associated with foreign direct investment, Litton clearly did not expand overseas to exploit any monopoly advantages it might have as a typewriter producer. If anything, it lacked experience and know-how in production and product development and would build on the experience that existed at the acquired companies. The Federal Trade Commission (FTC), for example, regarded the takeover of Triumph-Adler as "an alternative to original research and to developing a suitable machine based on the present state of the art."[15] The same could be said about the acquisition of Willy Feiler. Most plausibly, Litton's special advantages were based on its financial and managerial muscle as a multinational conglomerate—that is, its ability to cross-subsidize subsidiaries and to mesh together into a stronger unit parts that were vulnerable when isolated. As we shall see, however, Imperial did not receive vital resources and was kept in isolation.

The best we can say is that Litton collapsed the several stages involved in becoming an international producer into one. It entered the industry and ensured that it had an international range in production and marketing to match its main rivals on cost and in market shares simultaneously.

Factors Affecting the Development and Performance of the Subsidiary

Competition

Competition in all areas of the typewriter industry was severe.[16] However, differences existed in the features of the competition according to the period and market segment in which it occurred.

In the period to the end of the 1950s, the world typewriter industry, though on its way to being dominated by a handful of multinational producers, still consisted of many small- and medium-sized national producers. The manufacture of typewriters was, in the main, labor intensive and standardized. Therefore, barriers to entry tended to be weak and price competition severe.[17]

The 1960s saw the disappearance of several small long-established companies and the emergence of a handful of giant multinationals.[18] However, little slackening occurred in the intensity of competition. The Japanese, in particular, mounted an export effort directed mainly at the United States. For example, from 1964 to 1970, Japanese production increased fourfold from 302,000 to 1.2 million units, and exports increased tenfold with between 60 and 70 percent going to the United States. In response to such low-cost foreign competition and to the mature stage of the product cycle, the multinationals were compelled to seek low-cost production sites. As one multinational gained a cost advantage by moving to a low-labor-cost area, then others had to match the move or fall behind in profitability. Time after time multinationals shifted locations. For example, in the early 1960s, Sperry Rand Corporation transferred production from Britain to Italy;[19] Olivetti transferred production of portable typewriters from Italy to Spain in 1968 and in the same year closed a plant in Hartford, Connecticut and transferred its production to its Glasgow factory;[20] in 1975 Olympia transferred production of its portable models from Germany to Belfast,

Ireland;[21] and Litton transferred production from the United States to the United Kingdom over the 1969–1972 period.

Within the multinational form of organization, companies began to rationalize production, in particular, by increasing plant specialization and therefore economies of scale. This acted as an additional stimulus to relocation in the search for lower costs. Olivetti made note to this trend in the industry in its 1969 annual report. The report mentions, for example, the tendency for companies to decentralize assembly and part production in different countries. According to Olivetti, such decentralization would result in increased relocations of operations and an increased interflow of parts and semifinished products among various units of the multinational. These developments have produced two significant outcomes. First, much of the world trade in typewriters was and is of an intracompany kind. Second, the pattern of trade—that is, the quantity and direction of imports and exports—takes on a strange shape; many countries producing typewriters find themselves to be both heavy exporters and importers. I return to both these issues in later sections.

The 1960s also witnessed an important demarcation in the international market. Increasingly, the highly standardized and price-sensitive portable and manual models were replaced by more–technologically advanced electric models in the markets of the United States and Western Europe. In this top end of the market, competition is waged with technological innovations and patents. A technological breakthrough that is protected (either legally or by the high barriers that the cost and lead-in time of the research-and-development program and introduction of the innovation erect) enables the company to earn technological rents—a form of monopoly profits. International Business Machines (IBM) achieved dominance in this field in 1935 with the introduction of the electric typewriter, and it never relinquished its lead thereafter. In 1944 it produced the first typewriter with proportional spacing and in 1961 achieved a major breakthrough with the introduction of the Selectric heavy-duty office typewriter, fitted with a "golf ball" or single printing element. Throughout the 1960s, IBM reigned supreme, so much so that Smith Corona Marchant (SCM), a strong competitor, was forced out of the office-electric market in the United States.[22] As others began to produce their own versions of the single-element-printer typewriter (for example, Olympia and Litton), IBM was already pioneering a new concept in office machinery—word processing.

These patterns continued and were reinforced in the 1970s. The trend away from manual, and toward electric, typewriters continued, if unevenly, across the world. In the United States by the mid-1970s some ten electric typewriters were in use for every manual one. The ratio in Europe was 2:1, and the United Kingdom trailed with a 1:1 ratio.[23]

However, in much of the Third World, the extensive use of typewriters in the office had not yet begun or was in its infancy. This was a potentially large market for the now-mature manual models, but the competitive imperative for the multinationals was increasingly on finding cheap and docile labor forces. The tendency for companies to relocate to such countries as Brazil, Taiwan, and Singapore was still strong in 1975.[24] In between these two extreme ends of the market, the student population in the United States and, to a lesser extent, in Western Europe maintained or increased the demand for portable and, in particular, portable electric models.

Once again, in the mid-1970s, another crucial bifurcation in the industry took place. The field of word processing that IBM had pioneered in the mid-1960s, apparently too soon for the market, became important in the 1970s. Additionally, the technology that word processing employed, or could be allied to (computers and electronic microprocessors), took word processing out of the technical parameters of the typewriter industry and also out of the reach of many of the companies in the industry. The next major market battle would be fought on the field of the "office of the future" and would have much more to do with complete electronic systems for storing, editing, typing, generating, and distributing information. The established typewriter producers would now face not only IBM but also Xerox, Phillips, and International Telephone and Telegraph (ITT), companies with vast resources and extensive experience in electronic digital technology.[25] Although estimates indicate that only 2 percent of the 24 million typewriters in use worldwide in 1978 were word processors, the prize was a future share of a growth market with enormous potential.[26]

This brief sketch of competition in the industry sets the context in which we can examine Litton's experience. Litton entered the industry in 1965 and, by a series of acquisitions, captured some 30 percent of the world market for typewriters.[27] Little doubt exists that the acquisitions helped further the process of concentration, so much so that the FTC ruled that the acquisition of Triumph-Adler in 1968 violated antitrust law. On reviewing that decision in 1975, on appeal by Litton, the FTC reversed its decision but commented:

> Litton has a history of growth through acquisition in the typewriter market as well as in other markets. The need for a moratorium on this means of growth has been amply demonstrated.

It went on to order Litton, for ten years, to:

> desist from acquiring . . . the whole or any part of the stock, share capital, or assets . . . of any concern . . . engaged in the business of manufacturing typewriter products for sale within the United States without prior approval of the Federal Trade Commission.

However, despite the acquisitions, the large market share, and the trend toward concentration in the industry, the competitive struggle continued unabated, as we have seen.

In the United States, Litton had mixed fortunes. It trailed a long way behind IBM in the office-electric market and SCM in the portable market, but it led in the office-manual market with its Royal models.[28] However, this last sector was precisely the sector that was growing the slowest as the United States led the switch from manual to electrics in the office and that was most vulnerable to price competition. Litton responded to the competitive challenge in this sector by transferring the production of all its Royals to Imperial, citing "the need to compete more effectively against lower-cost foreign-made machines."[29] By 1972 Litton, like many of its competitors, ended up supplying the crucial U.S. market from overseas. Despite these moves, Litton cited losses on its sales of Imperial models in the United States as one of the main reasons for its decision to close the Imperial plants in 1975.

At the top end of the market, Litton had little early success. The FTC noted that Litton had spent $13.6 million on research and development in the 1964–1969 period in an effort to catch competitors in the heavy-duty office-electric range but that it had failed. That was a major reason for the acquisition of Triumph-Adler. Triumph-Adler provided Litton with the technological capability it so badly needed and proved to be a successful competitor in many model ranges in many parts of the world.

Competition within the British industry since 1966 can only be sensibly discussed when set in an international context. Not only are all producers in the United Kingdom foreign owned, but they also sell a very high proportion of their output overseas. Therefore, while conditions in the British market affected the competitive success of Imperial, they were overshadowed by the international market conditions (especially in the United States) and by the decisions of the parent. Calculating from the figures in table 6-1, we see that Imperial sold about 62 percent of its total production on an intergroup basis, mainly to the United States, 21 percent was exported mainly to the Third World, and 17 percent was sold on the domestic market. Two models were almost exclusively shipped to the United States on an intergroup basis.

Imperial's total production of 180,000 or so units was divided among three models (see table 6-1) and between two plants. Although exact cost comparisons are not possible given the unavailability of data, the low-volume runs at Imperial probably put it at a cost disadvantage as compared with the higher-volume producers on the continent, such as Olympia in Germany. The lower labor costs in Britain probably offset only some of the disadvantage. In any case, because Imperial tended to compete in the standard model range, many of its actual competitors were companies producing in even cheaper-labor-cost locations than Britain, again tending to undermine much of Imperial's advantage.

The British market for office typewriters, the only kind produced by Imperial, is estimated to have increased from 138,200 units in 1960 to a peak of 197,500 in 1973 and then decreased to around 180,000 in 1974. Within that

Table 6-1
Sales of Imperial Office Typewriters, by Type, 1974

Type	Model 790/95 Electric		Model 80 Manual		Model 470 Manual	
	Units	Percentage	Units	Percentage	Units	Percentage
Home sales	5,286	10.9	23,713	43.3	–	–
Export sales[a]	4,369	9	27,576	50.4	4,137	5.6
Intergroup[b]	38,869	80.1	3,444	6.3	66,477	94.4
Total	48,524	100	54,733	100	70,614	100

Source: Imperial Typewriters
[a]Mainly to the Third World.
[b]Mainly to the United States.

period the proportion of the market accounted for by manual and electric models changed. The manual share declined from 91 to 45 percent with a corresponding rise in the electric share.[30] Table 6-2 shows the market shares of the leading companies for the period 1971–1974. What stands out is the high market share of products imported from Adler, the German subsidiary of Litton, in both the manual and electric ranges, and Imperial's low share of the electric market in its home base, normally considered the easiest area in which to sell. What is more, Adler, a sister subsidiary of Imperial, outperformed the British company in its backyard, for whereas Imperial's total sales rose from 24,000 to 29,000 units in the period, Adler's rose from 27,500 to 40,000 units.

Much of the shape of Imperial's production and sales is the result of the decisions Litton took in the product-strategy area to which I now turn.

Product Strategy

Imperial's life from 1966 was intimately connected to Litton's evolving product strategy in a far more-comprehensive way than in the cases of Chrysler U.K. or Innocenti. Litton, by turn, rescued Imperial from extinction, built it up in terms of volume and employment, and finally committed it to death, making sure in the process that there could be little hope of reprieve. The case is particularly interesting in that Litton operated a truly international product strategy in the typewriter division. That strategy assigned very different roles to Imperial and Triumph-Adler. Whereas Triumph-Adler had substantial research-and-development capacity, Imperial had little; whereas Triumph-Adler produced several new models of good quality, Imperial produced only one new model of poor quality; whereas Triumph-Adler produced a diversified range of products, Imperial was

Table 6-2
U.K. Market for Office Typewriters—Shares of Main Companies, 1971-1974

Manufacturer	1971-1972		1972-1973		1973-1974	
	Units[a]	Percentage	Units	Percentage	Units	Percentage
Manual						
Imperial	19,400	23.4	22,400	24.1	23,700	24.7
Adler	15,300	18.4	18,000	19.4	17,000	17.7
Olympia	24,000	28.9	27,000	29	28,000	29.2
Olivetti	17,000	20.5	21,000	22.6	20,000	20.8
Others	7,300	8.8	4,600	4.9	7,300	7.6
Total	83,000	100	93,000	100	96,000	100
Electric						
Imperial U.K.	4,455	5.5	6,120	7.3	5,286	5.6
Imperial (imported)	2,406	3	2,524	3	2,141	2.3
Adler	12,200	15.1	16,500	19.6	23,000	24.5
IBM	16,000	19.7	15,000	17.9	16,000	17
Olympia	18,000	22.2	19,000	22.6	20,000	21.3
Olivetti	11,000	13.6	11,000	13.1	10,000	10.6
Others	16,939	20.9	13,856	16.5	17,573	18.7
Total	81,000	100	84,000	100	94,000	100

Source: Imperial Typewriters
Note: Years run from July to June.
[a]Unit equals one machine.

confined to the production of typewriters; and whereas Triumph-Adler sold in a balanced way to a wide range of markets, Imperial sold heavily to one market. Whatever other reasons may have existed for such an imbalance in the treatment of the two subsidiaries (for example, inherited differences that probably favored Triumph-Adler), a crucial one is the product strategy itself.

Imperial, almost from the very beginning, and certainly by 1969, was relegated to an offshore facility within the typewriter division. No serious research-and-development capability was located there. According to the consultants who investigated Imperial at the time of closure in 1975, the subsidiary did not possess any fundamental typewriter design, fundamental production-engineering development, basic research and development, knowledge of electronics for calculator development, or knowledge of technology for word-processing concepts.[31] However, if it made economic sense for Litton to concentrate its research and development elsewhere, we can still ask how it shared out the fruits of this effort.

Since Imperial was assigned the task of producing aging products in the mature phase of their life cycle, it was allocated few new models. The bulk of its production concentrated on two models—the 80 and 470 models. Both were manual and both had had long lives, although they were still marketable. The 80 was a machine introduced by Imperial in pre-Litton days, and it sold well in British and Commonwealth markets, though always at a discount above that offered by competitors.[32] The 470 was transferred for production at Imperial because of the cheaper labor costs there. Some 94 percent of production was exported to the United States on an intracompany basis for sale under the Royal name. By 1975 the design for the machine was based on a lever movement that was fifty years old, and it was considered "completely obsolescent." The two efforts Litton made to introduce electric models to Imperial proved to be dismal failures. The Willy Feiler design for a portable electric, which it had bought in 1966 and had apparently tried to produce at the Hull factory until the early 1970s, was abandoned because the machine was technically unreliable.[33] In its stead, Litton decided to market in the United States, an electric portable made in Japan by a company in which it had a minority interest.[34] In 1972, after the complete closure of the Royal plants at Hartford, Connecticut, Imperial began to produce the 790 model, or medium-priced electric. It was, in the main, sold to the U.S. market, again on an intracompany basis, and the hope was that it would help utilize unused capacity at Imperial. The machine was a disaster. The consultants noted its very poor reception in the trade because of its unreliability and added that it was "universally condemned as a virtually unmarketable product in the U.K." and was in need of a "complete redesign." These problems forced Imperial to sell it on a heavy-discount basis.[35] These examples hardly portray a picture of substantial technological benefits accruing to Imperial from the multinational connection. What is worse is that the good image of Imperial products in the trade was badly damaged by the aging products and the unreliable 790 model.

Imperial also fared badly in the battle for investment resources to improve production efficiency. When the 470 was transferred from the United States to the United Kingdom, "a complete set of tools and machine tools from both the U.S.A. and Holland" was also transferrred.[36] The British government went so far as to waive the import duty for three years on the understanding that production would be exported and employment at Hull increased. The Imperial workers contended that the quality of the product was adversely affected, a view partially endorsed by the consultants' report, which noted the need for "substantial expenditure to achieve improvement in machine condition."[37] One former manager at Imperial noted that, "many of the machine tools imported had little or no life left in them" but were used to "save the expenditure of fresh capital" and to save "experimental time" in using new tools.[38]

Finally, we have to examine how Litton allocated export markets among its typewriter subsidiaries. On the one hand, again Triumph-Adler was favored with the production of products with a high value-added content, exported to Western Europe and the United States. What is more, it was one of the main suppliers of manual and electric models to the British market (see table 6-2). Imperial, on the other hand, exported products with a low value-added content mainly to the United States, with a small share going to the Third World. Imperial was therefore heavily dependent on conditions in one market, the United States, which was in any case the market moving away from manuals at the fastest rate. Within the constraints of its product range, the only other possible strategy open to Imperial was to direct more of its exports to the Third World, a market in which it had traditionally been successful. However, even this avenue was increasingly closed off as competitors found cheaper-labor-cost locations to produce the standard models.

So, although Litton could claim that Imperial was a successful exporter because it had increased the value of exports from £1.8 million in 1969 to £6.4 million in 1972[39] and had been awarded the Queen's Award to Industry in 1970 for its contribution to the British balance of payments, for anyone scratching beneath the gloss, the picture was less convincing.[40] In many ways this was an engineered and unstable export boom, determined by the strategic decision to transfer production from the United States to Britain and to give Imperial a well-established market, rather than by the success of Imperial products in the marketplace. Imperial was producing models with little life in them and was essentially locked into a market with little long-term future.

The product strategy of Litton and other multinational producers of typewriters not only determined the fate of subsidiaries but also influenced the whole pattern of international trade in typewriters and the balance-of-payments position of many countries. For example, the United Kingdom in 1974 exported 415,638 units at a value of £15.5 million, two-thirds of which went to the United States, and imported 346,571 units at a value of £25.9 million, half of which originated from West Germany.[41] So although the United Kingdom produces enough typewriters in numbers to supply home demand, most of them are exported. Home demand is supplied by imports, which have a much higher value-added content. Whereas this might suit the economic and strategic designs of the multinationals, it denied Britain the capacity to participate in the production of technologically advanced products with good market potential, which might turn the balance of trade to Britain's favor and ensure long-term employment in the industry.

To sum up Litton's product strategy, I quote the Action Committee:

> The equipping of Imperial Hull with old machines from America, the use of Hull products as export leaders to the American market, and the failure to diversify production all suggest that the corporate plan of the multinational was, *from the outset*, to exploit British labor while this was profitable, . . . without putting down the kind of roots,

economically speaking, which would have committed the company to responsible permanent development of its English possessions.[42]

Industrial Relations

There was little industrial-relations trouble at Imperial during most of Litton's period of ownership. One contributing factor was the deep divisions among the work force. At Hull much of the work force was female—90 percent until 1972 and less thereafter.[43] At Leicester some 60 percent of the work force was of Asian ancestry.[44] These ascribed differences split the work force in the only two significant strikes at Imperial. In 1970, 700 women at Hull struck for one week to force the company to abandon its policy of paying some women under age twenty-one less than those age twenty-one and over for similar work. The men at the factory did not join the women on strike, thereby weakening the impact of the action.[45] In 1974 several hundred Asian workers at Leicester went on strike. Many of the non-Asian workers at the factory continued to work, again undermining the strikers' stand. The strike lasted twelve weeks and was particularly acrimonious, not so much because of the management/labor conflict but more because of racial antagonism and the differences between some union officials and the Asian workers. The strikers demanded more-equal and democratic representation inside the union and equal treatment from management in the payment of bonuses. The union refused to make the strike official and backed management in their decision not to rehire those who remained on strike.[46] Therefore, that the Leicester workers offered no opposition to the closure decision in 1975 is of little surprise.

If days lost from industrial disputes were not a serious problem at Imperial, Litton did claim that rising costs and the wage component of costs were putting Imperial in a noncompetitive position. I deal with the issue of costs and competitiveness in the section on profitability. Here I assess the contribution of productivity and labor costs to Imperial's problems. In their investigation of productive performance at Imperial, the consultants noted the following facts:

Productive performance as measured by the standard of the industrial engineers was better than planned in three out of the four comparisons made. They noted that the figures indicated "limited" scope for improvement in this area.[47]

The company had an absentee rate of 18 percent and a labor turnover rate that varied between 40 and 80 percent.[48] On the one hand, these very high figures would increase training costs and probably decrease performance. On the other hand, the high turnover rate probably weakened the union's bargaining position for higher wages and better work conditions.

A need existed for replacements or improvements in machinery and other equipment and for better workplace methods and materials supply.[49] All these are management's direct responsibility and suggest that productivity could have been improved by more capital investment and better management.

These facts paint a picture of a quiescent work force working as efficiently as the limited technical and managerial constraints allowed. There is no major or continuing conflict on the job-control frontier, although workers do not stay in the job for long.

The wages earned by the Imperial workers are a matter of some dispute. The Leicester workers claimed an average weekly wage of £25 for men and £20 for women in 1974. Imperial claimed the figures were £34 and £24 respectively. In any case, the average weekly earnings of Britons in 1974 was £47.7 for men and £26.9 for women, with comparable figures of £44 and £25 in Leicestershire and £46.2 and £24.8 in Humberside, which includes Hull.[50] Thus, in the context of British wages, Imperial was a below-average employer. However, Imperial's trading competitors were not only subject to British labor costs. Against machines from Taiwan, Spain, and other lower-labor-cost areas, Imperial was at a cost disadvantage on the international market.

Given that, on its own admission Litton was in Britain to take advantage of lower labor costs (relative to the United States, for example), it is no surprise that when the advantage disappeared with the challenge of machines produced in the developing countries, it decided to pull out. It could not improve its cost position by acting on the labor force. Wages were already below regional and national averages, and little room for improvement existed in labor efficiency without a change in method and techniques of production, quality of machines, and volume. Litton took few steps in these directions or in developing more-technologically sophisticated up-market products that might act to protect Imperial from low-cost competition.

Transfer Pricing

Did Litton manipulate transfer prices on Imperial's intracompany transactions, and if so, to whose disadvantage and with what consequences? Certainly the workers suspected transfer prices were manipulated to the detriment of Imperial, and not surprisingly, Litton denied all allegations. A considered judgment would require a careful examination of documents (for example, invoices) or detailed inside information. I was able to obtain neither.

Despite such a lack of data and information, three circumstantial points can be made. First, Litton had shown itself willing to manipulate transfer prices to its advantage in another situation. Two actions, one civil and one criminal, were brought by the U.S. Customs Service and the United States of America respectively against Litton for undervaluing imported merchandise from subsidiaries in Tijuana, Mexico, and Singapore. Customs charged:

> During the period from July 1968 through May 1972, 736 dutiable consumption entries from Triad De Mexico . . . and during the period from August 1970 through July 1972, 145 dutiable consumption entries containing merchandise shipped from Litton Components Private Ltd., Singapore were imported . . . utilizing false invoices.[51]

The criminal indictment charged Litton with:

> importing memory-core planes from Tijuana and Singapore . . . by means of documents which were allegedly false and fraudulent in that they reflected as entered value for the imported merchandise a value which was less than true value.[52]

The Customs Service demanded a penalty payment of $12,366,036. On 3 April 1974, a negotiated settlement reduced the claim to $1,106,238 on condition that a sum of $175,842 also be paid by Litton for loss of revenue on the importations.[53]

Second, Litton had ample opportunity to manipulate transfer prices. Some 60 percent of its total U.K. production was shipped on an intracompany basis to the United States. Therefore, most of Imperial's revenue depended on the internal price Litton decided to pay Imperial. In addition, some interflow of parts occurred among the European subsidiaries that were also amenable to transfer-price manipulation.

Third, there was a rationale for Litton to arrange the transfer prices to the disadvantage of Imperial. By undervaluing the invoices for merchandise shipped to the United States, it could deflate Imperial's profits and thus avoid U.K. taxes on repatriated profits and lower U.S. customs duty. Litton is reported as claiming that because it made such large losses in the United Kingdom it was, if anything, to its advantage to inflate the value of the invoices—that is, drain funds from the United States to the United Kingdom.[54] Of course, the very truth of the claimed profit-and-loss figures is what is open to doubt.

Without stronger evidence these points merely serve to reinforce the pervasive suspicion that surrounds such transactions. They also highlight the need for fuller disclosure.

Profitability

Litton claimed that the acquisition of Imperial had proved a financial disaster. Imperial, it was asserted, had made losses of £9 million since 1966, with £5 million of those losses occurring in 1973 and 1974, and additional losses of £4 million incurred in 1973 and 1974 on sales of U.K.-produced typewriters in North America.[55] No profits were reported for Imperial by Litton for any of the years from 1966 to 1975. As no published certified figures are available for Imperial's operations, and due to the suspicions aroused by the high volume of intracompany trade, skepticism must be directed at Litton's figures, in particular, at the absence of profits in any of the years prior to 1973.

Whatever the truth of these figures, and leaving aside the assignment of responsibility for them, Imperial had performed poorly. All models did not sell as well as expected, and some could only be sold by undercutting the prices of competitors who were selling comparable models.[56]

As table 6-3 shows, the consequence of the short fall in sales, and therefore volume, was unused capacity, which in turn helped to increase unit costs. For example, the consultants reported that in 1974 Imperial failed to meet its cost target by £3 million.[57] The variance was accounted for in the following fashion:

£500,000 for direct labor costs,

£2 million for overhead costs,

£500,000 for material costs.

In other words, two-thirds of the variance is due to the inability to spread largely fixed overhead costs (for example, lighting, heating, sales, and administrative costs) over large volumes. When this cost handicap is allied to the fierce competition in the market, which limits the ability to pass on cost increases, and the particular compulsion on Imperial to undercut some of the competition to sell models with a poor image, then quite conceivably Imperial operated at a loss, at least in the later years.

Table 6-3
Volume and Costs at Imperial Typewriters
(pounds)

Model	Three-Year Volume		Unit Cost		Percentage Increase in Costs
	Plan	*Actual*	*Plan*	*Actual*	
Electric	275,000	160,000	44.3	103.4	133
470	270,000	211,000	26	55.4	113
80	200,000	171,000	26	59.4	130

Source: Imperial Typewriters

Moreover, Litton argued that inflation and exchange-rate movement aggravated Imperial's financial plight. The higher inflation rate in the United Kingdom vis à vis those in competitor countries meant that Imperial was operating at a cost disadvantage, and the devaluation of the dollar in 1971 reduced the revenue from the large intragroup sales to the United States.[58] However, Litton failed to point out that the pound was also devalued in the period and that by mid-1975 the substantial fall in the relative value of the pound would have greatly assisted Imperial's overseas-trading position.[59]

The president of Royal-Imperial, who had supervised the closure, defended the decision to close in a letter to the government with seemingly impeccable business logic. He pointed out that an "exhaustive study" had indicated that Imperial's products were not competitive, could not be produced "in those factories" at a profit, and that "no amount of investment . . . could change that situation while still making economic sense."[60] The figures, to which neither the government nor the workers were privy, pointed to closure. The critical question, however, was not confronted: How could Imperial operate at a profit in the changed market and technological conditions of the mid-1970s without modern machines, high volumes, a well-designed and diversified product range, and diversified markets? Triumph-Adler, Litton's other major typewriter subsidiary, had these advantages and was consistently profitable, apparently paying out an unchanged annual dividend of 20 percent since 1969.[61] If Imperial was a hopeless case in 1975, it was only because Litton had consistently neglected to nourish it with resources. Although the proximate cause of closure was the recessionary conditions, the underlying cause was Litton's treatment of Imperial.

Reasons for the Decision to Withdraw

Although I have leaned toward the view that Litton closed Imperial as a result of strategic decisions that spanned many years, I am aware that other interpretations of the data are possible. In particular, because I was unable to obtain sufficient inside information on the reasons for closure, it seems wise to present three different interpretations, arguing each as best I can, and then explain why I am more convinced by one.

A Victim of Circumstances

One possible interpretation of the closure of Imperial is that it was a victim of circumstances. Markets for typewriters contracted in all parts of the world during the 1974–1975 recession. To make matters worse, Imperial produced in a country with a much higher inflation rate than those of many of its international competitors, thereby putting Imperial at a cost disadvantage. Moreover, its cost disadvantage was aggravated by the higher volumes or lower wage costs of its competitors. Given the severe price competitiveness in the segments of the market Imperial was in, increased costs could not be passed on but instead were absorbed by reducing profit margins. To compound the problems, the devaluation of the dollar decreased the revenue from sales to the United States.

In addition to the increased costs and reduced revenues, the sharp drop in sales in the recession produced spare manufacturing capacity in Litton's typewriter plants. Litton was forced to rationalize and chose to close its most peripheral plants. Imperial, with outdated products and machinery and little research-and-development capacity, was selected. What was left of Imperial's markets could be supplied by the spare capacity created by recession at the other Litton plants.

One other component can be added to support this interpretation. The claim could be made that Imperial was unfortunate because the recession and Britain's high inflation occurred at a time when Litton was in a weak financial position. Its record of fast growth and high earnings had been reversed in 1972 when, for the first time in its history, it made a loss. For the next few years, though it returned to operating profitably, it was bedeviled by a contract dispute with the U.S. Navy involving several hundred millions of dollars of claims by Litton on the Navy.[62] This situation may have damaged its liquidity and reduced its willingness to tolerate loss-making or stagnant subsidiaries. Instead, it carried out a comprehensive divestment process in the Business Systems and Equipment Group, one of the several product groups in the company.

Bad Management

Another plausible interpretation is that the closure was the result of bad management. Several management decisions could be classified as unwise. For example, Litton failed to rationalize production of typewriters sufficiently in the late 1960s, producing electric and manual models at both Triumph-Adler and Imperial, thereby foregoing the economies of scale from increased volume runs of each product. Management also failed to provide Imperial with sufficient research and development to support the development of a reliable electric machine and to update or replace aging manual models. The medium-priced electric was not only a marketing disaster but also seriously contaminated the image of the manual models. In the words of the consultants, the "opprobrium . . . rubbed off on the manual machines," which were themselves in need of redesign and restyling that was never carried out.

Management could also be faulted for poor organization of production, interrupted supplies that increased waiting time and hurt productivity, and excessive inventory levels that tied up cash and reduced financial liquidity. Someone at headquarters must have recognized these problems because in 1973 a management team from the United States was sent out to improve the situation.[63] The workers also claimed that frequent changes occurred in top management at the Hull factory with "the dismissal and replacement of nine general managers in the period between 1966–1975."

It would, however, be stretching credulity too far to assume that decisions to not make Imperial a more-balanced company by diversifying into related product areas, to not reduce its heavy dependence on sales to the U.S. market, to not replace old and unreliable machinery, and to exclude its products from Western European markets are attributable to bad management. More likely they were part of an overall centrally determined strategy, which is the interpretation of the closure to which I now turn.

A Central Strategy

Litton assigned Imperial the task of producing two manual models that were at the back end of their life cycle. These models accounted for over two-thirds of Imperial's production and were crucial to its viability. No serious effort was made to replace the two aging models or to significantly improve them. Although Litton did introduce two new electric models at Imperial, their design was flawed and they were never given the needed intensive design and production support to turn market failure into success. Also possible is that the medium-priced electric was introduced as an insurance cover in the event that the FTC forced Litton to divest Triumph-Adler.

Britain was seen as a temporary cheap-labor area well suited to the production of technologically unsophisticated manual models. The closure of the Royal plants in Connecticut, the transfer of equipment and products from there to Imperial, and the subsequent export of over 60 percent of total production to the United States suggest that Britain was also acting as an offshore-production site in Litton's corporate strategy. When the two aging models approached obsolescence, and when comparative labor costs changed adversely for Imperial, Litton ceased producing in Britain.

The limited function assigned to Imperial dictated that investment to improve production techniques or replace old equipment would be minimal. Moreover, there would be little incentive to diversify Imperial's products and markets since the long-term viability of the subsidiary was not a management priority. In the same vein, but more speculatively, Litton could have set transfer prices on the high volume of intracompany trade at an artificially low level, thereby draining profits away from Imperial for investment in subsidiaries allocated a future in the corporate strategy. In other words, corporate strategy at Litton's headquarters determined budgetary and operational decisions on the allocation of various resources, which in turn determined whether Imperial would be a victim of the recession.

Two other points can be made to support this interpretation of the closure, and both have to do with the conglomerate identity of Litton. First, Litton, like other conglomerates, tends to have a cavalier attitude toward subsidiaries, moving in and out according to the needs of the whole group. Litton's company report for 1972 makes very clear that the company would not "hesitate to sell all or part of a business area" when it decided that its growth path "differed significantly from the mainstream." True to its philosophy, Litton has an extensive record of acquiring and later withdrawing from companies whenever problems arose or the original advantage for the acquisition had disappeared. Unfortunately for many of the workers at those subsidiaries, the withdrawal would often mean a loss of jobs either because of closure or a sale that led to severe restructuring. Among the examples of this behavior are the already cited acquisition of the Royal plants in 1965 and their subsequent run down and closure in 1972 because labor costs made them uncompetitive, as well as the acquisition and closure of the Imperial plants within the space of nine years when the products reached the end of their life cycle. Other examples are the acquisition and then closure of a Dutch plant in 1974 because of high labor costs and the withdrawal from three Swedish plants in 1976 when the product they were producing, a mechanical cash register, was outmoded by the electronic ones. Again, in this latter case, Litton had acquired the Swedish company (SWEDA) for its expertise but had failed to adequately prepare it for changes in the industry. The subsidiary was supposed to have been profitable from the time that Litton bought the company outright in 1963. Litton, although withdrawing from production in Sweden, did not leave the field but kept the SWEDA brand name, moved the research-and-development department to the United States and located production in Pennsylvania and Massachusetts, and in Italy and Japan overseas.[64] Finally, the *Wall Street Journal* reported Litton as switching the production of electronic calculators from the United States to Japan because of Japan's cheaper production costs, and five years later, in 1971, of switching production back to the United States because the introduction of integrated circuits was supposed to have eliminated the advantage.[65] Litton, like many conglomerates, conducted its rollover strategy—that is, its movement into and out of product lines—on the back of a number of subsidiaries.

The second point is that managers of conglomerates, especially in the late 1960s and early 1970s, tended to stress the achievement of fast growth in sales, most often via acquisition, and growth in earnings per share. These twin management imperatives meant that many conglomerates did not undertake costly and long-term investments to develop new products and markets or to improve manufacturing facilities. Rather they attempted to grow and to keep up with technological developments by acquisition, which became especially attractive in time of depressed stock prices. On the operating side, management had an incentive to improve earnings by administering a ruthless cost-cutting operation to unhealthy subsidiaries. However, this could only cause a once-and-for-all increase in profits rather than provide the basis for a sustained period of profit-ability, which requires investment in machinery, research and development, and marketing.[66]

I think the last explanation is the most cogent because it is the most con-gruent with the available evidence. However, it should be obvious that some elements of each interpretation overlap. For example, bad management could account for some of the problems at Imperial. However, it is impossible that top management at corporate or divisional headquarters was not aware of the trends in the industry and the need for product development. A management seriously interested in the viability of Imperial would, for example, have redesigned the medium-priced electric machine. After all, its other subsidiary, Triumph-Adler, had diversified into advanced office equipment, producing a golf-ball typewriter, calculators, small computers, photocopiers, and word processors, all with an excellent reputation for quality. Management ignorance or incompetence, in this crucial respect at least, cannot explain the closure. On first sight, the inter-pretation proposing that Imperial was a victim of circumstance appears more convincing. However, many of the environmental difficulties' acting on Imperial affected many companies without causing their failure. Moreover, at about the same time Litton announced the closure, citing among other things the unfavor-able economic conditions in the United Kingdom (for example, high inflation, high wage settlements), Olympia announced the opening of a typewriter factory in Belfast, and Olivetti decided to expand production in Glasgow.[67] If the deci-sion to close had been a response to serious but temporary environmental conditions, one would expect Litton to have been less adamant than it was about its refusal to consider any sort of government aid, which could have helped it weather the difficult short-term conditions. Clearly, as the presdient of Royal-Imperial argued, the subsidiary was beyond saving. Also clear was that Litton's nondecisions on diversification into the dynamic areas of office products and on investment in new machinery and new products confined Imperial to the per-formance of a temporary function as the "Asia" or poor relation of Litton's office-equipment empire.

Process of Withdrawal

Litton planned and executed the closure of the two manufacturing plants so well as to draw the grudging accolade "brilliant" from one of the union leaders who fought the closure. Litton was able to withdraw from production in Britain, maintain market shares by supplying typewriters from elsewhere, and effectively scuttle any chance for a resurrected company based on Imperial to become viable and pose a threat to Litton.

Although the careful preparations for closure were a well-guarded secret, there were early signs that Litton intended to withdraw. In September 1974,

Litton announced a "$77.2-million reserve set up for operations to be discontinued," although no mention was made of specific subsidiaries. As late as 10 December 1974, a letter from the plant manager at Imperial to a member of Parliament outlines the company's difficulties noting, "There is very little time left if we are to succeed in reversing the present pattern of business trends in this industry" and suggests they meet "to discuss the problems and possible solutions" as soon as possible. Also, an Imperial circular to employees, dated 13 December 1974, refers to a "review of typewriter products and production capacity and facilities within Royal-Imperial." These signs prompted shop stewards to ask the Hull management, on 14 January 1975, to clarify the position of Imperial. Management replied that there was "no cause for panic."[68] On 17 January, Litton announced that the factories would close on 21 February, thereby giving the statutory notice. Two interesting points emerge from this preparatory phase. First, workers and politicians were kept in the dark as to the real situation, and even if they had correctly interpreted these signs, they would have gained but a few weeks' advanced warning. Second, a difference in objectives and knowledge seemed to exist between local and international management regarding the fate of the subsidiary. Local management seemed to seek government assistance to save Imperial, while top central management, as we shall see, was bent on withdrawing.

Friday, 17 January, was a day of much activity on the part of Litton. A senior Litton executive informed the government of the decision and asked it to "maintain the confidentiality of our discussions until 15:30 this afternoon."[69] At that time, a dismissal letter was delivered to each worker.[70] The unions were bypassed, probably in the hope of scuttling any organized response. Also on that busy day, a company called Office and Electronic Machines (OEM) circulated a letter to all Imperial dealers informing them, "that OEM is taking over the future marketing of Imperial products through a separate and distinct subsidiary, selling models from the Triumph-Adler factories and other sources."[71] Litton, by careful preparation, had safeguarded its interests by tying up the brand name and distribution and thus presented government and workers with a fait accompli.

Little resistance came from the workers at Leicester to these moves. One possible reason, as we have seen, was the deep division among the rank and file along the lines of race, which had been exacerbated by the racist National Front organization.[72] Other possible reasons are lack of leadership and reasonably good local labor-market conditions. Hull, in contrast, mounted a spirited and comprehensive resistance. Tactics were coordinated by an action committee composed of shop stewards, union officials, local politicians, and academics. Their first step was to appeal for:

a preliminary statement from the government which would contain an assurance that it is prepared to consider alternative plans for maintaining production and employment which the work people and union wish to submit, that the government will assist and participate in a study of such plans, and that the work force will be maintained intact for such time as a full study may take.[73]

The document argued that Imperial "is probably a victim of a purely company-oriented decision bearing no relation to British national economic interest," presented a cost-benefit analysis of the closure, and proposed tentative ideas on how to make Imperial viable. The initial response from the government was favorable, wholly due to the fact that the responsible minister, A. Wedgwood Benn, was sympathetic to workers' cooperatives and in favor of government intervention in the economy. He appointed a private consulting firm to examine, in "close consultation with the workers," the prospects for a profitable, viable, independent company that could provide secure employment "in the long term."[74]

For the next few weeks the Action Committee, the consultants, and various factions in government argued over the potential viability of a new Imperial. The first consultants' report, completed on 27 February 1975, reviewed two possible business strategies for a new Imperial. The first strategy, based on a low sales projection, forecast losses in the first five years of operation, and the second, based on a more-optimistic sales projection, forecast small losses in the first three years and small profits in the next two. The Action Committee immediately responded by proposing a third strategy that demanded a more-aggressive marketing approach to undermine Litton's arrangements in the U.K. market, either by taking over OEM or by imposing selective import controls against Litton products. The document urged that the government not adopt a "submissive posture in the face of Litton's present market control." In response to these criticisms, the Department of Industry asked the consultants to review the sales projections but did not agree to take any action against Litton's marketing arrangement. The second consultants' report, circulated on 26 March 1975, still forecast that the new company, operating without an established marketing network, would make losses in the first five years of operation and estimated the capital requirement for the new venture to be between £8.5 and £11.3 million.

The formal exchanges of documents and figures masked a great deal of political intrigue and a profound political disagreement. Whereas Benn and a handful of others supported extensive government intervention and support for economic experiments, many government ministers and senior civil servants in the Department of Industry considered such policies wasteful and commercially irrational. The turning point in the government's position toward the Imperial workers occurred when Benn was sacked from his position and transferred to the Department of Energy. Benn's replacement, Eric Varley, advocated a far more-commercial approach to the framing of industrial policy. According to some of those who participated in the top-level meetings that decided the fate of Imperial, civil servants, aware of the imminent sacking of Benn, were content to delay any decision until he had gone.[75]

The momentum for the creation of a new enterprise petered out in mid-1975, but not before the Action Committee had produced one more document on the viability of a new company in response to a request from the Department of Industry for detailed figures. The Union document, entitled "A Corporate Plan for New Harmony Enterprises," illustrates how far the workers were forced to scale down their demands to accommodate them to the market realities Litton's withdrawal arrangements had imposed. The document argued for the establishment of a small company employing 232 people in the first year and 808 after five years. However, it still projected losses for the first four years. No matter how the workers twisted and turned, they could not, without the willingness of the government to act against Litton's control of marketing, produce a plan for a commercially viable company. The document noted:

> From the commencement of our exchanges with government, it has been clearly recognized by all parties that marketing represented the key problem to be overcome in making our case for viability.

Nevertheless, the document represented another systematic example of the new socioeconomic rationality that workers and their allies were trying to introduce into the political arena. The document, though admitting that short-term losses would occur at the new company, pointed out that many costs, now not included in commercial decisions, would be saved and that new gains would be made in worker participation and in the ability of Britain to have an independent capacity to develop and sell typewriters.

The tactic of international worker cooperation was not seriously pursued by the workers given the initial favorable response from the government. In any case, the Action Committee was divided on the efficacy of such a tactic. One union leader noted that the closure of the British plants would benefit the German plants and that it was therefore naïve to expect practical help from workers there. However, another member of the committee, an academic, argued that if the German workers did not refuse to increase production to supply Imperial's old markets, then the Imperial workers could call on the solidarity of dockers to blackball typewriters from Triumph-Adler at British docks. In fact, dockers at the port of Hull did blackball a consignment of typewriters and parts from Germany. Litton was sufficiently concerned that it brought the matter up at one of the meetings with government officials, but it pointed out that the blackballing was hurting OEM more than Litton. One of the sad ironies of this case is to see how the mobility of conglomerate capital compels workers from different locations to benefit, often temporarily, at each other's expense; first the British workers benefited at the expense of the Americans, and then the Germans benefited at the expense of the British.

One other tactic was pursued. On the day that Imperial was to close (21 February), some workers occupied the Hull factory. The occupation was favorably reviewed in the press—for example, the *Economist* lamented the fact that Litton's behavior had turned "moderates into militants" and reported that among the sitters-in were supervisors, foremen, and methods engineers "eager to articulate the shortcomings of the Litton management."[76] Although the occupation was not fully supported by the work force, it did help to keep public attention on the case and pressured the government to consider possible rescue schemes. Much of the energy and leadership was provided by one female shop steward, Claire Tate. It was she who climbed the security fence, got the key to the factory gate, and let the others in. She kept the occupation going until she led a group out on 17 July, five months later, carrying a coffin draped with a sheet on which was written "LITTON—Lost in the Turmoil of a Multinational." Despite her efforts, only 70 to 100 workers ever participated, and many others turned against the occupation when Litton cleverly tied the payment of back pay and redundancy payments to the ending of the occupation. At most, the occupation caused minor inconvenience to Litton because it could not sell its assets (for example, machinery, work in progress, stocks) and had to continue paying rent on the land. Otherwise, Triumph-Adler and OEM carried on business as usual. Such is the imbalance of forces between labor and capital in divestment situations if labor is divided and cannot secure substantial political support.

Consequences of Withdrawal

Litton emerged from the process relatively unscathed. It abandoned or sold assets no longer necessary to its international strategy and yet managed to maintain its share of important markets. After the withdrawal, Litton, through its new marketing arrangement, had around 40–50 percent of the U.K. manual market and about 35 percent of the electric market.[77] Its nearest rival, Olympia, was some way behind with a 25 percent share of the total market. Into the bargain, by splitting off the marketing assets from the Imperial company, it effectively thwarted the birth of a new, viable, rival company. Looking back, Imperial had performed a useful bridging function for Litton at low cost. For several years Imperial had supplied the U.S. market with mature products from a cheap-production site. Little was spent on research and development and capital investment, and the British government subsidized some of the costs of training the labor force and of exporting.[78] With the recession and changing competitive conditions, Litton decided to rationalize its production facilities. Imperial's peripheral role was abandoned and its markets taken over by Triumph-Adler. Within days of the closure, imported models carrying the Imperial label were in dealer showrooms.[79]

The closure and the defeat of attempts to found a new company added to the growing numbers of unemployed in Britain. The laid-off men and women from Hull swelled an already high unemployment rate of 5.3 percent by about 20 percent. The rate in Leicester was lower (3.6 percent) but increased to 5.8 percent during the year.[80] Although no systematic follow-up study was made of these laid-off workers, the *Economist* reported that some 665 of the Leicester work force were still definitely unemployed on 1 July 1975, seventeen weeks after the closure, and that of the Hull work force, 450 had found jobs, 600 were on the dole, and 350 were unaccounted for.[81] Workers did receive money under the Redundancy Payments Act of 1965 and from a company scheme that provided from £35 for under two years' service to £270 for forty years' service.[82] In the absence of detailed studies, it is impossible to assess the full social, psychological, and economic impact of the closure on the workers, their families, and the local community. One serious and visible effect was on the Asian community in Leicester, where 10 percent of that population had worked for Imperial.[83]

An attempt to assess the economic costs of the closure to the national economy was made by the Action Committee at Hull. The committee calculated a cost of some £750,000 to the state through the social security system and a further unspecified sum in lost tax revenue for the first year. A further, unspecified sum would have to be added for Leicester.[84] Balance-of-payments effects, due to the loss of Imperial's exports and a rise in imports from other Litton plants, also need to be considered.[85]

Britain's dependence on the production and sales decisions of multinational companies in an important industry was highlighted by the closure. The National Economic Development Council Sectoral Party (a group of experts charged by the government to encourage industrial development on a sectoral basis) for the office-equipment industry observed that the ability of the U.K. office-machinery-manufacturing industry to meet sectoral objectives would rest, in large part, in the hands of foreign-owned multinational companies operating in Britain. It also noted that Britain's export share of a growing world trade in office-machinery products had declined from 11.5 percent in 1963 to 5 percent in 1973. Moreover, it pointed out that the British industry was ill equipped to benefit from the spectacular expected growth in the market for automatic typewriters and word-processing systems.[86] The clash between national and public plans and objectives and private multinational strategic decision making is vividly illustrated in this case.

Finally, a review of what lessons various parties drew from the case is interesting. Members of the Action Committee reacted differently to the defeat. One leading union official said the whole experience had helped him "grow up" and realize the futility of trying to battle multinationals with moral arguments. In the future he would gladly accept multinational companies in Hull for the jobs they would bring and had no reservations about Hull's benefiting from a

multinational transfer of production. An academic who was the leading researcher on the committee took a different view. While conceding the case was a
defeat, he felt it was essentially a political defeat and "a reflection of the defeat
of the interventionist forces in the cabinet." The Labour Member of Parliament
emphasized the "enormous power of multinationals and the inadequate response
of government to transfer pricing and other control mechanisms and the lack of
government resolution to take multinationals on," and he referred to the con-
temptible way multinationals dealt with government, as if they were just a body
one did "some public-relations work with."

On the whole, the press was critical of Litton. An editorial in the *Guardian*
attacked the "lack of accountability" of multinationals and castigated Litton's
behavior in first building up a work force of 3,200 workers, many of whom were
trained at public expense, and then nine years later telling them they were no
longer needed.[87] However, it stopped short of criticizing the rationality that
makes such decisions necessary and endorsed Litton's "right and duty to the
shareholders to switch production from one factory to another in order to maximize profits or to minimize losses." A writer in the *Financial Times* observed
that the Imperial case was different because it clearly illustrated how multinationals can deliberately close a subsidiary with the intention of supplying the
market from factories in other countries and concluded that government would
attach more-stringent conditions before allowing a takeover, especially if the
buyer owned similar factories elsewhere in the world.[88] The *Institute for Workers'
Control Bulletin* argued that in the struggle to protect their jobs and to establish
control over their work lives, the workers needed the "industrial armoury of the
sit-in method" and the "political power to command resources and control
market forces."[89]

Business International, on the other hand, held that Litton should not be
expected to adopt "a social-welfare role" and to provide jobs if those jobs do
not produce profits.[90]

Conclusion

Again, it is important to stress that although idiosyncratic features are evident
in this case, as with the others, Litton is but one example of the rapidly growing
conglomerate form of corporate organization. Therefore, many of the behaviors
identified in this case could be generalized to the conglomerate species.

Before we look at some of the typical behaviors of conglomerates, a few
facts need to be recognized. First, the conglomerate form appears to have become a permanent and important feature of the economic landscape. In the
twenty years after 1950, the proportion of single-business companies comprising
the *Fortune* 500 declined from 30 to 8 percent of the total.[91] The preferred
method of expansion for these companies was by diversification through merger

or acquisition. In fact, by the late 1960s, 81 percent of all corporate mergers in the United States were of the conglomerate type, with the remainder accounted for by horizontal or vertical mergers. This completely reversed the pattern of the late 1920s when only 19 percent of mergers were of the conglomerate type.[92] Despite the poor relative financial performance of many conglomerates in the 1970s, the trend toward diversification by acquisition has remained strong.[93]

This massive trend toward diversification by acquisition has had its malignant side, however. Many subsidiaries and plants belonging to conglomerate empires have been closed or run down in the process. One study shows that conglomerates have much higher rates of business closings than do corporations of a multiplant character but operating roughly in the same line of business. For example, the ratio of closings to openings of business establishments (for example, factories, offices, stores, hotels) in New England was 1.8 and 3.0 for conglomerates in the 1972-1974 and 1974-1976 periods respectively, as compared to ratios of 0.5 and 1.5 for multiplant corporations in the same periods. From 1972 on, the conglomerate ratios are higher even than those for independent enterprises, which are typically small and prone to failure.[94]

These large numbers of acquisitions and divestments do not seem to have produced the improvements in the productivity of capital that conventional economic theory would lead us to expect. Several studies show that representative samples of conglomerates have not, as a rule, achieved higher returns than nondiversified companies, nor have they achieved higher returns or a more-stable and less-risky earnings stream than could have been achieved by comparable portfolio investment. In fact, in most cases they did not perform as well.[95] Moreover, evidence exists that they do not "breathe new life" into "below-par" acquired firms.[96]

Certainly Litton did not breathe new life into Imperial; it was more like a kiss of death. Indeed, Litton's own economic performance is a vivid, if extreme, example of the dangers of rapid growth through diversification. For whereas Litton's total assets grew from $945 million in 1967 to $2.1 billion in 1973 and $2.2 billion in 1975, its return on assets and equity dropped substantially (the return on equity dropped from 19 percent in 1967 to 5.2 percent and 4.4 percent in 1973 and 1975 respectively).[97] Many conglomerates cannot, therefore, confidently claim their contribution to greater economic efficiency as a defense against the severe disruptions and dislocations in people's lives that they often leave in their wake.

One may well than ask why companies diversify into unrelated product areas. There are no theoretically agreed reasons. However, a convincing explanation can be built on the compulsion of all corporations to grow.[98] A company can expand by various ways. One way is to do so in line with the expansion in the market. Another way is by increasing its share of a particular market either by outperforming rivals or by acquiring or merging with them. Alternatively, a company can go beyond the limits imposed by the existing market boundaries by creating new markets with new products, opening up or invading markets across space, by exports and multinationalization, or by invading other product markets by vertical or conglomerate diversification.[99] Conglomeration turned out to be one successful growth strategy for young companies entering the industrial scene late and trying to expand quickly beyond the limits of their original industry.[100] Faced with many oligopolistic structures, they tended to invade product markets that were still relatively competitive and populated by relatively small companies. Acquisition was a quick and seemingly easy way to achieve "bigness," given that "bigness is a prerequisite to joining the game."[101] Therefore, the proposition that for the original conglomerates, diversification was more the by-product of growth by rapid acquisition than the dominant guiding strategy is worth entertaining. More-established companies in stable oligopolistic industries could, and are still able to, satisfy the urge to expand by multinationalization and by more-careful and -related product diversification.

To employ a biological analogy of the firm for a moment, we can say that the modern multi-unit company has found the means to repeatedly stave off death. It has managed to do this by increasing its financial, product, and structural flexibility in the context of an ever-changing environment. A popular managerial concept pioneered by the Boston Consulting Group can give a flavor of how this flexibility can be implemented.[102] The so-called product-portfolio strategy advocates that large multi-unit companies divide their enterprise into strategic business units (SBUs), each typically based on a related family of products. The company should then try to arrange the mix of SBUs in such a way as to take advantage of products, and often businesses, at various stages of the life cycle (birth, growth, maturity, and senescence). Businesses with new products, facing excellent growth potential, can be favored with cash siphoned off from businesses with products that have high shares of established but stagnant markets. The latter, known as "cash cows," are generators of cash for subsidiaries with new or improved products with low shares of fast-growing markets. This strategy has no place for what are called "dogs," businesses that have products with low or declining shares of stagnant markets. Litton quite possibly bought Imperial as a cash cow and turned it into a dog. Conglomerates, therefore, manage not only a "family of products" but also a "family of businesses," and sometimes, as in the Imperial case, the life of the business is dependent on the life of its products.[103]

Notes

1. Imperial Typewriters made profits every year from 1960 to 1966, but there was a decline from £571,000 in 1960 to £100,000 in 1966. The rate of return on capital employed was 11.5 percent in 1963, 11 percent in 1964,

and 10.5 percent in 1965. See Imperial Typewriters Ltd., *Annual Reports,* various years.

2. See the *Daily Mail,* 22 March 1966.

3. See D. Palmer, "The Rise and Fall of the Conglomerate Image," *Financial Times,* 28 May 1970.

4. By the late 1960s, Litton had acquired about 100 different companies, producing some 9,000 products spanning 17 product-market areas. See "What's Gone Wrong at Litton? Problems of Conglomerate Management," *Multinational Business,* no. 3 (August 1972): 40.

5. See Olivetti, *Annual Report,* 1964.

6. See United Nations, *The Growth of World Industry: Commodity Production Data 1964-1973, Volume II* (New York, 1975), p. 530.

7. The financial press was truly infatuated by Litton's early performance, referring to its "breathless" growth and to its ability to exploit the technological revolution with a massive staff of scientists. See, for example, *Financial Times,* 14 April 1967. The president of Litton is in fact quoted as saying, "where technological innovation can be expected to continue at a rapid rate, we're interested. If you can't innovate, we're not interested." See R. Heller, "The Legend of Litton," reproduced in *Business Strategy: Selected Readings,* ed. H. Igor Ansoff (Middlesex, England: Penguin, 1969), p. 361.

8. Charles Craypo, "Collective Bargaining in the Conglomerate, Multinational Firm: Litton's Shutdown of Royal Typewriter" *Industrial and Labor Relations Review,* no. 29 (1975): 9.

9. Ibid., p. 8.

10. See the trade-union publication, *Labour Research* (May 1975), p. 116.

11. Apparently, Royal's share of the U.K. market had dropped from 40 percent in prewar years to about 3 percent in 1965. See Heller, "Legend of Litton," p. 368.

12. The source of this information is an undated and untitled document submitted to the consultants. The author is not indicated but is almost certainly an ex-manager at Imperial. From this point it is referred to as "Ex-Manager."

13. See Urwick, Orr, and Partners Ltd., "Study of Imperial Typewriters Company Ltd." This is an unpublished report, conducted by private consultants for the Department of Industry in 1975, on the feasibility of maintaining a viable Imperial. The report notes that none of the other manufacturers had as complete and closely knit a network of dealers as did Imperial.

14. *Financial Times,* 25 May 1966.

15. As quoted in Craypo, "Collective Bargaining," p. 9.

16. The data on the typewriter industry are hard to find and inadequate when found. Unlike the automobile industry, about which an abundance of data and research exists, the typewriter industry has been badly neglected. There is a need for a published research project on this very interesting industry.

17. Surprisingly, Bain classified the industry as having high entry barriers and this at a time when typewriter companies were complaining about the intensity of price competition—a phenomenon not associated with high entry barriers. The classification can only make sense if import competition is excluded. See Joe S. Bain, *Barriers to New Competition* (Cambridge, Mass.: Harvard University Press, 1956), p. 170.

18. By the early 1970s, Olympia, Olivetti, Litton, and IBM were the main competitors in the international arena.

19. Roy Levine, "Battle of the Multinationals," *Financial Times*, 3 February 1975, p. 6.

20. Olivetti, *Annual Report, 1969*.

21. *Financial Times*, 22 September 1975.

22. Wilfred A. Beeching, *Century of the Typewriter* (London: Heinmann, 1974), p. 127.

23. Colleen Toomey, "Call for Electric Typewriters," *Financial Times*, 23 October 1978, p. 22.

24. Levine, "Battle of the Multinationals," p. 6.

25. Colleen Toomey, "Call for Electric Typewriters."

26. Ibid.

27. Levine, "Battle of the Multinationals."

28. Federal Trade Commission, "In the Matter of Litton Industries Inc.," USA FTC Docket #8778, April 1975.

29. The comment was by the president of Royal and is cited in "Hull Gets Jobs after U.S. Cutback," the *Times*, 24 August 1970.

30. Urwick, Orr, and Partners, "Study of Imperial Typewriters."

31. Ibid., p. 7.

32. Ibid.

33. Ibid.; and Ex-Manager.

34. See "What's Gone Wrong at Litton?" *Multinational Business*, p. 43.

35. Urwick, Orr, and Partners, "Study of Imperial Typewriters," p. 12.

36. See the Transport and General Workers Union (TGWU) Action Committee, *Threatened Closure of Imperial Typewriters, Hull: The Case for Government Aid to Maintain Production and/or to Establish a Co-operative to Assume Ownership and Management of the Plant: A Preliminary Statement* (Hull, 1975).

37. Urwick, Orr, and Partners, "Study of Imperial Typewriters," p. 3.

38. Ex-Manager.

39. The claim was made in a private document prepared by Imperial Typewriters and submitted to the Department of Industry in 1972 requesting "an extension of the waiver of import duty." The document is untitled.

40. In fact, the British government had helped finance some of the costs of this expansion. Many workers were trained partially at government expense, and much of the finance for export was raised under government guarantee.

41. See Department of Industry, *Business Monitor: Overseas Transactions, Series PQ 1005 Office Equipment* (London: HMSO, 1975); and Department of Trade, *Overseas Trade of the United Kingdom, Volumes 2 and 3* (London: HMSO, 1974).

42. See TGWU, *Threatened Closure of Imperial Typewriters, Hull.*

43. Ibid.

44. See Arthur Osman, "Union Blames Outsider for Strike that Ended in Fiasco," the *Times,* 17 October 1974, p. 2.

45. *Financial Times,* 29 September 1970.

46. John Wiles, "All Out Drive to Settle Discrimination Strike," *Financial Times,* 25 June 1974, p. 31.

47. Urwick, Orr, and Partners, "Study of Imperial Typewriters," p. 22.

48. Ibid., p. 24.

49. Ibid., pp. 23-24.

50. Department of Employment, *British Labour Statistics Year Book 1974, 1975* (London: HMSO, 1977).

51. See U.S. Department of the Treasury, "Notice of Penalty or Liquidated Damages Incurred and Demand for Payment," issued by the district director, U.S. Customs Service, San Diego, 21 November 1973.

52. U.S. Department of the Treasury, "Notice of Indictment," issued by clerk, U.S. District Court, Southern District of California, 10 December 1973.

53. U.S. Department of the Treasury, "Regulations and Rulings," issued by assistant commissioner, U.S. Customs Service, Washington, D.C., 3 April 1974.

54. See "When Economic Imperatives and Social Obligations Clash: How Litton Deals with the Dilemma in the U.K." *Business International Weekly Reports,* 14 March 1975, p. 82.

55. This claim was made in an untitled document Litton submitted to the press and to the consultants in 1975.

56. Urwick, Orr, and Partners, "Study of Imperial Typewriters."

57. Ibid., pp. 26-27.

58. Some of these points were made in a letter, dated 10 December 1974, from one of the Imperial plant managers, F.J. St. Clair to K. McNamara, member of Parliament for Hull. The letter attempts to show in what bad straits Imperial is in.

59. The pound-dollar exchange rate was fixed at £1 equal to $2.4 until 1971, at which time the dollar was devalued to £1 equal to $2.6057. However, by April 1973 the rate had changed to $2.4888, with further devaluation of the pound to $2.3279 at the end of 1974 and a larger drop in 1975. OECD, *Main Economic Indicators* (Paris, 1976).

60. Private letter to Lord Beswick, minister of state for industry, from J. Gilluly, 17 January 1975.

61. I could not find detailed figures on Triumph-Adler's financial performance. However, a recent article cites the 20 percent annual dividend and further notes that the subsidiary had doubled its domestic sales since 1974 mainly by moving into growth areas such as calculators, computers, photocopiers, and word processors. The article also reports that Volkswagen has bought a 55 percent ownership share in Triumph-Adler at a price Litton obviously could not refuse. See "Volkswagen Makes It Third Time Lucky," *The Economist,* 17 March 1979, p. 81.

62. See, for example, "Litton Wants More Cash from the Navy," *Business Week,* 15 December 1975, pp. 30–31.

63. Ex-manager.

64. Information on SWEDA obtained from telephone conversation with a Litton public-relations manager and from "SWEDA adds up to a loss for Litton," *Business Week,* 7 September 1974, pp. 27, 30. The International Metalworkers Federation, based in Geneva, Switzerland, submitted a document in 1977 to the OECD charging that Litton had violated the OECD guidelines for multinational companies in its treatment of SWEDA. This document contains useful information on the case and is titled, "Complaints on the Policy of Multinational Companies Calling for Application of OECD Guidelines for Multinational Enterprises."

65. See "Litton Says It Expects Quarterly Net to Turn Up by Fiscal 4th Period," *Wall Street Journal,* 5 March 1971, p. 14.

66. *Financial Times,* 28 May 1970.

67. See "Imperial Duck," The *Economist,* 15 February 1975, p. 89, in which it is reported that both Olivetti and Olympia will produce manuals in Britain for export at a profit.

68. As reported in the TGWU *Threatened Closure of Imperial Typewriters, Hull.*

69. Letter from J. Gilluly to Lord Beswick, 17 January 1975.

70. Each letter was accompanied by information on legal redundancy procedures and entitlements. They also promised that employment officers would visit the factory to help workers find alternative jobs.

71. Letter from the D.M. Markus, chairman and managing director of OEM, to Imperial dealers, 17 January 1975.

72. See David Clark, "The Day that Imperial's Empire Fell," *Manchester Guardian,* 31 January 1975, p. 17.

73. TGWU *Threatened Closure of Imperial Typewriters, Hull.*

74. Urwick, Orr, and Partners, "Study of Imperial Typewriters."

75. Three interviewees who participated in these meetings referred to this behavior on the part of the civil servants. One reported that they "ignored Benn's instructions because they knew he would be removed," and another noted the "enormous authority" they had to "frustrate ministers."

76. "Still Keyed Up," *The Economist,* 12 July 1975, p. 82.

77. See John Lloyd, "Secretaries Demand an Electric Typewriter," *Financial Times,* special section on office equipment, 3 October 1977, p. 15.

78. *Manchester Guardian,* 22 February 1976.

79. See "Typewriter Bombshell for Imperial Workers," *Daily Mail* (Hull), 3 March 1975, p. 1.

80. See the Department of Employment, *British Labour Statistics Year Book 1974, 1975.*

81. See "Still Keyed Up." *The Economist.*

82. Letter from Imperial to workers referred to in note 70.

83. See David Clark, "Day Imperial's Empire Fell."

84. The unavailability of detailed information on the length of unemployment and the level of payment precludes the giving of exact figures.

85. The balance-of-payments effects were mitigated by the increase in the exports of Olivetti and Olympia at this time. Nevertheless, exports dropped by some 70,000 units between 1974 and 1976. Imports also declined in the same period, but only by 30,000. See Department of Industry, *Business Monitor,* (London: HMSO, 1976).

86. Lorne Barling, "British Exporters Lag Behind," *Financial Times,* 3 October 1977, p. 23.

87. *Manchester Guardian,* 22 February 1975.

88. *Financial Times,* 1 February 1975.

89. *Institute for Workers' Control Bulletin,* September 1975.

90. *Business International Weekly Reports,* 14 March 1975, p. 81.

91. See Malcom S. Salter and Wolf A. Weinhold, "Diversification via Acquisition: Creating Value," *Harvard Business Review* 56 (July-August 1978): 166.

92. See Bluestone and Harrison, *Capital and Communities,* p. 123.

93. Salter and Weinhold, "Diversification via Acquisition," pp. 166–67.

94. Bluestone and Harrison, *Capital and Communities,* table 6, p. 43.

95. See Salter and Weinhold, "Diversification via Acquisition;" and R. Hal Mason and Maurice B. Gondzwaard, "Performance of Conglomerate Firms: A Portfolio Approach," *Journal of Finance* 31 (1): 39–48.

96. Mason and Gondzwaard, "Performance of Conglomerate Firms," pp. 45–46.

97. See Salter and Weinhold, "Diversification via Acquisition," exhibit 1, pp. 172–73.

98. See the interesting discussion on this in Paul M. Sweezy, *Capitalism and Other Essays* (New York: Monthly Review Press, 1972), pp. 43–45.

99. See Edith Tilton Penrose, *The Theory of the Growth of the Firm* (New York: Wiley and Sons, 1959).

100. See Alfred D. Chandler, *The Visible Hand: The Managerial Resolution in American Business* (Cambridge, Mass.: Harvard University Press, 1977), p. 481, for the same point.

101. The phrase is used by Richard C. Edwards in *Contested Terrain: The Transformation of the Workplace in the Twentieth Century* (New York: Basic Books, 1979), p. 77.

102. See Bruce D. Henderson, *Henderson on Corporate Strategy* (Cambridge, Mass.: Abt Books, 1979).

103. Ibid., p. 82.

7

Analysis of the Cases: The Growing Importance of the Internal-Political Economy

The development of giant companies has enabled them to replace not only the market determination of prices but also the market allocation of resources– national and international. This gives them a determining power. . .in the whole political economy of the nation and of the world. —Michael Barrat-Brown[1]

One of the advantages of the case-study method is that it permits the researcher to uncover many of the fine inside details involved in a case. However, the mass of details that surfaces in case studies can also make it difficult for the researcher to distinguish between what has wider import and what is idiosyncratic to the cases. In this chapter I simplify the task of analysis by focusing on the findings common to all three cases.[2] These findings are analyzed with two main questions in mind: Do they provide support for the conceptual framework presented in chapter 2? Do they bring to light any new insights about international divestments and the multinational companies that carry them out?

The coneptual framework I presented in chapter 2 argued that subsidiaries would be divested when they had, in one way or another, failed in the competitive-market battle. Failure would be indicated, most obviously, when they were sustaining losses or when the subsidiaries experienced a serious deterioration in their competitive position relative to their rivals. I also suggested that occasionally subsidiaries might be divested even if no relative deterioration had occurred in their competitive position as a result of some aggressive relocation by the parent. The case studies provided no evidence of such aggressive divestments, which of course does not mean that factor should be ruled out of consideration in future research.[3] There was, however, some support in the case-study findings for the market-failure thesis. This was most apparent in the case of Chrysler U.K. Its certified and published income statements did show a consistent record of low profitability or actual losses. In the Innocenti and Imperial cases, no certified profit-and-loss data were available, but indirect evidence indicated that they had become unprofitable. At first glance, then, we find strong support for the conventional wisdom.

Moreover, the reasons for the poor market performance of the subsidiaries seem consistent with the factors I specified in chapter 2. The three subsidiaries were operating in countries with relatively unfavorable business climates. Both Italy and the United Kingdom had weak economies with high inflation rates that handicapped the subsidiaries in their competition against rivals from countries with lower inflation rates. In addition, each subsidiary, in one way or another, experienced cost problems that could be related to the relations-of-production factor. However, the problem was not so much a deterioration in the cost position of the subsidiaries relative to their local rivals. The relations-of-production conditions at the subsidiaries were fairly well in line with the national norm. The problem arose because increasingly in the 1970s they were competing against foreign rivals that operated with lower costs.

The entrance of foreign rivals, occurring at a time when the world economy was slowing down, greatly intensified the competition between companies in the automobile and typewriter industries. The European automobile industry saw a levelling off in the demand for cars in the 1970s. Just at this time the Japanese companies began to successfully penetrate European markets, creating surplus capacity in the industry estimated at between 10 to 20 percent.[4] In this conjuncture, it is not surprising that some production facilities had to be closed. Chrysler U.K., operating with higher relative costs than its new rivals, was unable to generate sufficient cash to fund the development of new models or to mount aggressive marketing campaigns to counteract the competitive threat. Consequently, its market share dwindled and it was selected for divestment. Even Innocenti, operating in a relatively protected market and with a relatively well-differentiated product, was damaged by the intensified competition. The typewriter industry was also subjected to competitive instability throughout the 1960s and 1970s. At the advanced end of the market, technological change was continuous and rapid, and in the more-standardized-product segment of the market, the competitive threat came from lower-cost products manufactured in Japan and the Third World. Imperial, for a variety of reasons, could not counteract these competitive threats and was divested.

This combination of factors—that is, unfavorable business climate, poor cost and marketing performance, and intensified international competition—when allied to the weaknesses of the parents, in particular the cash problems they each experienced in 1975, seems to provide the necessary and sufficient conditions to account for international divestments. Yet this conclusion must be tempered by the following observations. Some companies operating in the automobile and typewriter industries in Italy and Britain performed well or at least survived the recession. Further, each of these weak parents owned subsidiaries that performed well at the same time and in the same industry as those that did not. The contextual factors (country, industry, and parent conditions) do not in themselves fully explain the decision to divest. This places a heavy and critical causal weight on the internal-cost and marketing factor, which certainly seems to make sense. The contextual conditions operate on many companies, but some extraordinary conditions such as a significant failure in performance will select out a subsidiary for divestment. We should then expect parents, acting in an economically rational manner, to select for divestment those subsidiaries with the worse cost and marketing performance.

The case-study evidence, however, cannot be invoked to provide unequivocal support for this contention. True, Imperial and Chrysler U.K. were very poor performers, but this is not at all obvious with Innocenti. It is certainly plausible to maintain from the evidence that Innocenti had been one of the star performers in the British Leyland group and did not have the worst cost or marketing performance at the time the decision to divest was made. Other factors were also at work. Indeed, Chrysler U.K., arguably the least successful subsidiary in the group and in the industry, was not divested in 1975. Although this was largely due to the rescue operation mounted by the British government, that was not the only reason. The parent had for several years supported a failing Chrysler U.K. and had actively sought government help to keep the subsidiary in operation.

It is, of course, possible to dismiss these examples by claiming they represent atypical irrational economic behavior, which would reaffirm the conventional wisdom.[5] Only more-empirical work will settle this question. However, in my view enough evidence is in the case studies to seriously undermine the conventional wisdom as it now stands. One fundamental problem has to do with the difficulty in evaluating the market performance of a subsidiary to determine whether it had in some sense failed. The superficial aspect of the problem concerns the accounting conventions utilized by multinationals. For example, although the ability of parents to artifically raise or lower a subsidiary's profits by manipulating transfer prices is a significant problem for workers and governments (since it can affect the wages and taxes paid), it should not prevent a parent from assessing the real performance of the subsidiary. The accounting distortion can simply be overcome by the parent's maintaining two sets of books. The deeper problem has to do with a subsidiary's lack of independence to make a whole series of operational and strategic decisions.

The cases revealed that it is not just a matter of the parent's allocating a certain amount of funds to the subsidary to spend as it determines. In this situation the subsidiary would have a real, if limited, independence and could be evaluated accordingly. The problem extends beyond the financial dependence of subsidiaries on the parents. The parents seem to have encroached upon the discretionary power of subsidiaries to the point at which they have little or no independent capacity to determine what products they will produce, from what suppliers they will buy, and in what markets they will sell their products. Such decisions, in addition to the control of financial and research-and-development resources, have been centralized at parent or regional headquarters. As one executive so correctly put it, "the profits of subsidiaries were affected by too many variables which were not under the control of local management and, . . . therefore, it would be a nonsense to use them as a measure of their success."[6] The same objection can be leveled at other financial indicators such as the rate of return on capital invested. The logical consequence of the resource dependency of subsidiaries should be for their performance to be

measured according to the tasks they are assigned in the plan and to the financial and nonfinancial resources they are allocated in the budget. This would
imply that some subsidiaries could be performing satisfactorily, even if they
seemed to be market failures. Conversely, of course, it also implies that successful subsidiaries could be divested because the overall plan so required.

Subsidiaries, then, could be said to operate and even compete in two environments. In addition to the external environment (the market), in which they
compete for sales and revenue, they are also embedded in a complex internal
environment. As part of a larger group, their interests become subordinated
to those of the whole group as reflected in the overall strategic plan and budget.
They find themselves allocated tasks that comprise only a piece of a grander
strategic design and thus are allocated resources accordingly. Further, they are
likely to find themselves engaged in a more-or-less overt political struggle over
their respective places in the overall design and over their share of the centrally
controlled resources. For example, Imperial was from the outset assigned a
marginal and short-term role within the Litton empire and was, therefore,
systematically denied vital resources. It is even possible, though no hard evidence
was uncovered to support this proposition, that any profits Imperial may have
made in the early years were channelled into central funds and allocated to
subsidiaries (such as Triumph-Adler) that were assigned a longer-term future in
the strategic plan. Innocenti, however, won a role for itself in the overall strategy
that belied its small size and marginality. This role was in no small part due to
the direct line of communication and influence that Innocenti management had
with top parent executives. However, when this coalition was ousted and and
the overall strategy changed direction, Innocenti was deliberately deprived of
access to vital resources in preparation for its contraction and subsequent
divestment.

The mediation of the relations between subsidiaries and external forces by
the internal environment does lend support to researchers who argue that
organizational and personal factors are important determinants of the decision
to divest. The evidence suggests that top parent management acquires a considerable degree of discretionary power in large multi-unit companies. The
parent can, for a variety of reasons, decide not to respond promptly to market
signals, even if those signals clearly indicate losses at the subsidiary. Some of
these reasons were identified by Caves and Porter. Managerial loyalty, for
example, was probably a contributing factor in the reluctance of Chrysler to
divest its loss-making British subsidiary. So, too, may have been the difficulty
Chrysler faced in trying to separate production and marketing assets, divesting
the former while maintaining the latter. In periods of low growth and surplus
capacity, parents are not reluctant to divest production facilities. The problem
is how to do that without losing market shares. However, such discretionary
power not only produces barriers to exit but also facilitates exit, even if market
signals do not clearly convey the need for such an action (for example,

Innocenti). Furthermore, I do not think such actions are necessarily economically irrational as implied by neoclassical theory. First, as we have seen, market
signals are not reliable or clear messages insofar as subsidiary performance is
concerned. Second, in terms of the long-term and strategic goals of the whole
group, such actions may be highly rational.

An overall assessment of the conceptual framework presented in chapter 2
indicates that though the factors I identified there as being associated with
divestment were present in the case studies, I did not anticipate how important
the internal environment would prove to be. The interaction between performance in the internal and external environments, such that success in one tends
to ensure success in the other, makes it very difficult to clearly assess the relative causal weights of the factors that influence divestments. More large-scale
research on this issue is obviously needed. However, abundantly clear is that
research strategies (and policies) that ignore the internal-political economy of
these organizations are doomed to miss a critically significant component of
the divestment issue and of the nature of these business giants.

Internal-Political Economy

In the remaining pages of this chapter I outline some of the essential features
of what I call the internal-political economy of multinational companies and
briefly discuss some of the wider implications of conceptualizing these organizations in this way. This phrase—internal-political economy—is particularly
appropriate because it emphasizes the political and conscious processes that
govern economic activity within the multinational company. Inside such companies, real planning goes on bargaining and conflictual relations exist between
various management enclaves over the distribution of resources, and conflicts
between labor and capital occur over the conditions of work and the distribution
of the income stream. Moreover, these activities take place within a social
structure characterized by hierarchies of power and influence. Such a con-
ceptualization also has the advantage of highlighting the contrast between
administered and planned activities and impersonal and unplanned market
forces.

This contrast has long been recognized.[7] In fact, Chandler has argued on
the basis of thorough research that "the visible hand of management replaced
. . . the invisible hand of market forces" in many sectors of the economy as long
as 1918.[8] The development of the internal-political economy has emerged
out of the process of growth that business enterprise experienced. With each
increase in size, more activities previously performed in the marketplace were
internalized and became subject to administrative control. Increased size and
the process of geographic and product diversification called forth a "complex
administrative structure to coordinate [the company's] activities and a larger

brain to plan for [its] survival and growth."[9] One of the key administrative problems multi-unit companies faced (for multinational companies are but one, albeit highly sophisticated, example of the more general form), was how to prevent the disintegration of the multi-unit structure into rival groups and how to impose a coherent and overall direction on the group.[10]

The case-study evidence and the work of other researchers suggest that the two favored mechanisms of control and coordination are centralization and strategic planning. A recent and detailed study of centralization in multinational companies, for example, concludes that, despite the rhetoric of decentralization among top managers, in reality a high degree of centralization exists in these companies.[11] Centralized control over a whole range of crucial resources tends to increase the dependency of the parts within the structure, and the dependency of the parts obviously constrains their operational freedom of action. Strategic planning actually conceptualizes the subordinate position of subsidiaries by defining the role each will have in accomplishing the overall goals of the whole group.

There is evidence that shows that large companies have increasingly adopted the formal apparatus of strategic planning.[12] According to one writer, a major reason for the rapid adoption of strategic planning was that it "promised managements that they could now control the destinies of their organizations and achieve corporate stability no matter what happened in the external environment."[13] Large companies attempt to make themselves into "permanent institutions" by pursuing two strategies.[14] One is to try to exercise control over the relevant economic and political environment. The other is to spread the activities of the company across many products, businesses, and markets. Because of the risks inherent in undertaking very expensive investment projects that will only yield a return after a number of years, large companies have a special compulsion to try to control or at least strongly influence prices, costs, sales, and the actions of government. According to Galbraith and others, large companies often succeed in acquiring this permanence.[15] Sales are obviously the most difficult to guarantee, but the companies try to reduce the probability of failure by extensive market research, vigorous sales efforts, and pressure on the state "to limit the oscillations in the economy."[16]

The strategy of product and geographic diversification also adds to these companies' permanence by providing them a degree of freedom to fail or make mistakes not available to single-product national companies. Diversified companies can adapt to environmental changes by altering their direction and shape. The death of products and the birth of new ones, the contraction and expansion of markets, the introduction of new technology, and the discovery of new sources of supply rarely strike at the "foundation" and "very lives" of companies, as Schumpeter believed.[17] Increasingly, the "perennial gale of creative destruction" takes place within the ambit of large multi-unit companies. The rollover out of old products and into new ones and the challenge of the new technology, market, or source of supply are all accommodated by the adaptive and restructuring behavior of large companies. Additionally, if one can generalize from the case of Britain, even "the expansion of new, and the decline of old, industries was achieved to a considerable extent through the change in the size and structure of firms and not primarily through new entrants and bankruptcy."[18]

Of course, not all types of companies will have a similar ability to restructure themselves in order to cope with environmental changes. For example, companies operating in capital-intensive industries (for example, Chrysler), where large sunk costs are typical, will have difficulty in displaying the nimble footwork of less-committed companies in labor-intensive industries. Perhaps the conglomerate type will prove to be the most footloose of all. The whole concept of conglomeration implies that such companies develop not only a family of products but also a family of businesses, each at a different stage in the life cycle (young, developing, mature, and old). This portfolio of businesses is then managed in such a way that some of the businesses are generating cash in their maturity (and prior to their death) for young units that appear to have a promising future in the marketplace.[19] According to Chandler, the managers of conglomerates have become "almost pure specialists in the long-term allocation of resources" (for example, Litton).[20]

However, much as centralization and strategic planning permit multi-unit companies to hold themselves together and to gain some stability in the environment, they cannot fully neutralize the forces that threaten to undermine their order and stability. One source of disorder is the internal conflict that seems to pervade large multi-unit companies. Conflicts can arise between various management enclaves over the formation and implementation of the plan and the allocation of resources. The business and sociological literature has long recognized that divisions and conflicts will exist between various functional departments (for example, production versus sales) over the distribution of scarce resources.[21] Cyert and March, in fact, conceptualize the large business organization as a coalition of bargaining or conflicting members and argue that "conflict is never fully resolved within an organization."[22] The parent/subsidiary form of relation is just a newer and perhaps, because of the added logistics and communication difficulties and the issue of nationality, a more-acute example of internal organizational conflict.

The degree of conflict within these organizations over the distribution of resources will vary. We can propose that it will vary according to:

The degree of central control over crucial resources,

The degree to which resources are scarce,

The degree to which the relations between parents and subsidiaries are rigidly hierarchical and authoritarian,

The degree to which subsidiary managers adopt a local frame of reference and the degree to which they act on it.

A rigidly controlled organization will attempt to prevent, by a system of carefully designed sanctions and rewards, subsidiary (and department) heads from pursuing local and sectional interests to the detriment of the whole group.[23] A weakly controlled organization will be less successful in preventing internecine conflicts from erupting. One way to prevent subsidiary managers from adopting, too strongly, a local frame of reference is to tie their success and security to a groupwide mobility channel. Against that, however, is the possibility that such managers will not care very much about the performance of the subsidiaries since they will see them merely as stepping-stones to other places. Also clear is that the more centrally controlled the resources (note that a subsidiary the size of Chrysler U.K. had to seek central approval before spending over $50,000) and the scarcer they are (in terms of the demands made upon them by subsidiaries), the greater the degree of latent conflict. As I have pointed out, whether this conflict becomes manifest depends on the actual relations between the parts of the organization.

One of the implications of this internal conflict is that resources will be distributed according to a combination of economic and noneconomic factors. As far as I can tell, little research has been done on the issue of what determines the internal allocation of resources. According to Wiles, a similarity exists between the so-called command economy of the Soviet Union and the large, complex company. In the Soviet Union, the allocation of investment funds is decided "by ideology," by "the political pull of local party bosses," and by "many other more-directly economic considerations."[24] So, if the experience of the Soviets can be used as a model, then allocative decisions in large companies may "eventually be taken on a rational basis, but in the short run and often the medium run, quite contradictory policies may be pursued."[25]

Building tentatively on the findings of our case studies, the following economic and noneconomic factors, at the least, seem to be important determinants of the distribution of internally held resources:

Differences in inherited assets and differences in past performances between subsidiaries; for example, the favored subsidiaries (Chrysler France, Innocenti until 1974, and Triumph-Adler) had better performances than others within the organization, and had better assets.

Differences in unit costs between subsidiaries—that is, the result of differences in labor costs and labor productivity; for example, Chrysler France and Triumph-Adler had better unit costs than Chrysler U.K. and Imperial had.

Differences in current and projected performances on the rate of return on investments, or on sales growth or market share, or more likely, given the dependence of these indicators on past parental allocative decisions, on budgeted targets; however, as we have seen, this determinant is particularly complex given the interdependencies between performance and allocative decisions.

The requirements of the strategic plan, which may be the product of the previous three determinants and/or developments in the environment as interpreted by top management.

The relative power of various subsidiaries that depends on all these elements but also on others such as preferences and coalitions at the head office and the vigor with which various subsidiary interests are pushed.

Whether we can still claim that such organizations seek to maximize profits is a question the case studies cannot resolve. What I can conclude is that the parents (which, after all, have the most power within the organization) will attempt to pursue policies and develop strategic plans to the benefit of the whole group rather than its many parts and that they must earn sufficient profits to enable the group to compete effectively with rivals. "Sufficient" here can mean at or just below the average rate of profit in the industry or market. Of course, companies the size of Chrysler and British Leyland can operate for a considerable period of time while earning below-average rates of profit. However, their competitive position will deteriorate, and at some point they will continue to survive only because the "central banks and the bourgeois state continue to bail them out."[26]

Perhaps even more important than the internal forces' undermining the stability of large companies are the external forces that remain outside their domain. For despite the control that flows from internalization, the order that is imposed by centralization, and the stability that is won by strategic planning, large companies cannot fully escape the dynamic forces of competition and technological change. Even giant multinationals the size of Chrysler and British Leyland can be brought to the brink of legal bankruptcy by such forces. The internal-political economy can do no more than provide large multi-unit companies with a degree of freedom from external forces. In the final analysis, the actions of companies are conditioned by the larger political and economic environment. The relatively uncoordinated actions of private companies produce cycles of boom and recession, which lead to unavoidable fluctuations in the conditions for profit making (for example, changes in aggregate demand). The mass of state regulations, which are the product of the continuous conflict and bargaining between classes and fractions of classes, can also act as constraining forces on the actions of companies. Thus, internal planning and external forces remain in a relation of tension. It is, at base, a tension between the internal- and external-political economy, between what Wiles calls the "domestic" and "foreign" policy of large companies.[27]

Implications

Several implications follow from the finding that multinational companies are internal-political economies operating in an unplanned, competitive world environment. First, we can expect divestments to become a routine part of the activities of multinational (and multi-unit) companies. Second, and as I have said before, the decision to divest will not simply reflect the operation of market forces. Too many other factors mediate the relation between subsidiaries and the market. Third, the internalization of economic activity and the development of an internal-political economy will subordinate the interests embodied in subsidiaries (for example, worker, community, and government interests) to those of guiding centers in other countries (a form of absentee control). This will tend to produce tensions between the two sets of interests. Further, insofar as subsidiaries compete for access to resources and a share of the income stream, then this will generate (at least in a latent form) a competitive struggle among workers, communities, and governments of various nationalities.[28] However, unlike the impersonal nature of market competition, this rivalry will be organized according to rules that are to a large extent set by the owners and top managers at the center. Finally, given that a few hundred multinationals now produce about one-sixth of the entire world's output of goods and services,[29] it does not seem too farfetched to conclude that substantial economic power resides in a few visible hands in a select number of key cities.

Notes

1. Michael Barrat-Brown, *From Labourism to Socialism* (Nottingham, England: Spokesman Books, 1972), p. 40.

2. For a more-detailed analysis of the findings, see Leon Grunberg, "International Divestments and The Multinational Company: Three Case Studies" (Ph.D. diss., Michigan State University, 1979), chapter 6.

3. Although Litton did engage in many relocations of production facilities, it was not clear if any were of the aggressive type.

4. Ernest Mandel, *The Second Slump* (London: New Left Books, 1978), p. 52.

5. The evidence presented by the work of researchers such as Sachdev, Torneden, and Caves and Porter indicates that such behavior is not atypical. Noneconomic factors do seem to heavily influence the divestment decision.

6. An executive quoted in Michael Z. Brooke and H.L. Remmers, *The Strategy of Multinational Enterprise: Organizational and Finance* (New York: American Elsevier, 1970), p. 114.

7. See the article by R.H. Coase, "The Nature of the Firm" in *Readings in Price Theory*, ed. G.J. Stigler (Chicago: Irwin, 1952).

8. Alfred D. Chandler, *The Visible Hand: The Managerial Revolution in American Business* (Cambridge, Mass.: Harvard University Press, 1977), pp. 1 and 455. Mandel also suggests that internal planning was systematized "shortly after the First World War." Ernest Mandel, *Late Capitalism* (London: Verso, 1978), p. 231.

9. Stephen Hymer, "The Multinational Corporation and the Law of Uneven Development," in *International Firms and Modern Imperialism*, ed. Hugo Radice (Middlesex, England: Penguin, 1975), p. 38.

10. The danger of rival groups is recognized in Bruce D. Henderson, *Henderson on Corporate Strategy* (Cambridge, Mass.: Abt Books, 1979), p. 50.

11. Michael Z. Brooke, "Centralization and Decentralization in the Multinational Firm: A Report to the Social Science Research Council," manuscript, International Business Unit, University of Manchester. I am grateful to Professor Brooke for allowing me to read the manuscript.

12. See the discussion in "The New Planning," *Business Week*, 18 December 1978, pp. 62-68.

13. Ronald N. Paul, Neil B. Donovan, and James W. Taylor, "The Reality Gap in Strategic Planning," *Harvard Business Review* (May-June 1978), p. 124.

14. "Permanent institutions" is an expression used by Alfred S. Eichner, *The Megacorp and Oligopoly: Microfoundations of Macro Dynamics* (Cambridge: Cambridge University Press, 1976), p. 21. Chandler cites evidence to show how large companies have become "self-perpetuating." For example, of the largest 278 industrials in existence in 1917, only 14 had been liquidated, dissolved, or discontinued by 1967. Chandler, *Visible Hand*, pp. 371-372.

15. See John Kenneth Galbraith, *Economics and the Public Purpose* (New York: Signet, 1973), p. 39 and chapters 10 to 15.

16. Mandel, *Late Capitalism*, p. 229.

17. Joseph A. Schumpeter, *Capitalism, Socialism and Democracy* (Harper & Row, 1976), p. 84.

18. Edith Tilton Penrose, in a review of Leslie Hannah, "The Rise of the Corporate Economy: The British Experience," *Journal of Economic Literature* 16 (1):147.

19. See the work of Henderson on *Corporate Strategy*.

20. Chandler, *Visible Hand*, p. 482. The *Wall Street Journal* reports the trend among some large companies to restructure themselves in an attempt to "clarify their image" and improve the price of their stock. Little is known about the employment effect of such divestments. See *Wall Street Journal*, 4 December 1980, p. 48.

21. For a brief review of the literature see Charles Perrow, *Complex Organizations: A Critical Essay* (Glenview, Ill.: Scott, Foresman and Company, 1979), pp. 153-60.

22. Richard M. Cyert and James G. March, *A Behavioral Theory of the Firm* (Englewood Cliffs, N.J.: Prentice-Hall, 1963), p. 43.

23. However, some have argued that centralization and rigidity will lead to vicious circles in which new bases of power and for conflict are generated, leading to even more centralization and so on. In other words, conflict is endemic to complex organizations. See Michael Crozier, *The Bureaucratic Phenomenon* (Chicago: University of Chicago Press, 1964), pp. 193-94.

24. P.J.D. Wiles, *Economic Institutions Compared* (Oxford: Blackwell, 1977), p. 353.

25. Ibid., p. 81.

26. Mandel, *Second Slump*, p. 81.

27. Wiles, *Economic Institutions Compared*, p. 63.

28. See the discussion in Alberto Martinelli and Eugenio Somaini, "Nation-States and Multinational Corporations," *Kapitalstate* 1 (1973):69-78.

29. Carl H. Madden, ed., *The Case for the Multinational Corporation* (New York: Praeger, 1977), p. 1.

8 Conclusion

Workers are not pieces to be added or removed from the productive machinery according to whether that machinery is going well or not. —Innocenti worker[1]

Competition has always produced instabilities in capitalist development. Workers, rooted as they are by social and personal bonds within the relatively inflexible structures of family and community, have had to adjust their lives to the mobility and cycles of capital. Some workers, at great human cost, have broken those bonds and migrated in search of capital and jobs. Many others have organized and pressured their governments to provide assistance so that they could better cope with the adjustment. Governments in advanced capitalist countries have responded with financial aid and by actually becoming employers themselves. This has been the favored solution to the dislocations produced by capitalist development and has been one of the primary forces behind the increased intervention of the state in modern times. This solution, of course, did not directly challenge the prerogatives of capital.

However, the accumulation of substantial economic power in a few visible hands and the recent waves of divestments have laid the basis for a direct and serious challenge to the freedom of capital. In the struggle against closures carried out by large multi-unit companies, workers (and others) have become aware that divestments are often consciously decided upon for strategic reasons. They therefore find it difficult to accept that they lost their jobs because of the operation of an impersonal, competitive market. The veil of the market is lifted and reveals efficient "accumulating machines" organizing their resources to further their interests at the expense of the interests of workers and communities. This demystification of economic laws presents ideological difficulties for the defenders of unfettered capital mobility.

The fundamental argument in defense of free capital mobility is that the market, if left to work unimpeded, will allocate capital in such a way as to ensure the optimum use of society's resources. One of the critical assumptions on which that proposition is based is that no major imperfections exist in the market. This assumption is untenable for a variety of reasons, one of which surfaced again and again in the case studies.[2] Large multi-unit companies exercise a considerable degree of market power and do not simply respond to market signals when making their allocative decisions. Another source of imperfection is that for many years now, capitalist societies have operated with unemployed resources. The closure of a subsidiary and the movement of capital elsewhere need not necessarily lead to increased social welfare if the workers and machinery remain unemployed for long periods of time. It really depends on what is done with the various resources that are freed up by the closure. Moreover, if one takes into account in the social audit the real-world facts of unemployment insurance, welfare payments, and costs that cannot be neatly calculated in accounting terms (for example, the damage to mental health, the disruption to people's family and community lives), then it is by no means certain that the mobility of capital always maximizes the societal welfare. It may maximize the profits of private capital, but that is not the same thing.

If the arguments of the neoclassical economists no longer jibe with the real world, some convincing, and more-pragmatic, arguments still can be raised in favor of capital mobility and divestments. The growing interdependence of the world economy, and the fierceness of the international competition that has accompanied that interdependence, have exposed the weaknesses of many industries and companies. Supporting such lame ducks indefinitely with public money is, in Thurrow's words, "a route to disaster."[3] If such companies and industries have lost their competitive edge because they cannot match the productivity of foreign rivals, the most sensible thing to do is to let them die, help the affected workers, and encourage the growth of young and dynamic industries. Only by following such an industrial strategy can a society prevent a gradual relative decline in its standard of living.

Workers have recognized the face validity of this argument and, in their struggles against closures and the unrestricted mobility of capital, have rarely made demands that were reactionary and parochial. They did not just demand that the company they worked for be saved and for things to go on as before. Where, for example, the demand for the product they produced clearly had declined, they included in their rescue plans suggestions for the production of new and more-socially useful products (for example, in the Innocenti case, school buses rather than cars). Workers and their allies were trying to shift the debate forward onto a more-progressive plane. In addition to mounting political campaigns in various countries to enact regulations that would moderate the effects of capital mobility (for example, longer notification periods, retraining programs, severance payments to the affected workers and communities), demands were made to increase public control over investment decisions. A variety of proposals surfaced, from having worker and community representatives on the board, to more-nationally based public control. The most imaginative proposal was developed by workers at the Lucas Aerospace Company in England. Faced with layoffs and possible plant closures, shop stewards prepared a corporate plan well in advance of what they believed would be a decline in the industry. Through a democratic process of consultation among the work force and in the community, they were able to prepare a 200-page corporate plan outlining some 150 products that Lucas, using the skills of the work force, could produce.[4] Similar, if less-comprehensive, plans were prepared by the workers in the three cases studied in this book. The central issue was therefore not the free market versus planning, but who would do the planning and according to what rationality it would be done. For if economic life is, in Habermas' words, becoming "repoliticized,"[5] both in the sense that the state is now an active participant in the economic sphere and that economic decisions are increasingly being taken by large visible hands, then we all need to recognize that reality and move forward.

Notes

1. Cited in John Fryer and George Armstrong, "The Cars Run Out of Road," *Sunday Times,* 2 November 1975, p. 53.

2. For a fuller discussion see Barry Bluestone and Bennet Harrison, *Capital and Communities: The Causes and Consequences of Private Disinvestment* (Washington, D.C.: Progressive Alliance, 1980), pp. 8-15.

3. Lester Thurrow, "Roundtable on Reindustrialization and Jobs," *Working Papers for a New Society* (November/December 1980), p. 49.

4. See the discussion in Martin Carnoy and Derek Shearer, *Economic Democracy: The Challenge of the 1980s* (White Plains, N.Y.: M.E. Sharpe, 1980), pp. 221-30.

5. Jurgen Habermas, *Legitimation Crisis* (Boston: Beacon Press, 1973), p. 36.

Bibliography

Books, Journals, and Official Publications

Aiken, M.; Ferman, L.A.; and Sheppard, H.L. 1968. *Economic Failure, Alienation and Extremism.* Ann Arbor, Mich.: University of Michigan.

Bain, Joe S. 1956. *Barriers to New Competition.* Cambridge, Mass: Harvard University Press.

Baran, Paul A., and Sweezy, Paul M. 1966. *Monopoly Capital: An Essay on the American Economic and Social Order.* New York: Monthly Reader Paperbacks.

Barnet, Richard J., and Muller, Ronald E. 1974. *Global Reach: The Power of Multinational Corporations.* New York: Simon and Schuster.

Barrat-Brown, Michael. 1972. *From Labourism to Socialism.* Nottingham: Spokesman Books.

Beeching, Wilfred A. 1974. *Century of the Typewriter.* London: Heinmann.

Blustein, Paul. 1976. "Another Chrysler Turnabout: But Is This One for Real?" *Forbes.* 15 November.

Bluestone, Barry, and Harrison, Bennett. 1980. *Capital and Communities: The Causes and Consequences of Private Disinvestment.* Washington, D.C.: Progressive Alliance.

Bomers, G.B.J. 1976. *Multinational Corporations and Industrial Relations: A Comparative Study of West Germany and the Netherlands.* Amsterdam: Van Goreum.

Braudel, Fernand. 1976. *Capitalism and Material Life, 1400-1800.* Translated by Miriam Kochan. New York: Harper & Row.

Brooke, Michael Z., and Remmers, H.L. 1970. *The Strategy of Multinational Enterprise: Organizational and Finance.* New York: American Elsevier.

Business International SA, in collaboration with J.J. Boddewyn. 1976. *International Divestment: A Survey of Corporate Experience.* SA Research Report.

Caille, Maurice. 1977. *Les truands du patronat.* Paris: Editions Sociales.

Carnoy, Martin, and Shearer, Derek. 1980. *Economic Democracy: The Challenge of the 1980s.* White Plains, N.Y.: M.E. Sharpe.

Castles, Stephen, and Kosack, Godula 1973. *Immigrant Workers and the Class Structure in Western Europe.* London: Oxford University Press.

Caves, Richard E., and Porter, Michael E. 1976. "Barriers to Exit." In *Essays on Industrial Organization in Honor of Joe S. Bain,* edited by Robert Masson and P. David Qualls. Cambridge, Mass.: Ballinger.

Central Policy Review Staff. 1975. *The Future of the British Car Industry.* London: HMSO.

Chandler, Alfred D. 1977. *The Visible Hand: The Managerial Revolution in American Business*. Cambridge, Mass.: Harvard University Press.

Coates, Ken. 1976. *The New Yorker Cooperatives*. Nottingham: Spokesman.

Coase, R.H. 1952. "The Nature of the Firm." In *Readings in Price Theory*, edited by G.J. Stigler. Chicago: Irwin.

Cobb, Sidney, and Kasl, Stanislav V. 1977. *Termination: The Consequences of Job Loss*. U.S. Department of Health, Education, and Welfare. Cincinnati, Ohio: NIOSH.

Craypo, Charles. 1975. "Collective Bargaining in the Conglomerate, Multinational Firm: Litton's Shutdown of Royal Typewriter." *Industrial and Labor Relations Review* 29:3-25.

Crozier, Michael. 1967. *The Bureaucratic Phenomenon*. Chicago: University of Chicago Press.

Cyert, Richard M., and March, James G. 1963. *A Behavioral Theory of the Firm*. Englewood Cliffs, N.J.: Prentice-Hall.

Deadman, W.B., and Wells, G.G. 1975. *Taxation in Europe*. London: Farringdon.

Dunning, J., and Pearce, R.B. 1975. "Profitability and Performance of the World's Largest Industrial Companies." London: Financial Times.

Edwards, Richard C. 1979. *Contested Terrain: The Transformation of the Workplace in the Twentieth Century*. New York: Basic Books.

Eichner, Alfred S. 1976. *The Megacorp and Oligopoly: Microfoundations of Macro Dynamics*. Cambridge: Cambridge University Press.

European Ecoomic Community. 1973, 1975. "Report(s) on Competition Policy." Brussels.

Fayerweather, John, and Kappor, Ashok. 1976. *Strategy and Negotiation for the International Corporation*. Cambridge, Mass.: Ballinger.

Federal Trade Commission. 1975. "In the Matter of Litton Industries Inc." USA FTC Docket #8778. April.

Galbraith, John Kenneth. 1973. *Economics and the Public Purpose*. New York: Signet.

Gamba, Marino. 1976. Innocenti Imprenoitore, Fabrica e Classe Operaia in Cinquanti'Anni di Vita Italiane. Milan: Mazzatta.

Great Britain. Department of Employment. 1975. *British Labour Statistics Year Book 1974, 1975*. London: HMSO.

_____. 1977. *British Labour Statistics Year Book, 1974, 1975*. London: HMSO.

Great Britain. Department of Industry. 1971. *Business Monitor: Overseas Transactions*. London: HMSO.

_____. 1975. *Business Monitor: Overseas Transactions*. London: HMSO.

_____. *An Approach to Industrial Strategy*. London: HMSO.

Great Britain. Department of Trade. 1974. *Overseas Trade of the UK*, vols. 2, 3. London: HMSO.

Greenwood, John. 1977. *Worker Sit-Ins and Job Protection: Case Studies of Union Intervention*. London: Gower.

Gregory, Gene. 1976. "From Nissan with Love." *MSU Business Topics* 24: 47-59.

Grunberg, Leon. 1979. "International Divestment and the Multinational Company: Three Case Studies." Ph.D. diss. Michigan State University.

Habermas, Jurgen. 1975. *Legitimation Crisis*. Translated by Thomas McCarthy. Boston: Beacon.

Heller, R. 1969. "The Legend of Litton." In *Business Strategy: Selected Readings*, edited by H. Igor Ansoff. Middlesex, England: Penguin.

Henderson, Bruce D. 1979. *Henderson on Corporate Strategy*. Cambridge, Mass.: Abt Books.

Herron, Frank. 1975. *Labour Markets in Crisis: Redundancy at Upper Clyde Shipbuilders*. London: Macmillan.

Hollingworth, F.D. 1975. "Divestment-It's Tough to Bite the Bullet." *Business Quarterly* 40:29-32.

House of Commons. 1975. *Fourteenth Report from the Expenditure Committee. The Motor Vehicle Industry*, vol. 1. London: HMSO.

_____. 1976. *Eighth Report from the Expenditure Committee together with the Minutes of Evidence Taken before the Trade and Industry Sub-Committee in Session 1975-1976 and Appendices. Public Expenditure on Chrysler UK Ltd*. London: HMSO.

_____. 1976. British Leyland: The Next Decade. London: HMSO.

Hymer, Stephen. 1975. "The Multinational Corporation and the Law of Uneven Development." In *International Firms and Modern Imperialism*, edited by Hugo Radice. Middlesex, England: Penguin.

_____. 1976. *The International Operation of National Firms: A Study of Direct Investment*. Cambridge, Mass.: MIT Press.

International Metalworkers' Federation. 1977. *Facts about Spain's Motor Industry*. Geneva. IMF World Auto Councils Release.

Johnson, H.G. 1970. "The Efficiency and Welfare Implications of the International Corporations." In *The International Corporation*, edited by C.P. Kindleberger. Cambridge, Mass.: MIT Press.

Kelly, Ed, and Webb, Lee. 1979. *Plant Closings: Resources for Public Officials, Trade Unionists and Community Leaders*. Washington, D.C.: Conference on Alternative State and Local Policies.

Kindleberger, Charles P. 1969. *American Business Abroad, Six Lectures on Direct Investment*. New Haven: Yale University Press.

Knickerbocker, F. 1973. *Oligopolistic Reaction and the Multinational Enterprise*. Cambridge, Mass.: Harvard University Press.

Lall, S. 1973. "Transfer Pricing By Multinational Manufacturing Firms." *Oxford Bulletin of Economics and Statistics* 35:181-84.

Madden, Carl H., ed. 1977. *The Case for the Multinational Corporation.* New York: Praeger.

Mandel, Ernest. 1978. *Late Capitalism.* London: Verso.

_____. 1978. *The Second Slump.* London: New Left Books.

Marcus, Matityahn. 1967. "Firms' Exit Rates and Their Determinants." *Journal of Industrial Economics* 16:10-22.

Martinelli, Alberto, and Somaini, Eugenio. 1973. "Nation-States and Multinational Corporations." *Kapitalstate* 1:69-78.

Mason, R. Hal, and Gondzwaard, Maurice B. 1976. "Performance of Conglomerate Firms: A Portfolio Approach." *Journal of Finance* 31 (1):39-48.

McKenzie, Richard B. 1979. *Restrictions on Business Mobility: A Study on Political Rhetoric and Economic Reality.* Washington, D.C.: American Enterprise Institute.

Mick, Stephen S. 1975. "Social and Personal Costs of Plant Shutdowns." *Industrial Relations* 14 (2):203-08.

Mukherjee, Santosh. 1973. *Through No Fault of Their Own: Systems for Handling Redundancies in Britian, France and Germany.* London: MacDonald.

Multinational Business. 1972. "What's Gone Wrong at Litton? Problems of Conglomerate Management," vol. 3.

_____ . 1976. "The Multinational that Wanted To Be Nationalized: A History of the Chrysler Rescue," vol. 1.

Organization for Economic Cooperation and Development. 1975. *Economic Outlook.* Paris, July.

_____. 1976. *Economic Survey: Italy.* Paris, January.

_____. 1976. *Main Economic Indicators.* Paris, December.

_____. 1977. *Economic Survey: Italy.* Paris, March.

Paul, Ronald N.; Donovan, Neil B.; and Taylor, James W. 1978. "The Reality Gap in Strategic Planning." *Harvard Business Review* 56 (3):124-30.

Penrose, Edith Tilton. 1959. *The Theory of the Growth of the Firm.* New York: Wiley.

_____ . 1978. Review of "The Rise of the Corporate Economy: The British Experience" by Leslie Hannah, *Journal of Economic Literature* 16 (1): 146-48.

Perrow, Charles. 1979. *Complex Organizations: A Critical Essay.* Glenview, Ill.: Scott, Foresman and Company.

Pontarollo, Enzo. 1975. "The Truth about the 1,700 Sackings." In *Alternativa Produttiva.* Milan: FLM.

Pratten, C.F. 1976. *Labour Productivity Differentials within International Companies.* Cambridge: Cambridge University Press.

Reynaud, Jean Daniel. 1975. *Les syndicates en france,* vol. 1. Paris: Seuil.

Robinson, Geoffrey. 1975. "Italian Fiasco." *Spectator.* 6 December.

Rollin, Henry, 1977. *Militant chez Simca—Chrysler.* Paris: Editions Sociales.

Salter, Malcom S., and Weinhold, Wolf A. 1978. "Diversification via Acquisition: Creating Value." *Harvard Business Review* 56 (July-August):166-76.

Schein, Virginia E. 1977. "Individual Power and Political Behaviors in Organizations: An Inadequately Explored Reality." *Academy of Management Review* 2 (i):64-72.

Schumpeter, Joseph A. 1950. *Capitalism, Socialism and Democracy*. New York: Harper Torchbooks.

Scott, Richard W. 1965. "Field Methods in the Study of Organizations." In *Handbook of Organizations*, edited by James G. March. Chicago: Rand McNally.

Securities and Exchange Commission. 1975. *Form 10-k Reports*, Chrysler Corporation. Washington, D.C.

Society of Motor Manufacturers and Traders. Various years. *The Motor Industry of Great Britain*.

Stern, Robert N.; Haydenwood, K.; and Hammer, Tove Helland. 1979. *Employee Ownership in Plant Shutdowns: Prospects for Employee Stability*. Kalamazoo, Mich.: W.E. Upjohn Institute for Employment Research.

Sweezy, Paul M. 1972. *Capitalism and Other Essays*. New York: Monthly Review Press.

Thurrow, Lester. 1980. "Roundtable on Jobs and Industrial Policy." *Working Papers for a New Society* 7 (6):47-59.

Torneden, Roger L. 1975. *Foreign Divestment by U.S. Multinational Corporations: With Eight Case Studies*. New York: Praeger.

Turner, Graham. 1971. *The Leyland Papers*. London: Eyre and Spottiswood.

United Nations. 1973. *Multinational Corporations in World Development*. New York.

_____. 1975. *The Growth of World Industry, 1973 Edition, Volume 11. Commodity Production Data 1964-1973*. Department of Economic and Social Affairs, Statistical Office, New York.

U.S. Department of the Treasury. 1973. "Notice of Penalty or Liquidated Damages Incurred and Demand for Payment." Issued by the district director, U.S. Customs Service, San Diego. 21 November.

_____. "Notice of Indictment." Issued by clerk, U.S. District Court, Southern District of California. 10 December.

_____. 1974. "Regulations and Rulings." Ruling issued by assistant commissioner, U.S. Customs Service, Washington, D.C. 3 April.

_____. 1979. "Statement of G. William Miller before Subcommittee on Economic Stabilization of the House Committee on Banking, Finance and Urban Affairs." Washington, D.C.

Van Den Bulcke, D. Undated. "Existing Data." In *Investment and Divestment Policies of Multinational Corporations in Europe*. ECSIM, Saxon House.

Vernon, Raymond. 1977. *Storm over the Multinationals: The Real Issues.* Cambridge, Mass.: Harvard University Press.

Wallender, Harry W., III. 1973. "A Planned Approach to Divestment." *Columbia Journal of World Business* 8:33-37.

Wiles, P.J.D. 1977. *Economic Institutions Compared.* Oxford: Blackwell.

Young, Neil, and Stephen Hood. 1977. *Chrysler U.K.: A Corporation in Transition.* New York: Praeger.

Unpublished Documents

Brooke, Michael Z. 1979. "Centralization and Decentralization in the Multinational Firm: A Report to the Social Science Research Council." Manuscript. International Business Unit, University of Manchester Institute of Science and Technology.

Chrysler Action Committee. 1975, 1976. The Workers' Document. Coventry, England.

Chrysler U.K. 1976. "C6 Comparison, CUK vs. Chrysler France." 4 September.

———. "Relief Allowances: Ryton and Poissy Assembly Plants." 25 November. Coventry, England.

———. 1978. "Our Future with P.S.A. Peugeot-Citroen."

Former Manager. 1975. Untitled document submitted to Urwick, Orr and Partners Ltd.

Innocenti Leyland. 1972. "Note per la Presentazione alle Rappresentanze Aziendali." Milan. May.

International Metalworkers Federation. 1977. Document submitted to the Organization for Economic Cooperation and Development. Geneva.

Litton Document. 1975. Submitted to the press and consultants. Untiltled and undated.

L'Union Departmentale des Syndicatas CGT des Yvelines. 1974. "Press conference. 29 October 1974. #42 December.

Manpower Services Commission. 1978. Chrysler (Linwood) Redundancy Study. London.

Sachdev, Jagdish C. 1976. "A Framework for the Planning of Divestment Policies for Multinational Companies." Ph.D. diss. University of Manchester.

TGWU Document. 1975. "A Corporate Plan for New Harmony Enterprises Ltd." Prepared for presentation to the Department of Industry by the Action Committee of Imperial workers.

Transport and General Workers Union (TGWU). 1975. Threatened Closures of Imperial Typewriters, Hull: The Case for Government Aid to Maintain Production and/or to Establish a Cooperative to Assume Ownership and Management of the Plant: A Preliminary Statement. Hull: TGWU.

Urwick, Orr and Partners Ltd. 1975. "Study of Imperial Typewriters Company Ltd." Document for Department of Industry Special Report.

Villiam, Mariot. 1975. "Come Una Multinazionale puo Esportare la Crisi: Il Caso Leyland Innocenti." Ph.D. diss., University of Milan.

Index